Going with the Grain

This Large Print Book carries the
Seal of Approval of N.A.V.H.

Going with the Grain

the Grain

A Wandering Bread Lover
Takes a Bite out of Life

Susan Seligson

Thorndike Press • Waterville, Maine

page 53: Recipe from *Traditional Moroccan Cooking: Recipes from Fez* by Madame Guinaudeau, reprinted with permission of publisher, Serif, London.
pages 88–89: Recipe from *Build Your Own Earth Oven* by Kiko Denzer, Hand Print Press, P.O. Box 576, Blodgett, OR 97326, Phone: 541-438-4300. Reprinted with permission.
page 174: Excerpt from "Sunlight" from "Mossbawn: Two Poems in Dedication" from *Opened Ground: Selected Poems 1966–1996* by Seamus Heaney. Reprinted by permission of Farrar, Straus and Giroux, LLC.
pages 425-427: Personal recipe of Lora Brody, reprinted with her permission.

Published in 2003 by arrangement with Simon & Schuster, Inc.

Thorndike Press Large Print Nonfiction Series.

The tree indicium is a trademark of Thorndike Press.

The text of this Large Print edition is unabridged.
Other aspects of the book may vary from the original edition.

Set in 16 pt. Plantin by Elena Picard.

Printed in the United States on permanent paper.

Library of Congress Cataloging-in-Publication Data

Seligson, Susan.
    Going with the grain : a wandering bread lover takes a bite out of life / Susan Seligson. — Large print ed.
      p. cm.
    Originally published: New York : Simon and Schuster, 2002.
    ISBN 0-7862-5068-2 (lg. print : hc : alk. paper)
    1. Bread. 2. Cookery, International. 3. Seligson, Susan — Journeys. 4. Large type books. I. Title.
TX769 .S3987 2003
   641.8′15—dc21   2002038424

For Howie

Acknowledgments

For their encouragement and enthusiasm I thank Sara London, Sinan Unel, Suzanne Strempek Shea, Vivian Bower, Janice Allee, Lois Griffel, Madeline Miller, Seth Bauer, and my parents, Rhoda and Jack Seligson. Thanks to those whose generosity made my work easier, especially Omar Douad, Mazen Hamadeen, Tim Allen, Bob Walsh, Michael London, and Lora Brody.

I extend my deepest gratitude to my editor, Sydny Miner. I knew we were going to hit it off as soon as we compared hairdos; the journey's been a pleasure from start to finish. For her endless hard work, friendship, and wisdom I am forever grateful to my agent, Susan Ramer.

Finally, I thank my best friend, coach, underwriter, dance partner, dishwasher, publicist, jester, therapist, and muse. They are the same person — my husband, Howie Schneider. Long may he nudge.

Contents

Introduction:

No Samples Today

> *On n'arrete pas le murmure*
> *Du peuple quand il dit: "J'ai faim,*
> *Car c'est le cri de la nature:*
> *Il faut du pain. Il faut du pain."*
> — CHANSON OF PIERRE DUPONT,
> BOHEMIAN POET

My husband invited a new acquaintance and his wife to dinner at our house. "We heard you're writing a book about bread!" they exclaimed. Their eyes darted around our kitchen; their hands patted their bellies. "We were hoping for some samples!"

Alas, the only "samples" I was equipped to offer were writing samples. It's happened time and again in the last two years — folks expecting to sink their teeth into some stupendous bread, courtesy of the lady penning a "bread book." In truth, I'm no baker. I don't even make cakes or pies, though if my craving is strong enough I'll bake cookies. The only bread I make at home is challah, a nod to my Jewish heritage. Challah is easy. The dough is crammed with so many eggs it rises as predictably as the tide and is nearly impossible to ruin. Also it makes a wicked French toast.

People who write about bread — and there are many doing a terrific job of it — tend to be professional bakers or seasoned food writers. I am neither. My lifelong love affair with bread has less to do with crust, crumb, and the vagaries of sourdough cultures and more to do with bread as a reflection of people's varied beliefs, daily lives, and blood memories. Bread captivates me for many reasons. But most of all I love bread because I never tire of traveling to new places to learn how people nourish their bodies and spirits, how they rejoice, mourn, and manage in the face of adversity. Native bread can teach us these things, and more. Visit a village bakery or a matron tending a clay hearth to feed her family. Watch, listen, inhale — the bread tells the most essential human stories. And because a person's desire for that homespun bread doesn't diminish when he or she emigrates from Delhi to Astoria or

Amman to Atlantic Avenue, in the middle of New York City I can close my eyes and take a bite, and the bread, like a tune or a scent or a face in the crowd, carries me far away. That's how it is with bread and me. So you'll forgive me if I don't bake the stuff. No samples today.

Bread is personal. Without leaving New York City an enthusiast may partake of Silesian potato bread, South Indian *dosa*, Finnish *rieska*, Ethiopian *injera*, and Italian *grissini*. But witness the disgust, even outrage, on the face of a resident foreigner biting into some feeble imitation of his native bread. An Iranian acquaintance travels from upstate New York to Brooklyn to buy flat breads the size of welcome mats in which to wrap kebab. Long after his family migrated to Florida, my friend Peter makes annual treks to his Long Island birthplace to buy out Bambi's onion rye, with which he stocks his freezer for a year. Cashing in on a tidal wave of transplanted New Yorkers, an enterprising Cape Codder flies in fresh bagels from the mother church, H & H, on Manhattan's Upper West Side. The first time after many years that I sank my teeth into the eggy flesh of a genuine onion roll I felt as if I were reunited with a cherished old friend. For baby boomers of

11

my vintage even a slice of Wonder Bread delivers fond childhood memories.

I've done a healthy amount of traveling. Were I asked to distill the culture and spirit of a faraway place into one tangible object, it would be a hunk of bread. I never tire of flour in all its incarnations. A crusty baguette, a dense slab of black bread, a round of pita, chapati, country biscuits, matzo, lavash — these are a few of my favorite things. Whether I'm slogging up a mountain or snuggling against the cool leather of a long-distance train compartment I've taken to keeping my pockets full of the local bread. And when I open my mind, heart, and palate to another culture its bread is as resonant as the national tongue or currency.

Bread *is* a form of currency. What other food approaches its variety and endurance? Consider the pleasure, pain, and general havoc attributable to the result of a simple union of flour, water, and salt. Throughout its eight-thousand-year history bread's value has been measured in hope and despair, power and subjugation. Clerics sermonize on it, poets rhapsodize over it, beggars pine for it, and the masses agitate for it. Saints have been beatified in its name. Every year in September the ancient

Greeks honored Demeter the bread goddess with nine days of egalitarian hoopla including parades with plows and scythes sculpted entirely of dough. Ever since the people of ancient Jericho baked crude cakes of wheat and barley in the desert sun, bread has been man's most persistent entitlement. People will suffer any number of indignities, but triple the price of bread and whether it's contemporary Jordan or eighteenth-century France, they take to the streets in angry hordes. As Roman lawyer Juvenal famously wrote in A.D. 110, "bread and circuses" are what keep the masses pacified. Nearly 1,900 years later, Herbert Hoover would remark that "world peace means a peace of bread." I don't know what happens when the powers that be start messing with circuses, but bread revolts have helped shape the course of history. In eighteenth-century London protestors pillaged grain stores. In France's "flour wars" of the 1770s, people convinced of a conspiracy to raise bread prices seized grain from barges and tossed grain merchants into ponds. This supposed secret, grain-exporting *pacte de famine* — perpetrated, the people believed, at a time when aristocrats were patting their wigs and faces with precious flour — led to the storming of the Bastille prison. And though the majority of the attackers wielded axes and muskets, some, historians say, carried ears of grain.

Bread is spiritual. Hindus visit temples with offerings of bread for their gods; Muslims lay bread on the graves of loved ones. Native Americans adorn themselves with ceremonial breads for harvest dances. Jews say a Sabbath blessing over the bread and shun all leaven for the festival of Passover. Jesus at the Last Supper took some unleavened bread and declared to his disciples that the bread had become his own body, his precise meaning to remain a source of eternal debate. Both Muslims and Hindus consider it blasphemous to take a knife to bread. Several cultures bake coins into bread in a symbolic gesture of gratitude to the land and its gift of grain. In Uzbekistan, when a family member ventures on a long journey or joins the army he takes a bite out of a fresh *non* bread, which is hung on a hook and left untouched until his safe return, which he celebrates by sharing the bread with friends.

My unabashedly whimsical, haphazard journey was an initiation into these enduring rituals as well as catapulting me from the sacred to the profane. In the coiled stainless-steel innards of the Wonder Bread factory my guide plucked one loaf, then another off the assembly line to illustrate a point, then flung the bread in the trash. A week later, in southern Ireland, a miller palmed no more than a tablespoon of whole grains to explain the grinding process, then carefully returned every grain to the drum.

Bread is fundamental. Swift's "staff of life," bread is synonymous with survival. From Canadian seafarers' hardtack to Saharan nomads' pita, bread is an emblem of human adaptability and imagination. Before the world morphed into a place of blurred borders and continents raised the global flags of Nike and Coke, bread was a strictly local invention crafted from whatever the land could produce. Wildly abundant during good times and the crudest sustenance in bad, bread is born of the flours of wheat, corn, lentils, barley, rye, rice, and manioc. With little more than lard, water, and anything that withstood drying and grinding, for centuries the poorest women put bread on the family table, even if that was all they could put there. Extending grain flours with finely ground chestnuts or hazelnuts worked out so well the French continue the practice.

Over the centuries the desperate have also improvised with grape seeds, pine bark, clay, straw, even human bones. None of these caught on.

Almost from the start, all bread was not created equal. Wheat, of course, is the aristocrat of grains. In America wheat wasn't cultivated successfully until 1621, when the Jamestown colonists succeeded where Columbus had failed. Wheat demands coddling; oats can survive the most unforgiving rocky terrain. European nobility feasted on real wheat bread while the destitute chewed on "gruel bread" from rye, millet, or any reasonable or unreasonable facsimile they could muster. Ancient Romans named breads according to their grains and the quality of the flour milling. As Bernard Dupaigne writes in his wonderful *History of Bread*, coarse and mixed-grain breads consumed by slaves and the poorest peasants were called *panis sordidus*, consisting of whole meal and bran. *Panis plebeius* was made with crudely sifted flour laced with milling waste. The slightly more fortunate would partake of *panis secondaris*, prepared with low-quality wheat flour. And then there was the prized bread of nobility. It was the whitest and the softest to the bite: *panis palatius*.

When the industrial revolution spawned a shift from handmade to bakery bread the trend was considered scandalous. What mischief would attract women's newly idle hands? And the bakers were up to their own mischief, tipping the scales and "duping" flour with alum or worse. The rapid evolution of milling technology took its aesthetic toll. "What a strange, fortuitous course does the history of man pursue," wrote H. E. Jacob in his rambling opus, *Six Thousand Years of Bread*. "The technological crisis of the Middle Ages made men eat splinters of stone in their flour; the technological progress of our industrial age has produced machines so precise that they grind away the living strength of our flour."

Jacob wrote these words in the early 1940s. He would be heartened by the return of *panis sordidus* to the American table. Despite the vast availability of cheap, overprocessed replacements, handcrafted indigenous breads aren't disappearing as Jacob might have predicted. These breads reflect one tradition that refuses to be diluted or globalized out of existence. Lamenting the decline of its signature baguette, which was headed the way of the genuine New York bagel, the so-called panivorous French have bolstered and enforce with renewed vigor laws compelling bakers to maintain that nation's *haute* standards when it comes to bread. Here in America, prosperity and health consciousness have brought a renewed passion for handcrafted breads. Today's gourmet mavens and "slow food" enthusiasts are embracing coarse stone-ground flours and wood-fired hearths. They're forking over three dollars for a round of Tuscan peasant bread of the humblest ingredients. On supermarket shelves dense, nutty alternatives — or engineered impersonations of them — crowd out standard-issue white bread. Not since the time of Sylvester Graham, the temperance crusader whose *Treatise on Bread, and Bread-making* raged against the evils of nutrient-depleted, refined flour, have Americans been so alert to the virtues of wholesome bread. The efforts of Dr. Atkins and his disciples' demonization of "carbs" notwithstanding, we are rediscovering bread and the versatility of grains, the glory in the flour.

My odyssey took me into the bakeries, homes, and in one foray, a tent of people for whom preparing the daily bread is an act of love and faith. There is Michael London of Saratoga Springs, New York, who believes the bread and the fire are alive with spirits and likens his firebread to a fine wine. There is Parisian baker Max Poilâne, the unsung brother of world-famous Lionel. In the bread world Lionel's *Pain Poilâne* is Gucci, Hermès, and Chanel rolled into one. But Max is as much poet and philosopher as baker, content with his little corner bakery, tenderly kidding with his loyal clientele. In a tent in the Jordanian desert village of Wādī Mū-sá I knelt beside a Bedouin woman named Fatima as she turned a flat bread in a pit full of glowing embers. I encountered people with a passion for bread and a gift for teaching, men like the gentle Tim Allen in Shanagarry, Ireland, and Idaho biologist Ed Wood, a wild yeast expert and master baker who collects and distributes exotic sourdough cultures. And there were many others, dispensing bread and wisdom from locales as exotic as India and Morocco, and as homespun as Blodgett, Oregon, and Huntsville, Alabama.

My journey illuminated and reinforced what I've long believed to be true about bread. It is best expressed in Arabic — *aysh*. For in that language the words "bread" and "life" are the same.

The Bread Mystery:
Fès, Morocco

*Bread is the main thing to understand:
the staple of speculation, the food for
all theories about what happens next.*
— HILARY MANTEL,
A PLACE OF GREATER SAFETY

In the name of Allah give me bread.
— FESI STREET BEGGAR

My husband and I spent Christmas 1997 in
Morocco. I'd been pestering Howie for years
about escaping for the holidays to an Islamic
country, somewhere we could get through
the thick of the season without ever hearing
dogs bark "Jingle Bells" or the words "great
gift idea." As our base we chose the northern
imperial city of Fès. We'd visited this chaotic, ancient metropolis the year before.
Both of us were smitten and sad to leave it so
soon. Also, I had some unfinished business

there. I longed to solve the bread mystery.

A person doesn't blithely stroll into the ninth-century medina of Fès. Stepping through the gates of the old city, Fès-el-Bali, is more like being pulled into a raging river; you catch your breath and surrender to the current. How strange, I thought, that this sensory extravaganza is as familiar to Fesis as a suburban mall back home would be for me. It seems unthinkable that anyone, even over a lifetime, could fail to be startled by the dancing colors, the pungent air, the bone-rattling insistence of this thousand-ring circus. Howie and I step over the cobbled threshold from extremely old to ancient, and we're pelted with the sweet-savory smells of cooking fat, jasmine, orange blossom, musk, and mud-crusted pack mules. Allergic mess that I normally am, I don't even sniffle. It's as if every receptor cell in my body is already on overload.

From the din I make out the ageless entreaties of street commerce. The common denominator is bread, universally required, perpetually produced. A new day yields about one fresh loaf for every inhabitant of the old city. Carted in sacks, perched on the tops of heads, balanced precariously by mischievous toddlers, nearly identical Moroccan round loaves crisscross the narrow streets like Federal Express packages on Seventh Avenue.

The medina bakeries offer no bread for sale. Their business is to immerse the homemade loaves in gaping wood-fired hearths, after which customers retrieve the fresh-baked breads, each a fragrant pillow. By the time a typical Fesi family tears off hunks of semolina loaf to dip into the lemony juices of the supper tagine, or stew pot, the breads have made a round-trip journey at the behest of a system sustained not by lists and figures but by dogged attentiveness, faint nods of the appropriate heads, and sheer faith. Few words are exchanged, nothing is written down. No one with whom I spoke would change a thing about the system. My tagged luggage has been waylaid to cities I've never visited, the photo store has sent me home with snapshots of a stranger's family barbecue, and I once lost an entire outfit at the dry cleaners. But in Fès it's an unspeakable rarity for a baker to misplace or misdirect a single bread. How is it possible?

Morning seems the best time to make sense of what appears to be a bread-centered conspiracy. In the company of a sullen young translator from the Arabic Institute named Karim, I survey the bread traffic from the vantage point of a café, in Place Nejjarine, near the henna souk. The proprietor produces a rickety spool table and laborer's bench, which I drag beside a mosaic fountain framed by elaborately carved cedar. In the carless square a gaggle of children are playing tag. One tiny girl carries a wooden slab with two loaves on it, and as the children sprint and giggle, she just manages to save the shaped dough from slithering off the tray to the rank stones under her feet.

I gulp my second espresso and, to Karim's frustration, bound off in a misguided attempt to shadow these trays of loaves as they come and go. A native of the medina, Karim knows it's a futile enterprise. The loaves and their bearers materialize seemingly out of nowhere. On their one-arm pedestals floating above the crowd, loaves emerge from ominous alleyways or the discreet doorways of aristocratic homes, the wealth of their inhabitants betrayed only by the elaborate frivolity of colored tiles called *zellijes*. The bearers are just as abruptly swallowed up by dark stairwells or shadowy depressions in windowless stone facades. Foreboding as seawalls, these conceal uncounted labyrinthine worlds of private courtyards and sun-baked rooftops. On the streets in winter, the faces of medina men are in shadows inside the pointy hoods of their woolen over-robes. This prevailing style lends a conspiratorial air to their every move as they dart here and there like figures out of a game of Dungeons and Dragons.

It is a world tauntingly out of bounds to the casual visitor. But I was able to do some serious spying from a strategically placed rooftop café. I saw drying laundry in candy colors, smoke curling skyward from Macbethian cauldrons, women bent over washbasins, and men folded in prayer. Beyond the high walls lining the medina streets and alleys are updated harems from which women venture out only for hurried shopping errands or a trip to the *hamam*, or community bath. For pubescent girls and restless young wives, a sheet of uncooked round loaves perched on a shoulder is a welcome license to dawdle in public. Young girls' yearnings aside, why not bake bread at home? It's not possible in the old city; there are no proper ovens, Karim tells me, though his own mother bakes bread at their apartment in the *nouvelle ville*. Other than a few holes in a tiled kitchen stove, most Fesi homes contain only a *kanoun,* or freestanding charcoal-burning brazier of sun-baked clay. Here sauces, couscous, and tagines simmer on glowing coals. Buying bread is considered almost sacrilege. True, the cafés and food shops of the *nouvelle ville* serve up their signature croissants and baguettes, but the feisty, transplanted country people who populate Fès-el-Bali consider these French staples second-rate. Morocco has been independent since 1956. To cultural purists, the croissant, the essence of *nouvelle ville* yuppie fare, is an affront to precolonial authentic Morocco, whether Arabic or Berber. And why, they wonder, would anyone buy bread when they can avail themselves of a nearly flawless communal baking system that does the trick today as well as it served people in the time of Moses?

Medina women prepare bread dough every morning without exception. They knead the dough in a *gsaa,* a round dish, big as a café table, crafted locally of unglazed baked clay or carved oak, olive or walnut wood. Every day they turn out several loaves of the simple bread called *ksra.* The typical bourgeois Fesi family feeds thirty or more people. Laborers who won't return from work for a proper lunch set out with a hunk of bread, which they eat at midday along with olives and sour milk.

"Why do you care so much about *bread?*" the meticulously Euro-clad Karim grouses as we take our third espresso break at a sidewalk café, by the Bab al Jaloud gate. Here is why: Man has been making bread for eight thousand years, and Fès is a rare living museum of the last millennium. Here bread is the glue of community and the currency of human relations; Muslims place bread — *xoobz* — not flowers or stones, on the graves of their loved ones and that bread is the traditional sustenance in the holy month of Ramadan. Toiling before our eyes are descendants of the ancestral chain of bakers and millers born to what truly may be the planet's second-oldest profession. Here a person can see the world in a grain of wheat. I've answered his question, but Karim feels we've hounded enough bakers for one day, and hails a cab.

Karim takes me to the stylish Café Aswan in the *nouvelle ville*. Arranged like an orchestra pit, its tables face the busy Boulevard Mohammed V and draw its traffic with magnetic regularity. I could certainly linger here, nibbling on almond pastry and watching elegant Arabs murmur into cell phones. But every minute I spend here is a minute apart from the drama of the medina. I can't bear to be away from it. I have stood on snowy alpine summits and ocean bluffs, I've trudged through rain forests and paddled a kayak through schools of dolphin, but nothing holds my senses hostage like the pungent mob scene of the bazaar. And Fès-el-Bali is the mother of them all.

The bakeries are spread generously and reliably throughout the old city, and I suspect my nose could lead me easily to any one of them. But I'd never find my way back. Foreigners do not enter the medina alone; it simply isn't done. There are no proper maps of the maze of streets and alleyways that make up Fès-el-Bali, which dates to its establishment in 809 by Idriss II, a member of Morocco's first Arab dynasty. (The Karaouinyine Mosque, founded in 862, is one of the world's oldest universities and remains the pride of Fès.) The medina has been continuously inhabited ever since. But no one ever got around to naming the streets, or even drawing a proper map. "Our medina streets were narrow, dark and serpentine — filled with so many twists and turns that cars could not enter, and foreigners could not find their way out if they ever dared to come in," writes Fès-born Fatima Mernissi in *Dreams of Trespass*, her memoir of a harem childhood. "This was the real reason the French had to build a new city for themselves; they were afraid to live in ours." The medina's centuries-old refusal to bare itself for visitors' convenience is part of what makes the place irresistible. In a time when data collectors are poking into every natural and manmade nook and cranny I'm grateful for the few locales that elude them.

But it's frustrating, too. I long to wander on my own, to get lost and found and lost again, the way I have in Venice or Calcutta. No one knows how many people live in the medina, named by UNESCO as a Heritage of Mankind City, sharing the honor with the Old City of Jerusalem. Old Arab Fesis die off and their children and grandchildren migrate to the *nouvelle ville* while a stream of Berbers, who make up about half of Morocco's population, descend from the surrounding mountains. Once an exclusively rural tribal people, the Berbers are to Morocco what Indians are to North America. Non-Arabs, they dominated all of northwest Africa before the Arab conquest in the seventh century A.D. Though most Berbers speak Moroccan Arabic, their own language dances among three hundred dialects and is rarely, if ever, written. I fell in love with their colored robes and garish headscarves. They look as if they've come bearing frankincense, licorice, and myrrh, and, in fact, many of them do. From the desert and the scrubby highlands the Berbers brought with them a variety of unleavened specialty breads, including the kind of flat bread that can be baked by burying the dough in the hot desert sand. In the medina, Arab-owned bread stalls employ only Berber women to stretch crepe-like dough over a hot globe. "Only Berbers know to work the dough this way," one shopkeeper told me, motioning to a dark woman with leathery hands.

A self-contained hive in perpetual flux, the medina is home to anywhere from a hundred thousand to three hundred thousand people, depending on the whims of *les guides,* the government-sanctioned guides who lurk outside Fès's hotels clad in white robes and red fezzes. These passive-aggressive entrepreneurs have at least one quality in common: their talent for fabrication. When Howie and I stopped to browse in one of the medina's Judaica shops our guide, Benani, instructed us that each of the menorah's nine candlesticks represents one member of the family. "You have a big family, you light more candles," he explained. Howie and I nodded wearily, not in the mood for launching a lecture. Besides, we're a bit hazy on the details ourselves. It wasn't long ago that I thought a Maccabee was a type of cookie.

Still, *d'aller sans guide* is a risky proposition. Even if we were equipped with some primal homing device preventing us from being defeated by the medina's dense coil of look-alike streets, having a licensed guide in tow is the only effective way of scaring off swarms of would-be guides, referred to as *les faux guides*. False guides are as wisely avoided, and ultimately a lot more irritating than false prophets. Official guides are easy to spot, if not for their operatic costume then for the laminated identification cards that swing from their necks. But *les faux guides* run the gamut from enterprising wannabes (many official guides got their start this way) to money-grubbing predators, to the universally vilified *fumeurs de hashish*. Most ubiquitous are the ragged prepubescents promising a *petit* price in keeping with their stature. These are the hardest to shake off. They buzz around you with the tenacity of mosquitoes until you either hire them, which is ultimately the same as adopting them, or beat a breathless retreat back to the sanctum of the hotel. Nothing amuses an official guide more than watching the poor slob who spurned his services being harassed by a *faux guide* of any age.

Within the apparent insanity of the medina there is a surprising level of order. Its confounding sprawl is really a mosaic of distinct squares, each with its own mosque, Koranic school, fountain, *hamam,* or bath, and, of course, a bakery. One guide put the number of these squares conservatively at 150, another told me 800, but most sources point to the lower number. Wrapped around the squares are districts specializing in a particular form of commerce or craft. I suppose I could eventually orient myself by the districts — the tanners, woodworkers and metalsmiths, millers, the gold souk, the henna souk, and the textile districts, where weavers toil as they have for centuries. And there are always the distant mountains, the minaret of the great mosque, and the ramparts of the king's humble pied-à-terre, an eighty-two-acre palace at the edge of Fès-el-Jdid, the Andalusian quarter that once was home to thousands of Jews expelled from Spain. There is still a synagogue and a well-maintained Jewish cemetery there.

The medina's communal bakery system functions in perfect sync with the work at home, performed by an army of prep cooks. In every household in the medina matriarchs, daughters, or servants devote part of their day to kneading the bread they'll enjoy fresh with each supper. This enterprise is not the relaxing ritual familiar to Vermont earth mothers or upwardly mobile owners of Williams Sonoma bread machines. Like everything pertaining to Fesi cuisine it's a labor-intensive proposition. Many families first buy the wheat itself, which they lug home in sacks from crammed narrow stalls in the medina market. Picked over, rinsed, and laid to dry on sunwashed terraces and rooftops, the wheat is then hauled back to the local miller, who grinds it into four flours, each with its special purpose. Howie and I stood mesmerized at the millers' stalls as coarse and fine powders rained from stone grinding mills we'd witnessed only within the precious confines of the ye olden theme parks scattered about our own New England. From the cleaned, groomed whole wheat comes a soft pure flour for the bread, a white semolina for couscous, a coarse golden semolina from the bran, or coating, and the bran itself, destined not for muffins but for the family mule. Aside from what floats into the atmosphere not one speck or kernel is wasted.

In a culture haunted by blood memories of deprivation and famine, bread embodies the blessing of sustenance. As it is to Jews, to Muslims bread is a gift and a blessing. Even the kneading of the dough in the immense *gsaa* is preceded by an invocation to Allah.

Though all were originally built for this purpose, some of the bakeries still share their immense hearths with the *hamam*, the public baths. To visit the inner sanctum of the medina's bakeries, most of which are below street level, is to descend into an ancient, deliberate world. At these bakeries hundreds of identical, rounded durum semolina loaves, each the size of a dinner plate, are hurriedly plunked down on a table near the entrance. The baker or his assistant snatches the trays of loaves. When the loaves emerge baked, each is fetched by a member, friend, or servant of the families who will dunk the bread into their evening *harira* (soup). Nothing is written down, few words are spoken, nothing is labeled.

Karim grudgingly obliges me as we troop into one bakery after another. My feeble attempts at research resemble a Sid Caesar routine. I ask a basic question and Karim rolls his eyes and launches a lengthy harangue that makes the baker roll his eyes as well. The baker offers an equally lengthy reply, which Karim translates back to me in four words or less. I am close to becoming the laughingstock of the old city. Later that day when I sack Karim, he makes an initial show of being bewildered. But he's clearly relieved. Fortunately I've got other names given me by a contact at the Moroccan Tourist Bureau in New York. How I wish my Arabic weren't confined to hello, please, thank you, I'd like some water, and God is Great.

From our hotel I phone Brahmin Snikah, the man I hope will be Karim's replacement. An official guide in his thirties, he's a friend of a friend of a helpful man at the Moroccan Embassy in Washington. When I reach him he's just returned from a vacation in Spain, and agrees to act unofficially, in plainclothes, as my interpreter. We'll meet him the next morning, but as he's helping us on the sly we must go to a café in the *nouvelle ville,* and from there enter the medina surreptitiously, far from the Palais Jamai and its gaggle of notoriously competitive *guides officiel.*

Tourists tend to return home with grim tales about Morocco, but those tales seem never to apply to Fès. Perhaps too many foreigners experience only the port of Tangier, which they reach by ferry from Spain and march off the boat's gangway like lambs to the slaughter. Tangier is all the things squeamish travelers fear: it is grimy, predatory, noisy, and conspiratorial. But it is cleaner and no more dangerous than many parts of New York City. In truth, Morocco is one of the cleanest countries I've visited. Its airports and train stations are glaringly immaculate, perpetually swept and polished. A random piece of litter on a Moroccan train platform stands out like a fly in an operating room. In the medina, sweepers emerge in force each dawn to relieve the dank alleys and market streets of cigarette butts, animal dung, and flotsam from fruit and vegetable stalls. Okay, so they dump a lot of the stuff in a shallow stream of septic sludge known as the Fès River. The guide had led us there and with a sweep of his arm announced *"Oued Fès"* with obvious pride. Howie paused to make a drawing and I started to gag.

But the stink of Morocco, where it rears its head, is not the stench of sulfurous heavy industry. Slightly larger than California, Morocco is a country of farmers and artisans. A leading producer of sugarcane and sugar beets, it exports wheat, tomatoes, potatoes, oranges, melons, olives, grapes, and dates, and its three mountain ranges and fertile valleys are home to some 17 million sheep, nearly 6 million goats, and 3.5 million cattle. It is a country that persists, fairly successfully, in producing goods that are edible, wearable, decorative, or utilitarian. And its artistic heart is the blue city, Fès.

I ask Nadjia, the secretary at the Arabic Institute, to take me shopping. Fluent in English and French, she grew up in the medina and will take me to the gold market where I hope to buy a small Islamic charm, the ubiquitous hand of Fatima, a symbol that pays homage to the great cross-dressing warrior and Mohammed's favorite daughter.

Walking the medina's market streets is a sensory extravaganza on the level of snorkeling. Your mind seesaws from minute detail to overall, kaleidoscopic sweep. Here an airborne chorus line of candy-colored *djellabahs*, there an Everest of polished dates. Your nose rivets you to a bucket overflowing with neroli blossoms tended by a portly Berber matron wrapped in what looks like magenta crepe paper. But soon something else flashes at the corner of your vision and you pivot to face a palette of red, orange, and brown spices and soon the scent of cumin and neroli perfume are battling for your nose's undivided attention. Eyes trained down or skyward there are things to marvel at — carvings and mosaics and friezes and rugs and teapots and doorways revealing the contours of men bowed in prayer. It's a medieval world without the pestilence — everything bared for the consumer, the head and hoofs of the slaughtered beast beside its meat, the woodworkers' lathes and rugmakers' looms clicking and humming in the shadow of the goods themselves. Metal and leatherworkers ply their trades while squatting in crammed cubbyholes, on perpetual display like windows on an advent calendar. Most stupefying are the tanneries, ground zero of all the medina's anachronistic enterprises. Breathing in fumes so acrid visitors hack and gasp, turbaned bare-legged men pop up and down like jack-in-the-boxes as they use their bodies to dredge wool and hides within a vast many-hued honeycomb of stinking tubs. Drying skins cover all the surrounding rooftops. Gnarled heaps of wool resemble the aftermath of some ghastly massacre.

As I lurch cluelessly onward veiled strangers yank me out of the path of oncoming mules and handcarts. Ragged children flash their teeth and call *"Bonjour, madame!* Hello!" "Hold on tight to your purse," says Nadjia.

"I do all my shopping in the medina; the quality is so much better and you get much more for your money here," says Nadjia. "But you have to know what you want." Here is a fraction of what you can buy: flat bread, pastry, sesame candy, flour, henna, kohl, pots and pans, teapots, fresh mint, orange blossoms, gold, silver, wood, brass, copper, leather, embroidered trousseau towels and sheets, tobacco, yogurt, newspapers, combs carved from bone, calculators, televisions, boom boxes, and tape cassettes of music from Morocco, Spain, Syria, and Egypt as well as American country-and-western. There are stalls whose merchants peek out from behind great surging buttes of fresh fruit, figs, dates, pine nuts, almonds, and pistachios. In rapid succession like flipped pages of a *gastronomique* are Berber soft cheese, chicken necks, goat heads, snails, and towers of silvery fish the size of peapods. There are shoes, sweaters, and ready-to-wear *djellabahs* and tailor shops at every turn. Too, too many eggs beckon from every food stall. Vermicelli overflows from sacks as huge as couches, and herbal pharmacies peddle painted deserts of cumin, coriander, saffron, cinnamon, paprika, and chiles. An earthen-colored mix combining anywhere from ten to a hundred spices, the *ras el hanout,* or "head of the shop," differs from stall to stall, each of which uses its own secret recipe. There are preserved lemons; pots of *harissa,* a tongue-searing paste of garlic, chiles, olive oil, and salt; and black olive–oil soap cakes, and for buffing the skin, palm-sized pills of sandalwood wrapped in wooden snoods. I linger spellbound by one of several stalls offering just fat, a Fats-R-Us crammed with vats of lard and gristle, and something else dark and gooey and unidentifiable. "What is it?" I ask in French, and the proprietor motions for me to stick my finger in and take a taste. I'm relieved to find it is sweet, some kind of fig and nut compote. (It is probably what condemns me to violent intestinal eruptions that will last through the night.)

Howie is fixated on the lack of refrigeration. He cannot stop harping on the fate of those unsold hunks of beef and goat meat, those chicken and pigeon carcasses that bake in the sun.

"I hate shopping," a politically correct friend of mine always insists. I find the statement nearly as shocking as if she'd said she hated animals. There is nothing more human than the marketplace, and the teeming bazaars and souks of the East and the farmers' markets all over the world are reminders that commerce is the oldest most enduring universal language. When a nation's in crisis we see images of babushka-clad matrons bargaining for a bruised potato or a rotting turnip. Commerce is the first sign of life after a calamity. Consider the concession stalls sprung, as if by spontaneous generation, from the primordial despair of the refugee camp. In Fès shopping for staples can easily fill the day. It sounds like everyone's fighting but it's just the routine spirited dialogue of buyer and merchant. A woman may spend hours — as long as it takes — marching indignantly from stall to stall, retracing her steps until she gets the price she wants on a sack of tomatoes. Foreigners tend to be mystified by this. But just imagine the ruckus if, say, the price of smoked salmon at Zabar's were negotiable.

Twenty-nine and unmarried, Nadjia lives with her invalid mother in the *nouvelle ville*, not far from the Arabic Institute. A pleasantly buxom woman with heavy lipstick and styled hair, she wears tight Western clothing and high heels half chewed by gravel and cobblestones. Does she hope to marry? "I have a friend in Casa," she tells me over coffee at a rooftop café in the medina. "Casa" is Moroccans' nickname for Casablanca, the nation's most modernized city and the one offering the most employment opportunities for young professionals. This "friend," a salesman Nadjia met when he had some business with the institute, is as immersed in his career as Nadjia is in hers as administrative secretary, an enviable post for a young Moroccan woman. Sometimes they meet up with friends for a long weekend in Marrakesh, but neither can envision moving for good. As for the local men, Nadjia dismisses the situation as hopeless. "Either they're young and they don't want to marry, or they're young and have no money, or they're old and have money and want someone as a second wife," she says.

As Nadjia and I roam the tunnel-like

medina streets at random she points out the many incarnations of bread. We side-step miniature matterhorns of fried, honey-glazed pastry. This is a seasonal treat. It is a week before the eve of the month of Ramadan and these sweets are to Ramadan what fruitcake is to Christmas. You just glance at the stuff and someone is urging a sticky wad of it on you, no charge for mademoiselle. Nadjia has a stomach ulcer and can be excused from the month of dawn-to-dusk fasting. But I'm surprised to learn that when she keeps the fast she tends to gain as many as eight pounds. Do explain, I say, expecting vindication. I can't even bring myself to stop snarfing down food for the twenty-four hours of Yom Kippur, a day when Jews are required to fast.

Ramadan falls on the ninth month of the Islamic calendar, when God first revealed the Koran to the prophet Mohammed. Most non-Muslims tend to think of it as the glum, self-flagellation fest, and in fact sub-Saharan nations refer to the holiday grimly as the "month of thirst." Pre-pubescents and menstruating women as well the old, sick, or traveling are exempt from the fast, which forbids not just eating but smoking, drinking, sexual intercourse, lying, and malicious gossip. But Nadjia explains that the month actually revolves around eating. It's a kind of daily Thanksgiving feast, every table perpetually cluttered with candies and cakes. After sunset, or that moment when, according to the Koran, the light has waned enough that a black and white thread appear the same, the eating begins, and it doesn't stop until first light. Looking forward to another foodless, smokeless, even drinkless day, people observing Ramadan tend to eat like there's no tomorrow.

The guide Brahmin Snikah has returned from vacation in time to be with his family for Ramadan. He is a soft-spoken, articulate Fesi whose passion for the medina rivals our own. There is no census of bakeries, he says, but he guesses the number to be at least three hundred. He guides us to the granaries, where we peer through the grainy dust at the millers, squatting and lost in the rhythm of their task. All day long in the medina, groaning millstones spill forth sack after sack of coarse yellow wheat and cornmeal, dusting the stone floors and the street and the mustaches of the mostly Berber laborers.

There is no inhabitant of the medina who is not within walking distance of a bakery. The bakeries are close enough so that even tiny children can carry the tray of uncooked loaves there and deposit them wordlessly just inside the baker's door. We often saw such children dawdling in the souks or horsing around with each other as the loaves slid precariously to one edge of the tray and then to the other. Brahmin, son of a typical Moroccan matriarch, assures us there'd be hell to pay if the loaves were lost. And what about those few married women whom tradition confines to the home? If there is no husband or child to spirit away the day's loaves, how do these women manage? A Fesi man told me the women simply set the tray outside the door. "Someone," he said, "an acquaintance or neighbor, will take the bread to the bakery, and return it later to that same spot."

It would be nearly accurate to say that if you've seen one of the medina's bakeries, you've seen them all. Most are built back to back with the *hamam*, the public bath, which draws its heat from the bakers' deep stone hearth. Behind its veil of chaos the medina is a model of conformity and predictability. The bakers never try to undersell each other. From the banks of the Oued Fès to the Bab al Jaloud gate the baking charge per loaf is five dirhams, about forty cents. No bakery promises swifter service than his nearest competitor. It takes Ahmed as long to bake a bread as it takes Abdul, and some mystical market force appears to ensure that no one baker has more loaves than he can handle.

If there was a difference in ambiance from bakery to bakery, it eluded me. Descending into one such establishment after another I witnessed the same tableau: makeshift shelves of round loaves, a worker or two crouching by the wood- or dung-fired hearth working the baking breads with an immense ramallah, or peel.

On the eve of Ramadan, the bakeries also produce tray upon tray full of *chekbakeit*, the ubiquitous holiday sweet. These are also cranked out by small-scale bakers scattered throughout the souks. Selling directly from their stalls, these bakers offer a variety of crepes, pancakes, and flat breads. In the hottest and narrowest of market stalls I watch a Berber woman with henna-stenciled hands pour batter on hot globes for *gneunboura*, a spicy pancake that must be peeled off the globes with expert delicacy. "It's a uniquely Berber skill, passed down from generation to generation," says Brahmin, echoing what another shopkeeper had told me about this being, now and for always, an exclusively Berber craft. There is also the *trid,* or crepe, and *milhoui,* a semolina flat bread that's cousin to India's nan. "But when we say Moroccan bread, we mean the bread you see here," says Brahmin, gesturing to a waiting line of round loaves at Mohammed's bakery.

Most of Mohammed's customers drop off their loaves in the morning, and some may return for them in as soon as an hour. If the breads aren't all collected by closing time — eight in the evening — Mohammed or his son Abdul will carry the loaves to the family's home or leave the bread in the coffee shop next door or pass it on to some other intermediary. By suppertime customers are reunited with their loaves, which may, like a friendly cat, have traveled among many hands. Women prepare the dough, of course, but there is not one woman baker in all of the medina. "The bakery is man's work," says Mohammed. "Home work is for the ladies, outside work for men."

Though only some carve their initial into the bottom of the loaf, and the marks are often indistinguishable, it is extremely rare, if ever, that a customer returns home with the wrong bread. "People would get really furious," says Brahmin. "Oh, that would be just terrible," said Nadjia when I asked her about it. To hear them talk of it, the gaffe would be less like getting the wrong shirt from the Chinese laundry and more like getting the wrong dog from the kennel. The notion is utterly unacceptable.

But how can this be? I watch a stream of Mohammed's customers come and go, depositing trays of uncooked loaves and snatching up cooked ones. All the while his baker is rearranging the loaves in the "modern" hearth, one of only twenty-one in the medina with crude heat controls. "My bread is cleaner and baked more evenly," says Mohammed, who learned the trade from his father and passed it along to his son. "In other bakeries the bread is close to the wood; in this one it is close only to the brick." Mohammed's modern hearth is lit from within, an unusual feature even though the medina has had electricity for nearly a century. It's not Mohammed's snazzy hearth that stirs my awe. It's the fact that his baker must do more than recall which loaves ended up where to begin with, but where he moved them to — a kind of bakers' three-card monte. I'm trying to pay attention and already I've lost the game.

"Come," says Mohammed, and I obey. He places a bread on my outstretched left palm, another on my right. "Feel," he commands. Though they look identical, one bread is crusty and dry, the other soft and springy to the touch. It occurs to me briefly that I'm busy pawing the bread that will accompany someone's evening meal, but Mohammed takes the breads away and replaces them with two others. Mohammed needs no further identifying characteristics than the weight, hue, and feel of the bread, all of which differ from loaf to loaf. "See the difference in color," he says. Howie joins in, and so does Brahmin, and soon we're all earnestly sniffing, palpating, and tossing around various breads of which, I concede, no two are precisely alike — not even to the baker who blithely rearranges them deep in the hearth, some beyond his vision. A bread, explains Mohammed, is as individual as a person's face, or voice. Mrs. X's dough is dense and heavy, Mrs. Y's overkneaded and airy. Mrs. K's loaves are as perfectly round as if shaped with a ring mold, Mrs. P's faintly elliptical. Not that Mohammed would ever critique the loaves to these women's faces. "Everyone wants hers to be the lightest bread," he says, winking at me.

So, I inquire, rather stupidly, as it turns out, "What if someone new comes in? How will you knew that person's bread?" Mohammed groans and rolls his eyes in disbelief. "If it's someone new, of course I'll remember," he cries. "We always remember what is new!"

Howie and I hand a bundle of dirhams to Mohammed and some pens to his young helper, and Mohammed sends us off with a sticky clump of *chekbakeit*. As we wend our way home I ask Brahmin to let me navigate. With great confidence I march us in the exact opposite direction of our hotel, the Palais Jamai. I'm angry with myself. Mohammed has me thinking about the virtues of attentiveness to the subtlest detail and here I am unable to distinguish one narrow street from the next. But that is why Mohammed does what he does, day after day, keeping alive a system in which Fès's bustling communities are woven and interwoven as tightly as those Berber carpets thrust in our faces at every turn.

Sore and spent from a day of pounding the medina's uneven pavement, I decide to treat myself to the *hamam* at the hotel. Palais Jamai's *hamam* is to those frequented by the medina's masses what a Harley Davidson is to a rickshaw. I had visited a public *hamam* in Kusadasi, Turkey, and was treated like an inmate in a medieval asylum. Pummeled, doused, and rubbed raw with something like Ajax, I stumbled onto the street feeling as if I'd been violated by a gang of sailors and tossed into the sea. I felt certain that at these inflated prices, the Palais Jamais *hamam* would be, by contrast, a luxurious experience.

Imagine my surprise when, after stripping down to my underpants, I was led to a steamy cubicle and ordered by a feisty Berber woman named Fatima to lie face down on the soggy tiles. Fatima scoured me with black soap and then, like a deranged physical therapist, yanked my legs this way and that. "Sit up," she commanded, after which she jammed the small of my back down to the floor in what we yoginis call *pachimotanasana,* probably Sanskrit for ouch. Then her strong, hennaed hands went to work on my buttocks and limbs, which she kneaded precisely as if I were, well, a lump of bread dough. I had to smile. We left Fès and headed south into the Middle Atlas, settling in at a chilly mountain guesthouse in the village of Azrou. From there we drove northeast toward Algeria, stopping at the strange whitewashed city of Taza, which appears from afar to be slowly sliding down the mountainside. Then we returned to the Sheraton Fès for a few days before flying home.

As for Christmas, it came and went without a peep.

Madame Guinaudeau's Traditional Moroccan Bread

From Traditional Moroccan Cooking: Recipes from Fez, *by Madame Guinaudeau*

INGREDIENTS:
Two pounds sifted white flour
A handful of salt
One to one-and-a-half pints water
Yeast (dried or cake)

In a deep earthenware pan, mix the flour, salt, and water quickly, stopping before it is a solid mass. After softening the yeast with a little water, place it in a corner of the pan, mix it with the dough, and knead the dough vigorously for at least 20 minutes.

Separate the dough into four parts, reserving one dough ball for the next day's starter. With the palm of your hand, work the remaining dough balls into disks about 8 inches in diameter. Cover the dough with a cloth and allow it to rise until, when pressed lightly with a finger, it springs back to its original shape.

Fesis send the dough to the wood-fired communal oven for baking. In a regular oven bake the bread for about 45 minutes at 375 degrees.

Bread Is My Path:
Saratoga Springs, New York

I will make for you a bread so good that it will never again be used as an accompaniment for other foods; it would be a nourishment in itself, a food for gourmands. One would never again say, "I have eaten a tartine of cheese on some bread." One would say instead, "I have savored a tartine of bread underneath some cheese."
— *LA FEMME DU BOULANGER*
(*THE BAKER'S WIFE*),
MARCEL PAGNOL FILM

Bread is being rescued from oblivion. It's as if it had been locked up in a closet somewhere for years.
— MICHAEL LONDON,
QUOTED IN *TIME*

Bakers tend to be a passionate breed, fond of waxing poetic about their craft. I spent time with two bakers for whom the crafting of the simplest loaves is an act so soulful and so consuming that any discussion of leaven or wood fire is infused with religious and metaphysical fervor. On opposite ends of the country, oblivious to each other's efforts, they turn out what may be the best bread in the country. Or, at least it should rightfully be the best in light of the integrity of its ingredients, the joyful fanaticism of its creators, and the inspired choreography of its preparation. These are not monks, but theirs is breadbaking as an act of love, gratitude, and penance. And the stuff tastes incredible too.

What led me to Michael London was an item in the "Food Stuff" section of *Dining In*, in the *New York Times*. The item described the debut of Rock Hill Reserve, a bread whose creators sought to market it like fine wine. This *pain au levain* was very special. A five-pound loaf costs $18. Intrigued, I arranged to travel to Saratoga Springs, New York, and meet the man behind this bread.

"Bread is my inner path."

Michael London holds forth at a corner table in his Saratoga Springs patisserie while my dog Louie and I share a buttered *pain au levain* slab that could double as the insole of a men's size-ten shoe. The completely, utterly-from-scratch pastries crafted here by London and his wife Wendy are deservedly famous. The late George Balanchine confessed an addiction to Mrs. London's, sustenance for him and his company in this summer home of the New York City Ballet. Married in the lull between an apple crumb tart and a cheesecake, the Londons are the Steve and Edyie of the trade, belting out harmonies in gâteau and ganache. Their vacations amount to bakery tours of the great capitals of Europe. But the pastries are a dalliance next to London's profound, almost mournful love of bread. When it comes to leaven, crust, and crumb the possibilities tug at London's soul, offering no respite. He feels your *pain.* The most respectable homemade or bakery bread is to London's loaves what Astroturf is to a poppy field in Provence. Once a professor of poetry, he speaks of bread in a torrent of allusion and metaphor, quoting William Carlos Williams, Henry Miller, and the Kabbalah. His bread is alive, his bread has its own primal rhythm, his bread is "the guru." The baker needs "real fire," well water, and grains possessing the life force. The bread's loving preparation, akin to the "birthing process," must be made to coexist with the rising of the sun, the cycles of the moon. The baker cannot hurry the bread. Like wine, 90 percent of which is "made on the vine," the bread "makes itself," opines London. The baker is nothing more than "an attendant priest, a steward." The true baker's fire is nothing less than sacramental.

On outward appearance London doesn't look like the kind of man who cavorts with bread fairies. Tall and solidly built, with a gourmand's paunch, he's a youthful fifty-three with a zealot's bottomless energy for thoughtful, allusion-crammed banter. His small spectacles and healthy crown of combed-back salt-and-pepper hair make London look like the college professor he used to be and the country gent he is today. His features are kindly, small, and intent, like those you'd prefer in a therapist.

"One night years ago, close to Thanksgiving, I went out at about eleven to make the starter for the morning's bread," a rapt London recalls, his body arched forward over the tiny café table. "That afternoon I'd said the Hebrew prayer for the dead. And that night, under a full moon I saw a cartoonish mandala, made of forms dancing around the roof of the bakehouse. I ran back to the house to wake Wendy, but when we got there the forms were all gone. The next day I told our baker about this strange experience — those shapes dancing in a circle like Casper the ghost. He told me he'd seen the very same thing that night, after he threw a sacrificial bread into the fire. I learned that there are salamander spirits, elemental beings behind the fire. And I think it's important as a baker to get these elemental beings as your allies."

I have no idea what London is talking about. When he is on a roll, so to speak, there is nothing to say. "Uh-huh," I murmur, scrawling away. Would a layman dare comment to Michelangelo on the nature of marble? Would a Cordon Bleu student point out to Jacques Pepin that his delicately whittled kiwi looks more like a frog than a swan? What do most of us, listening to NPR while keeping vigil at our pathetic, PAM-stained gas ranges, know of real fire, of the awesome, fragile power of the hottest heat, of the virtues of brick crafted from volcanic ash native to the palisades of a range somewhere in the wilds of Germany?

I am still working on this slice of bread, or, more accurately, The Bread. At the time of its conception, the late 1980s, this same firebread was like no other in New York, if not the entire U.S., says London, with characteristic modesty. This was the bread of the European countryside. But, like all things *sauvage,* the bread was unpredictable, a risky venture. It took London two years of tinkering to approximate a *pain au levain* equal, or nearly so, to that of the exalted Parisian Lionel Poilâne. "Our bread came out of *us,*" says London. "It had big holes and a tangy flavor. It wasn't made with yeast. When our bakery closed for a few years Wendy told me to do what was in my heart of hearts, and that was, of course, crafting the bread. I bought a $27,000 oven without a single account. But we knew we had the bread. We'd send a few cartons to the city with shipments from a local smokehouse. Soon the phone calls came, from Balducci's, from Dean & DeLuca."

As it turns out, the ethereal realm of salamander spirits and the Visa checkout aisle at Dean & DeLuca are not far apart. At Manhattan's Union Square Greenmarket, this same bread — London's Rock Hill Reserve five-pound firebread — sells for $18 a loaf. The loaves sell on Mrs. London's Web site for $20. To handle the increased distribution Joshua London, London's son from a previous marriage, joined the business along with a stepbrother and a friend. When people balk at the price, London reminds them that the finished product reflects the passion, sweat, and science of a fine wine. Compared to that wine, says London, the bread is a steal. For one thing, left in a paper bag at room temperature it can keep for weeks. And there is the matter of supply and demand. With a sixty-ton oven said to be unique among all the hearths of North America from the Arctic Circle to the tropics, the Londons can't turn out more than a hundred five-pound loaves a day. They use only certified biodynamically grown wheat the cultivation and harvesting of which ensures not only the health of the soil but "the creative shaping forces of the cosmos on the plant." I half expect London to boast that the grain is irrigated with the tears of angels, the harvest consummated by virgins under a full moon. "To make bread you need real fire, pure water, and the grain must be alive. In Holland, you know, they've done tests to confirm the life force of foods."

To skeptics, for whom the Bakehouse Hill spiel might arouse the appetite as much as a flask of ipecac, I say, just taste it. Wrap your jaw around a hunk of that bread. London's firebread is exquisite, a dense crusty pillow bearing lines and scars like a tribal chieftain. Inside, the crumb is a fragrant moonscape of shaped peaks and shallows. Each slice bears the fingerprints of fresh yeast cultures harvested from the dewy glaze on wild grapes with a tenderness and vigilance approaching the attentions paid to a beloved puppy. It's true. This bread is alive.

To London the mass production of bread — of all food — is a personal affront. Who can deny that our palates have been raped and violated, that our assembly-line culture deprives us of any sensual memory of the earth's true gifts? Like his hero Rudolf Steiner, who put forth a "science of the spirit" and dubbed it anthroposophy, London sees his bread as an affirmation of the deepest self-knowledge. That it makes a mean crostini seems to concern him less. Though its taste may please us we don't know whether our food is delicious in the way nature intended because we have nothing with which to compare it. We poor schmoes don't even know what we're missing. We dwell within reach of the proverbial banquet and we're starving to death. We've been eating the ersatz form our entire lives. "How many people know the taste of a real raisin?" asks London. I joke with him about the "vegetables" we consumed at our postwar suburban family table. They flopped listlessly out of cans in an odious yellowish liquid. Broccoli, string beans, peas — all were equally mushy and khaki-colored. The first time I saw a bright green broccoli floret I thought there was something wrong with it. I could not conceive of people actually laboring to remove great numbers of fresh peas from pods. And bread? These days were full of Wonder, with fresh bagels and onion rye on Sundays.

Ever the inquisitive child, London wondered why any self-respecting Jewish boy in the heart of Brooklyn should have to consume bland, mass-produced bread. Right there on the miniature Eastern Europe that spread across Eastern Parkway and along Flatbush Avenue were bakers following the recipes of the Polish and Romanian shtetl. The young London coveted their onion *pletzel* and their cinnamon *babka*. While his peers focused their energies on making lots of figurative dough, London lusted after the real thing.

Okay, this could be any baker's made-for-*Biography* story. But what possesses a man to produce bread so labor-intensive that the endeavor ends up costing him money? I have to wonder: What would I think of this bread had I not known Michael London's journey, from a feisty youth haunting the bakeries of Brooklyn's Eastern Parkway, to the owner of a custom-built oven costing as much as a second house? The reluctant visitor prowling the galleries of the Museum of Modern Art sees only a vast canvas of black and groans dismissively, but would he react the same way if he could see the artist sparring with the canvas in his studio, working the brush, the textures?

The son of deaf parents, Michael London likes to talk, which is fortunate for me. The more he talks, the more time I have to sample the bread, a croissant, and the pastries in the place. I'm starting to feel a little queasy but the tartlets and tortes keep appearing at our table. Louie's conked out under my seat. London's childhood neighborhood, Brooklyn's Eastern Parkway, hasn't changed all that much in the half century since he was born. In the late sixties London taught literature and poetry at Saratoga's Skidmore College. He'd returned from a pilgrimage to California to meet his inspiration, the novelist

Henry Miller. What spoke to London most was Miller's essay lament, connecting the decline of America's spirit to the fall, the "demoralization" of its bread.

Miller's words lodged themselves into London's brain with such tenacity a *New Yorker* cartoon–style cross section of that organ would have revealed a separate and distinct lobe labeled "bread." Back in New York and living in Manhattan, London paid the rent by balancing platters of burritos at a Mexican place in the Village. The rest of the time he tinkered in his tiny kitchen like a medieval alchemist, experimenting with bread. By popular demand (his friends gobbled the stuff up) he narrowed his scope to the daily production of a whole-wheat soy loaf inspired by a World War II recipe in *Vegetables for Victory*, by Ambrose Heath. The bread was so beloved he developed a clientele, regulars who awaited the fruits of London's minuscule oven in an apartment not much bigger. He'd deliver the breads on his bicycle. In a surreal twist, his future, second, and forever wife Wendy was also baking bread in her apartment and cycling sacks of it around the Village. How many times did they just miss each other, their mutual view blocked by a passing moving van, their attention waylaid by an approaching siren?

In the Village there was a Sufi-run bakery called Ananda East, which, like Tassajara on the West Coast, blended flour, eggs, and Eastern spirituality. It was the mother church, the largest natural foods bakery in the East. London would hang out there, pestering the bakers for advice and pleading for a job. "Eventually I offered to work there for nothing, to learn," says London. "I wasn't a baker at all." It turned out the owner was on the verge of calling London about a maintenance position at Ananda. "I took the job," said London, who recalls his first night there in inescapable, almost visceral detail. "That night," he says. "That night my brother drowned off Big Sur." The loss fractured London's life into Before and After. With his brother gone in an instant, London's dreams took on a new urgency.

London was baking at Ananda after a month, helping develop a high-protein, nutrient-dense loaf called Cornell Bread. But London was seduced by images of himself at the next level. The way London tells the story I can imagine his life as a Broadway musical. He set his sights uptown and was poised to insinuate himself, Zelig-like into the most high-falutin' kitchens of the bread universe. He was a pest, but who could resist a guy willing to slave away without pay, just to learn? You'd think anyone who wants this badly to bake professionally should be allowed to; it's not as if London decided to become Secretary of State. But no. At the bakers union they delivered the humbling news: you don't ask to be an apprentice, pal. Someone has to come looking for you. London ignored the warning and promptly showed up at Maurice Bonte and wedged himself into the closet-sized bakery hoping to make himself indispensable. From there he made his move to the famed Greenberg's. "I spoke to Mr. G.," says London. "And he told me I was out of my gourd. I kept on going back to him. He told me I was crazy." But five months later, perhaps out of sheer exhaustion, Mr. G., the Mozart of cheesecake, sighed and told the young acolyte, "You can start Monday at four p.m." London was ecstatic. Then he remembered he'd been called to jury duty, starting Monday. If there was a God, He must have wanted London to become a baker. If not, why arrange for the former manager of Sutter's Bakery — one of the few men in New York City able to empathize with

London's plight — to be jury master on that fateful day? London was excused.

For most of that year he padded around Mr. G.'s bakery earning next to nothing, and took vocational classes at a high school on Sixty-eighth and Madison, where he was most certainly the only pupil with a master's degree. The years brought the end of one marriage and the start of another, the birth of a child, then another, and another. Named for London's mother, who now lives in California, Mrs. London's bakery prospered from 1977 until 1985, when they closed it and decided to retreat to the things they loved most. They reopened the bakery at a new location two years ago, after the christening of the firebread oven, which, next to his family, is the love of London's life.

I leave London to his business but he makes me promise I'll be back for lunch. I'm already stuffed to my eyeballs with rich pastries but London has a way of decriminalizing this kind of eating, and I go for it. Just two hours later, at one of Mrs. London's café tables in the sun Louie and I share a warm spinach, pine nut, and Parmesan on focaccia — and then (what else?) dessert.

London's baker Bernard will be making

firebread tonight. I've got enough time to return to the motel and process the ten thousand grams of fat I've consumed. Before long it's time to rouse myself and drive out of town along thirty miles of gently curving country roads, to London's residence and the inner sanctum: the firebread oven.

London has drawn me a map that bears as much relationship to reality as the salamander spirits. What he's drawn as a hairpin turn is a simple left, his interpretation of certain intersections is freer than the curriculum at a Waldorf school. And the Londons' hamlet of Greenwich is not close to Saratoga, it's way out in the middle of nowhere. I backtrack several times, assuming I've missed the house, and Louie is seated upright on full alert in the back of my Jeep. At last I pull up at a white farmhouse nestled in a generous acreage of impossibly green velvety hills. Despite the scourge of slam-bam development, upstate New York still cradles what must be some of the world's most serene, photogenic farms. I feel like I'm in Ireland's County Clare. The air is cloyingly sweet with freshly mowed grass and honeysuckle. London had warned me about his dogs, advising me almost sternly to keep Louie in the car, so I was surprised to encounter not a pack of snarling Omen hounds but a salt-and-pepper shaker set of yapping spaniels, one of them geriatric. The dogs announce my arrival at the main house, a two hundred-year-old Federalist design. It must cost a fortune to keep a house looking this old. I follow London to the cavernous kitchen, comprehensively re-tooled to look more ancient than the one it replaced. The long immaculate room is chock-a-block with marble slabs and butcher block and the serious-looking stainless-steel accoutrements of folks who cook entirely from scratch. Everything is oversized. Fruits and vegetables are arranged like Cézannes in bowls the size of kiddie pools. There is something about foodie kitchens like these that makes me feel a mixture of shame and defiance. I want to seek refuge at the nearest hot dog stand.

Here on the free-range paradise of Rock Hill Farm the cows, chickens, and horses are treated as family and fed fare better than the children at most American public schools. Emma the dairy cow lives contentedly on a diet of eight loaves of whole-wheat and rye breads — the genuine article, from the bakehouse — with some cornmeal and bran thrown in for variety. London discovered the diet in an old French farm journal. This cow may live by bread alone, but she produces at least two gallons of rich creamy milk each day and her offbeat diet has the blessing of the farm's veterinarian.

Bakehouse Hill stands about an eighth of a mile from the main house, halfway up the highest hill for miles around. The barnlike structure appears simply, even hastily built. This is a deception. The bakehouse was built to the specifications of an oven that is to ovens what a Stradivarius is to violins. Constructing it was a complicated, major pain in the ass involving a crew of elite masons and a German master oven setter, and insanely expensive shipments of stone called tuff (pronounced *toof*). Volcanic stone formed from naturally compressed ash, tuff was used to build the old ovens of the Alpine region and throughout Italy.

"You've heard of Pirandello's *Six Characters in Search of an Author*," London tells me as I gape into the mouth of the vast yawning hearth. "Well, I was a baker in search of an oven." There is a cult of masons and through them London learned of a "mythic figure" called Ernst Heuft, a master oven builder living in the Pacific

70

Northwest. "This is a man who dreams about ovens the way I dream about bread." A fifth-generation oven builder whose son is carrying the torch, Heuft was born in the German hamlet of Bell, "Town of Oven Builders." London's friend Dale, the mason who first spoke reverently of Heuft, told London that "If I live to be a hundred I won't know on my little pinky what Ernst knows. You've got to call this fellow."

It began as a telephone courtship in which Heuft rhapsodized about the tuff ovens he'd known, though to his knowledge no one had built one in more than three decades. Heat moves slowly through tuff, formed by the ash of cooled lava, pressed into rock over twenty thousand years. The wait seemed like geological time to London: three long years, after which they got the funds together and sent a first fax to a tuff quarry in Germany. "We sent Ernst back to his homeland to supervise the quarrying," says London. "He was there for about a month."

Because of the grinding the tuff arrived damp. The endeavor wasn't just horrendously costly; it mystified the folks of Washington County, which is known for an abundance of blue stone, perfectly suited to hearth building. Michael and Wendy's oven weighs sixty tons, its thermal mass a layered construction of tuff, sand, and gravel. (By firebread oven standards it is petite, measuring six feet by eighteen feet.)

During its installation London had to work out a last-minute glitch. "Ernst is very exacting — he teaches masonry science," says London. But Ernst thought the oven wouldn't weigh more than ten tons, fifteen at the most. And he'd never before built an oven above the ground, one with a cellar below it. The way the bakehouse was originally designed the finished oven would've crashed through the floor. Unlike most brick or stone ovens, the oven at Bakehouse Hill derives its cooking heat from a wood fire built right on the hearth rather than in a separate firebox. "It took a couple of months to get things right because the cement was curing," says London. "I had to make very slow fires every day, and wrench the steel tie bars tighter and tighter because everything was settling."

A large part of the baker's craft is building and baby-sitting the fire until the heat from the spent embers is the right temperature for baking. The heat is good for no more than a hundred loaves a day.

Inside the bakehouse I find London's

partner Bernard Castellani busy tending the fire. At forty, Bernard shares London's religious devotion to the bread. As for Castellani's origins, a God-playing geneticist could not have engineered a more suitable hybrid for the job: half-Provençale, half Tuscan. Bernard's tousled curls and moody features are a cross between a Michelangelo and a pugilist. In addition to the bread, he and London share a reverence for Rudolf Steiner, particularly Steiner's belief in country bread as a "complete food" embodying the life-giving forces of all the elements. The fermentation of the leaven should always extend over midnight. London and Bernard choose firewood according to which best suits the grain — beechwood for wheat breads, pine for rye — and even the time of year in which the tree was felled. Steiner had much to say about the actual milling, too. He believed the miller should maintain "harmonious proportions" between water flow, the size of the wheel, and the size of the millstone, according to London. Also, the milling itself should be done by the grains "rubbing and jostling each other and that the transmission from the cogwheel to the spindle be in the proportion of seven to twelve or twelve to seven."

Passing the time with London and Bernard even as they sniff rising dough and tinker with the fire, bread is almost irrelevant, a by-product of a marathon, ritualized communion with the forces of nature. That a loaf of Rock Hill Reserve is likely to grace the table of a celebrity dinner party at a prewar duplex in Gramercy Park is of little interest to London, and utterly irrelevant to Bernard. Dusted with flour and wearing a trading bead strung on a rawhide choker, he looks rather *sauvage* himself.

Both men are obsessed with the fire. Bernard is just as busy chopping and carting firewood as he is with the rising loaves. "We realized we shared a similar path and passion," London says of Bernard, who ran a bakery in the Luberon region of Provence called *Le Fournil de Merindol,* known for its fragrant herb, nut, and olive breads. Bernard takes his instruction from the writings of Steiner and his belief in "etheric forces." "We both discovered that, all things considered, bread makes itself, in the same way 90 percent of a great wine is made on the vine," London says of Bernard. "And we realized we were stewards of bread, attendant priests, so to speak, and the degree to which we were attuned to the breadmaking process was the extent the bread revealed itself to us." A purist who dismisses even most so-called American artisan bread as "dead as chewing gum," Bernard is equally disgusted with the bread in France. *"Le problem c'est le ble,"* the wheat, says Bernard, who bakes for London three nights a week. The wheat isn't fresh, or organic, its nutrients are depleted. "My mother-in-law once lost my grain and I have to hide my anger," says Bernard. "I have true passion for the grain." The biodynamic wheat used in the firebread is grown in North Dakota according to the phases of the moon. For the hallowed dough Bernard uses water from a pure spring two hundred feet deep, unrefined sea salt, and a small amount of chestnut flour.

Though both London and Bernard know bread like a surgeon knows the belly, they are willing for their efforts to be complicated by the hardness, or high-protein level of the biodynamic flour. The higher the protein level the higher the gluten content. The biochemical soul of leavening, gluten is the elastic component of flour that captures bubbles from the fermentation of the yeast. Most artisan bakers prefer a lower-gluten flour with a protein content of about 12 percent. London's breads tend to be more dense. "That's fine," says London. "I don't give a flying fuck about those specs. We're not looking for voluminous bread. We're looking for delicious bread. And I want the bread to be a certain color, that's all I'm looking at. These organic mills don't have sophisticated enough equipment to come out with the right extraction for us. But look," he says, inviting me to plunge my fingers into a small flour bowl. "This is beautiful, maybe even lighter than we need."

Commercial yeast is another scourge. Most breads are far too yeasty, says London. As it is with wine, fermentation should be slow. When London speaks of his levain starter, he waves an arm to encompass the sweep of his farm. "We have wild grapes growing here," he says. "Ever notice the cast of musty color on an organic grape? That's wild yeast, and that's all it takes. There are these wild spores in the air, and all we do is to lasso these spores and get them into a starter or culture. People speak of inoculating the bread," says London. "But I prefer *seeding*." Any flour-and-water made with wheat flour, which contains the protein gluten, will rise if it's left exposed to the outside air, which abounds with the spores of wild yeasts. Given time, fermentation will progress without the warm temperatures at which most bread bakers are taught to nudge the yeast along. When he joined a *National Geographic* project to recreate the first leavened bread of the ancient Egyptians, Idaho sourdough scholar Ed Wood captured wild yeast cultures from the terrace of his hotel in Giza. London extracts some starter from the fridge to offer me a sniff. I have grown to love the beer-like odor, and I'm prepared to discuss such visceral matters as relative pungency, but London has rocketed once again into outer space.

"Culture. It's an interesting word, culture, because it really has to do with inner culture, like Ezra Pound's journal *Cultura*, it has to do with the bread's inner culture. If you take a bread raised with this culture and you go like this," he says, grabbing a round of dough and smacking it like someone's plump behind, "it won't collapse." Using wild, untested strains of yeast, London and Bernard must determine the sugar levels of the grape. As it is with wine, the use of laboratory-bred yeast spawns a very boring, generic product, one, says London, "lacking depth." "It has very limited parameters. There are no surprises. But when you use things *sauvage,* wild cherries, there are more surprises and as a consequence the baker or vintner takes risks. Our culture tends to be largely predictable as long as we don't take it for granted." This last statement has me perplexed, but I let it pass. I ask London if he's ever lost a starter, inadvertently allowed it to perish. "We've waited too many days but we haven't lost it," he replies. "It's part of my inner culture."

The key is to maintain a thriving balance between the mold (yeast) and the ambient bacteria. "We were taught early on that everything should be warm, warm, warm," says London. "But in fact, the yeasties like it warm but the bacteria like it cold, and longer fermentation periods develop depth of taste. You want the culture to be fresh. There's a fine line between fermentation and putrefaction. I mentioned this to Julia Child and she agreed. She thinks a lot of bread is just sour, period."

But London is after something subtler, more mysterious. "It's not like people bite into it and say, oh, this is sourdough bread. What Bernard and I would like to achieve here is *terroire.* With wine that means the ground it comes from. To us it means

78

something with character as opposed to something generic."

London and Bernard discuss fire the way some men talk baseball. Who would imagine that a hearth fire could be so packed with drama and nuance? No one, Bernard insists, can expect to produce real country bread without the right fire. Baking time won't begin until midnight, when the stone is permeated with radiant heat. On broad shelves along one wall of the preparatory section of the bakehouse — it reminds me of a potter's studio — a hundred waiting round loaves sit nestled in baskets. After a brief gestation behind the iron doors — these, too, forged by German smiths in the land of the oven builders — the crusty breads will emerge, scooped one by one onto Bernard's long broad palette. In the spirit of Steiner and his fellow bread mystics Bernard will return one bread — "the best bread" — to the fire. It's an offering steeped in humility and respect for the fire. It's also a perfectly good loaf down the tube. But at this point nothing London says or does surprises me. "I bring my bread to restaurants because it's so important to me with good food to eat good bread," says Bernard. "We have good food and good wine. But good bread is very, very hard to find."

I can't keep myself awake until midnight, and so I slip out into the starry night and leave Bernard to his labors. Early the next morning at Mrs. London's, London presents me with a round loaf the size of a chair cushion, which I place in the front seat of the car nearly as tenderly as I would a child. After all the philosophizing and preaching there is ultimately this: a large, dense, faintly charred crusty peasant loaf, a lusty, consequential bread out of a Brueghel canvas. But it is a bread nonetheless, nothing more, to be torn or sliced and dispatched to the gullet.

Most of America lies between Michael London's gentleman's farm and Kiko Denzer's converted hunting cabin in Blodgett, Oregon, a town so sparsely populated and rural people in Portland never heard of it. Along with his wife, Hannah Field, Denzer bakes bread with a sense of mission equal to London's. The bread is equally fine. Welsh-born Hannah is a professionally trained baker and she's lived on a succession of working farms. Hannah possesses an artist's temperament. With her knowledge of grains and sourdough (she uses one culture that's been in her family for fifty years) she likes to vary her breads depending on her mood, something she wasn't free to do when she was on someone's payroll. Like London's, the Denzers' breadbaking is informed as much by their spirituality and Steinerian view of nature as it is by craftsmanship. But the Denzers go even farther. Hunkered down on the soggy bank of Grant Creek at the edge of Oregon's great Willamette forest, they are staging a quiet revolution, and the bread is its guiding metaphor.

Kiko and I had been corresponding by e-mail for months. In those messages and the few times we spoke on the phone he was so helpful and good-humored I decided to include a visit with him in my research. I'd ordered his book, *Build Your Own Earth Oven*, after I got it in my head to build my very own earth oven. That head needed examining. There I was (a) mechanically inept, (b) pathologically impatient, (c) living on a coastal barrier spit with nothing resembling clay or even rich mud, and (d) residing in a resort community with so many zoning strictures our dogs may soon require permits to pee here. I let go of that particular fantasy but I was fascinated by Kiko's book, and the ovens depicted in its pages. Some are striking for their simplicity and others, especially those crafted with Kiko's guidance by groups of children, are sculptural, molded into creatures including a rabbit, squirrel, gorilla, turkey, and gargoyle-like "mud man." By helping people create such lovable basic ovens, Kiko inspires in those people an intimacy with bread. It often doesn't last; these ovens are only kept alive by use. But Kiko, forty-two, can't be granddaddy to earth ovens all over America. Those projects are just a sideline anyway. Kiko's real work is at home on Grant Creek.

After a succession of abrupt turns along unsigned country roads I pull up to where the Denzer house absolutely must be, according to Kiko's exacting e-mailed directions. But all I see is a funky shack, practically hugging the road. Hesitantly I get out of the car, and Kiko unbends himself from a woodpile to wave me in. This tiny place is so many miles from anywhere and before I realize Hannah is on the premises I feel as if Kiko is marooned there. "If I had known," I say, gesturing toward the lonely landscape, "I would've called to see if you needed anything, like Q-tips." Kiko laughs. I let myself through the gate and the homestead unfolds before me. Yes, the property is quite small. But this is no shack. This is a laboratory for the Denzers' fierce anticonsumerism. This is self-sufficiency asserted with humor and an artful touch: the homemade cob-house studio, the outhouse with composting toilet, the densely sowed vegetable garden, the shack itself, and, of course, the domed mud oven standing beside it. Hannah emerges from the studio and shakes my hand. "We have enough Q-tips, thank you," she says. Kiko and Hannah, who's twenty-nine, have lived here together for three years, Kiko for ten. They look to be identical in age and they comprise one of those couples who are in such intellectual sync they can deliver a manifesto in spirited tandem. Popular culture is an anathema to these two. Their idea of entertainment is singing old English ballads. "I used to play the oboe but I quit," says Hannah. "The instrument is just too bourgeois." They are the kind of people who make me feel guilty for buying Chanel lipstick. Seated on a rickety chair at the cabin's one table, I feel as if my Bloomingdale's charge is emitting incriminating gamma rays from inside my purse. "I try to leave this place as little as possible," says Hannah. Like Kiko she is energetic, slender, and fit, with a bushy head of hair.

"Guess how old this bread is?" Hannah says as she lays out a green salad and toast.

I can tell by the mischievous smirks on their faces the bread's been around for a while. The rest of the *pain au levain* sits on the table, uncovered, as it has for guess how many days. It's delicious, crusty outside and chewy within. It's fourteen days old. Hannah and Kiko waste nothing. Bread is their main food and its incarnations include bread pudding or even a lasagna. "We pretty much keep a sourdough culture going from week to week and store it in the fridge," says Denzer. "Sometimes we feed it rye, sometimes wheat, sometimes whole flour, depending on what we're making. Hannah occasionally uses commercial yeast for special bread or pizza dough."

Hannah tosses a salad of homegrown greens and fresh goat cheese. A narrow slice of rich earth extending from the road to the streambed, the garden is small but prolific and she'd like to live almost completely off its bounty. "There is no such thing as waste, only gifts we fail to be grateful for," says Kiko. He is full of ideas about the corruptness of our economy, our misguided view of what constitutes wealth, our pillaging of the planet, and the loss of community. These ideas gel in the "action" the pair has chosen: to be self-sufficient and to live in accordance with a simple creed. "We hold food as a simple value of very little real worth, especially compared to the immense value we bestow on so-called economic growth or, God forbid, professional sports," says Kiko. "That mis-placed value is, to me, an indicator of the real poverty of our culture. Food and land and labor and human dignity are the only real sources of value but we trade those for cash hardly giving a thought for our chil-dren, our air, our water. But we can't eat cash, no matter how much we make! So the value of bread is not in the price, but in the inherent integrity of the cycle, from seed to grain to mill to dough, into my stomach and back out to the soil, via my composting toilet." Baking in a wood-fired earthen oven restores the simplicity of bread by returning you, Kiko writes, to the essentials: earth, water, air, and fire. These beliefs reflect the philosophy of Rudolf Steiner and explain why Kiko is invited to impart his craft and philosophy to children at Waldorf schools. Kiko hasn't heard of Michael London. So I tell Kiko about London the poet-philosopher, London the baker, London the proprietor of a custom-made tuff wood-fired hearth, London the purveyor of Rock Hill Reserve firebread at

$18 a loaf. Kiko sneers. "Simply putting a price tag on the loaf brings the whole discussion back into the sewer mentality which rules our overconsuming Western culture."

The Denzers fire up their earthen oven once a week or every two weeks and spend an evening baking a dozen or so breads for themselves and also to barter for eggs, fresh-killed meat, or produce from neighboring farms. When I arrive, the couple is preparing to bake. In Denzer's earth-scented studio, loaves in canvas-lined baskets sit in a row on top of a narrow guest bed. Hannah allows me a turn on the hand-grinder they use to make cornmeal to coat the loaves. "We don't need a gym," she says as I massage my throbbing bicep. Though he lacks Hannah's training Kiko grew up with a reverence for handmade bread. He watched his mother, the artist Ann Wiseman, unwind in the kitchen. She was a gleeful baker who liberated herself from recipes to conjure her own quirky breads. He loves to quote her: "There are no mistakes, just new ways to make bread." When Kiko was twelve his parents sent him to a farm in Brittany where he studied French and worked in the fields and subsisted largely on *pain au campagne*.

After college, where he earned a degree in Humanities, Kiko's job history reads like a career guide for the nonprofit sector. He worked in urban homesteading, community development, cooperative education, drug and alcohol abuse prevention. For part of those years he also worked for a Boston sculptor making molds and castings for the Museum of Fine Arts. All these pursuits were grooming him for life on Grant Creek, sculpting, making mud ovens, baking bread, growing food. "I need to be actively and physically involved in making life," is how Kiko puts it. "Participation is the key, to bread, to community, to culture, to life."

To life. I take a last gulp of tea, pay a visit to the composting toilet, which is truly a work of art, and drive off with Kiko and Hannah waving in the mist. Could I live like this? For a time, perhaps, and then I'd feel antsy, claustrophobic, and lonely for the full human catastrophe, beautiful or not. If I lived in this place I'd probably take to driving thirty miles for a cappuccino. It would be interesting, I think, to pop in on Kiko and Hannah again in ten or fifteen years. By then, they will surely be out of Q-tips.

Kiko Denzer's Ten Steps to Real Sourdough

From Build Your Own Earth Oven,
by Kiko Denzer

FRIDAY EVENING:
1. Make a wet "sponge" of flour (preferably organic), one quarter to one half cup starter or one teaspoon commercial yeast, and water (one to two cups per loaf).
2. Let yeasts grow overnight.

SATURDAY MORNING:
3. Save a few tablespoons of sponge to start your next batch. Feed it a bit of flour and water and store in refrigerator.
4. Add flour and salt (one teaspoon per loaf) to the remaining sponge.
5. Knead vigorously for fifteen minutes.
6. Let dough sit for two to five hours.

NOONISH:
7. Shape dough into loaves.
8. Proof loaves (poke with finger; dough should be impressionable but springy) and let them rise about two hours.

9. Bake!
10. Let bread sit twenty minutes before eating. The bread is still cooking!

The Bedouin Way:

Jordan

*If you bake bread with indifference, you bake
a bitter bread that feeds half man's hunger.*
— KAHLIL GIBRAN, *The Prophet*

*He deserves paradise who makes his
companions laugh.*
— THE KORAN

"You are welcome."

All over Jordan the scene repeats itself.
In the rubble of the desert, in the crush of
the bazaar, on the rich man's farm, or in
the poor man's hovel: we say, "*Salaam,
Marhaba.* May we watch you bake the
bread?" Old or young, the Jordanian bows
his head and says, "You are welcome." He
finds some crates or pillows and sits us
down with a cup of tea, perhaps an orange
soda. His children and his neighbors' children appear out of nowhere to giggle and

gaze at our pale skin and eyes, to gawk with disbelief at our masculine lace-up boots. Cousins materialize in twos and threes. "You are welcome," they say, each touching a hand to his heart. It occurs to us that these people have other things to do, and our presence is causing a commotion. Is it okay? We ask once, twice. *"Mish Mushkele,"* they reply. No problem.

In the bakeries a well-meaning helper tries to hand us a round of bread from the cooling table but the owner swiftly intercepts it with a look of exasperation. No, no. Not that bread, but this one, the one just being scooped out of the oven, is for our honored guests. And here is a bag of breads for later, and try this sweet roll. I ask, pointing at something unfamiliar, for instance, a giant, doughnut-shaped sesame bread, *"Shu hada?"* What is this? "Ah, *baygalah!"* and before we can blink one is added to the bag. We reach into our wallets for a few dinars. Our innocent gesture has the men gesticulating in horror. No, no, no. Please, no money. And can't you stay a bit longer? Drink more tea? *Ahalan wa sahlan fique,* you are most welcome.

I am generally a person of extreme highs and lows, not grouchy but someone who can shut down like a garage door, my patience with the entire human race temporarily depleted. In Jordan, where I traveled with my friend Vivian, I was open, content, and placid as a Buddhist monk. The place agreed with me. My Jordanian romance began in Amman with a smitten hotel clerk's generosity and blossomed from there. I fell in love with the landscape. Jordan's mountains look as if they were poured from above or thrust like rockets from below. For a desert country its valleys are surprisingly verdant. The desert itself is vast, pink, and dotted here and there with the camels and the fabled black tents of my Scheherazade reveries. I fell in love with the bread, and the mushy beans called *fool*, even, in time, with the bitter cardamom coffee. I found the call to prayer hypnotic as it cascaded across valleys and hills from muezzin to muezzin, cries of "Allah" overlapping like a mournful fugue.

Unless you're a guest in someone's home, the Arab world is a world of men. My worries about this quickly evaporate. I warm to the Jordanian men. The ones we meet laugh a lot and go in for good-natured teasing. A few grace me with an Eastern variation of "Got your nose!" which makes me feel like a five-year-old but doesn't anger me. The men treat us with a paternal kindness, which, in the context of our surroundings, we find not at all insulting. My notebook is filled with the names of these men: Omar, Ahmed, Ali, Hissam, Samir, Mazen, Hussein, Sayeed. One chaste fling spills into the next (there are a few marriage proposals, some talk of camel trades, but all in good fun). Jordan is one place where I can forgive a man who asks me to drape my headscarf across my face; he wants to see what I really look like. In my travels abroad I've been hissed at, goosed, chased, and beckoned like a dog. In the Louvre Museum a man tweaked my breast. Jordanian men flirt with far more nuance and restraint. Also I have never seen such handsome men on parade anywhere.

The staples of rural Jordanians' diet are bread, goat's milk, yogurt, rice, and tea. We sank our teeth into pillowy bread baked in earthen pots. We tore into bread thin as sackcloth peeled off steaming domes, bread birthed from the coal and ash of a simple pit fire, pita tossed like skimming rocks along the infernally hot floor of a brick oven. Here, as in most of Arabia, domestic baking methods haven't changed much over the centuries. Leavened or not, the bread is simple and tastes of nothing more than wheat and fire. As it is in Egypt, Syria, Lebanon, and Yemen, here is a land where breadmaking is a labor of love and gratitude. In some Muslim cultures coins are baked into the first bread from the annual grain harvest, an offering of thanks. In Arabic, bread is often called *aysh,* the same as the word for "life." To take a knife to bread is considered an act of violence. If bread falls to the ground an Arab will pick it up and place it to his lips and forehead before setting it aside. So intrinsic is daily bread to the quality of Arab life that as recently as 1996, when taxes on imported wheat had driven the price of bread up an intolerable 250 percent, Jordanians took to the streets. But the disturbances served their purpose, and then-King Hussein slashed the price of bread to one within reason.

For Jordanians in the countryside, who far outnumber those in the city, baking bread is as habitual and sanctified as the call to prayer. Outside the city families eat fresh bread with every midday and evening meal. The baking falls seamlessly into the rhythms of the day; you could set your clock by it. Arabs distinguish between Arabic bread and *aysh fino,* which is foreign (literally French) bread. Following our noses to breads reflecting the baking traditions of Jordan, Egypt, Syria, and Iraq, we had neither the time nor the appetite for anything but Arabic bread. This we ate everywhere, morning until night, and everywhere we received one or more breads as gifts. Vivian and I couldn't finish them but we couldn't bear to throw them away. As a result the backseat of our rental car came to resemble a picnic for the world's luckiest pigeon.

Though the geographical details eluded me as sovereign borders swelled and contracted in my short lifetime, Jordan had long been an object of my desire. As a teenager, while my suburban New York friends succumbed to the lure of the kibbutz, I fell hard for the other side of the Jordan River. I wished myself inside the dreamy expanse of Arabian Desert in *National Geographic* foldouts. These are the things that seized my imagination: carpet-draped dromedaries, jasmine and neroli-scented anything, jangly jewelry, the notion of men and women not so much dressed as wrapped in blazing circus colors. I was obsessed with tents. Using bed quilts, broomsticks, and safety pins I'd construct a semblance of one in our suburban backyard and beg to sleep out there under what light pollution had spared of the night sky. Growing up inhaling the lingering fumes of onions and potted meat, I was captivated by the cumin-spiked hole in the wall that was Mahmoud's on MacDougal Street in Manhattan's Greenwich Village. At fifteen I'd travel to the city by train, head straight for the Village, and park myself at Mahmoud's to drink sweet tea with an almond in it and listen to the alien lilt of the Arabic spoken by Mahmoud and his friends. With other transportation at my disposal, I preferred getting from here to there on foot. I was a Jewish Bedouin girl.

Long overshadowed by imperious Egypt, Jordan is compact and gentle, a bit player in the global drama. Its citizens seem genuinely tickled that you came so far to be there. When I mentioned I was planning a trip to Jordan acquaintances flashed me stern looks and warned me to be careful. Careful of what? Expect rabid anti-Semitism, they said. Steer clear of bands of roving militants bearing ancient tribal grudges. Don't get kidnapped! Relatives and friends worried that as women — especially Jewish women — traveling alone, Vivian and I were asking for trouble. "I just didn't feel comfortable in Jordan," a friend of a friend declared at a Bar Mitzvah gathering. I dared to ask: "How much time did you spend there?" Less than one day. She didn't even spend the night. "I wouldn't *want* to spend even one night there," she added defensively. "They hate Israel, you know." This isn't exactly a news flash. Jordan is a nation populated largely by Palestinians, many of them refugees. Every spring on Israeli Independence Day Jordanians flock to demonstrations of mourning to commemorate *Nakba*, the catastrophe. Yet King Hussein's efforts toward normalization are what put Jordan on the tourism map. Israelis were first in line.

As it turns out, no one seems to care whether we are Jews, Unitarians, or Jehovah's Witnesses. On the rare occasions the subject comes up the news has zero discernible effect. Only one sour moment occurs. We set off for a walk under the ramparts of the Crusaders' castle in Kerak, when it suddenly begins to hail. We look up to see teenage boys hurling rocks at us. Why? Our idyll is shattered. What makes us targets? Did they spot us for infidels? Distraught, we complain to the hotel manager. "They throw the rocks always," he tells us with a pained look on his face. "They throw the rocks at *us*. They are very bad people." In fact, elsewhere in Jordan we neither notice nor collide with any of the unemployed male youths whose combination of menacing energy and self-loathing, according to observers such as Robert Kaplan, are the true scourge of the developing world. In their e-mails my friends in Amman tell me it's all going sour now, but we were there in the economically promising ripples of the Oslo peace accords between Israel and the Palestinians, when minds if not hearts were looking to the future with optimism.

Twelve years older and a great traveler, Vivian agrees to join me knowing nothing about Jordan. An artist with a sharp eye and insatiable curiosity, she admits she confuses Jordan with Lebanon and Syria and that to her the Middle East is an inscrutable haze of obscure conflicts and numbing newsbabble. Hardly anyone we speak with before the trip knows much more, but I was lucky to meet up with Kathleen Abdallah, an economist for the United Nations and a sister of my old friend and newspaper colleague Mary Ellen O'Shea. She and her Egyptian husband lived in Amman for five years. At a coffee shop on Manhattan's Second Avenue she looks over my short list of hotel recommendations — most of them from former tourist packages — and dismisses them as overpriced, overhyped, and lacking local flavor. I mention hiring someone as a guide and driver. "You won't need one," she tells me. "You'll be fine."

When we arrive, Jordan had only recently lost its cherished King Hussein after a forty-eight-year-reign. Hussein was the only ruler Jordan had known since it gained independence in 1946 after a quarter century of self-government under the British Mandate. When the news came of his death after a seven-month fight with cancer Jordanians flocked the streets to mourn the loss of the man they called their father, their dear. Women slapped their faces and wailed. "Al Hussein is Jordan," people's handwritten placards read. At the time of our visit his son and successor, the London-educated Abdullah, was still searching for a comfortable and effective ruling style. He'd taken to disguising himself as an ordinary Jordanian and venturing out among the masses, wrapped in a contingent of plainclothes bodyguards. Vivian and I entertain ourselves with Abdullah sightings. "I think that's the king," I whisper to Viv in the pocked courtyard of a skeletal desert castle. I motion to the disheveled caretaker, who follows me from chamber to chamber asking "Is good, Jordan? You marry? You marry?" Another day we spy our Abdullah at the edge of a busy Amman street pouring coffee from a samovar. We also spot him standing frozen, about to puff on a water pipe, in a life-size diorama at Amman's historical museum.

The size of Indiana, Jordan is a tapestry of parched desert, steep sculptural hills, jagged mountains, gorges, canyons, and the lush Jordan River valley. On all but five percent of this land little thrives except desert grasses, sage, juniper, and scrub pine. From its arable patches Jordanians coax modest harvests of wheat and barley, and the tomatoes and cucumbers accompanying nearly every meal. For export Jordan grows olives, figs, apricots, grapes, and, of course, almonds. There are herds of longhair goats and sheep, sturdy Arabian horses, and the most enduring desert cliché come to life, the sunlit profiles of grazing camels.

We drive miles in and around towering *jabals* (hills) and sage-studded desert flats giving rise here and there to clusters of stunted olive trees. Something dark, unsightly, and puzzling grows from these trees. A nest of some kind? Mutant gypsy moths? In fact, Jordan is under siege by black plastic bags. With the tenacity of the body snatchers they affix themselves to every protuberance in their path, to tree branches, boulders, highway signs. They gust across the desert, dipping and weaving like a flock of migrating birds. Once you see them you can *un*-see them. Perhaps someday a massive army of schoolchildren can fan out among the hills, valleys, and plains, grabbing the odious sacks as they go, stuffing them into the mother of all plastic bags and recycling them into flip-flops for everyone.

"You are welcome in Jordan."

To cross into Jordan from Jerusalem we hire an Israeli taxi at Damascus Gate to drive us across the West Bank and a Jordanian cab to take us over the King Hussein Bridge and into Amman. Israel-bound travelers cross the Allenby Bridge. They are the same bridge and the traveler's first lesson in the region's loaded use of language. To Israel it's East Jerusalem, to Jordan, who lost that territory in the 1967 war, it will forever be Occupied Jerusalem. Jordanians visit relatives in Palestine. Israelis acknowledge no such place. The arcane procedures at two border posts and a brief complimentary bus ride across the limbo zone in between make an all-morning journey out of a distance of about forty-five miles.

I'd booked us a room at Amman's Hisham Hotel, reputed to be a small quiet place frequented by foreign journalists. *"Fonduq Hisham,"* the driver repeats, rubbing his chin. He has a pained look on his face. As soon as we enter the seething core of Amman he is completely lost and takes to jerking the cab this way and that to attract the attention of passing drivers. I commit my first Arabic words to memory: *"Wayn fonduq Hisham?"* Where is our hotel? The phrase will come in handy. One lengthy exchange after another and our driver still cannot find someone who has heard of the place. We pull out maps and plead with the driver, who is practically in tears, not to unload us to another cab. After far too long a time, sweaty and exhausted, we pull up at the Hisham. We are relieved to find it exists.

There was nothing unusual about this cab ride. "Is very difficult city, no signs, always something new," Omar Douad, Hisham's manager, tells us. "In Amman everyone is lost."

Like Rome, Amman was originally built on seven hills. Like Dante's hell, it is comprised of circles. But the underworld itself might be easier and about as pleasant to navigate as the Jordanian capital, even on a day when traffic isn't clotted by university protests, construction, or the apparent need of every driver on the northern side to get to the southern side, and vice versa. A village of two thousand at the turn of the century, Amman has exploded in dimensions and population with all the orderliness of an earthquake. Though it isn't beautiful and borders no scenic mountains or bodies of water, and though one Middle East hand described it as "the most boring city in Arabia," today's Amman is an international hub as lively as prewar Beirut.

The city is in the throes of another kind of war, an all-out assault on every last shred of open space. Its battles are waged with bulldozers, cement mixers, jackhammers, and cranes. Every few blocks a new office tower or hotel hatches from the last vacant squares of rubble, and when these structures are complete they all look exactly the same, which is to say they resemble a succession of multistory parking garages. We learn soon enough that half-built office buildings make lousy navigational markers. "Every day in Amman is a new building," a Palestinian cabdriver told us as he veered this way and that to avoid knots of construction. "Makes you crazy." Scores of minarets poke skyward from the bedlam as if gasping for air. The city layout is so herky-jerky that at times it seems the only sane way to orient oneself is to await the afternoon prayers and note in which direction people are bowing.

The good news is that your Amman cabdriver is likely to pull over and buy you a cup of coffee to sip while you ride. The bad news is, well, when it comes to the Amman roads, it's all bad news. For example, the Hisham is on Zahran Street, just off the Third Circle. But it's little use counting circles. Of Amman's eight "circles," some really are, some are just off-kilter intersections, and at least one spits you into a tunnel that emerges so far below or above where you want to be that you are clueless how to proceed. Street signs are semi-hidden at curb level with cursive too small to read. And even if one could make them out their names change frequently, though the rule of thumb seems to be: when in doubt, call it Hussein. Amman's secondary roads loop under and around with the logic of loose threads in a clothes dryer, so once you screw up (and you will), you may be slouching toward the real

Bethlehem before you're able to find your way back to the city. We have breakfast at the Inter-Continental coffee shop with Kathleen Abdallah's daughter Alyce, a Fulbright fellow living in Amman for the year. She is stunned that Vivian and I plan to drive ourselves around Amman. We hold our heads high, assuming our bravado impresses her. She tells us we are lunatics.

Jordan sits across the Gulf of Aqaba from Egypt, which you can reach by ferry from the lively Port of Aqaba. To the south this sliver of a nation is a vast infernal sandbox spilling into Saudi Arabia, to the north a hop and a skip from Damascus. Thanks to the efforts of American-born Queen Noor and the Oslo peace accords, there has been a surge in tourism, though most visitors are bused directly to the ancient city of Petra. There they gape in slow moving clumps, advancing past the excavated temples and tombs like a big blob of protoplasm. Vivian and I take to referring to tour groups as "the clumps." They are mostly Europeans. The few Americans we meet are in Petra on brief jaunts from Israel.

Jordanians hold no grudges toward Americans. With a population of only 5 million Jordan received $543.2 million from the U.S. for military training, natural resource development, family planning, and food aid, in the form of nearly $50 million worth of wheat. Literacy in Jordan is high, at least 85 percent, but jobs are few and the population is climbing fast. Among both its government and its people, most Sunni Muslims, Jordan agonizes over the hopeless Palestinian-Israeli conflict and its conflicting loyalties to Arabia (including Iraq), and the West. Between 1996 and the following year the United States increased aid to Jordan by 1,800 percent, just our way of saying thanks to the King Hussein's valiant efforts, in his ailing final days, on behalf of the Orwellian "peace process." Jordan's biggest headache is the one endemic to desert nations: too many people, too little water.

In the city Vivian and I don't attract much attention. I despise my short, shapeless legs so keeping them covered as a show of respect is about as much of a sacrifice as giving up borscht for Lent. Though all Jordanian women dress modestly they range from indistinguishable pillars of black to matrons in colored headscarves to stylish women with western-style suits and coifed hair. Outside the city women wear shapeless bell-sleeved ankle-length shifts with embroidery curling around the neckline. Many men continue to wear the traditional white *djellabah,* or floor-length tunic, their heads wrapped in signature Arabian keffiyeh headdress or crowned with skullcaps. Somehow, in spite of all the air pollution, dust, and greasy dinner fare, the men's garments remain spotless and blindingly white. Somewhere unseen, their wives and daughters are doubtless bent over basins clutching bars of laundry soap, wringing and scrubbing, wringing and scrubbing.

On Fridays, the Islamic holy day, Amman's main streets are closed to traffic, and the entire expanse of its downtown is a sea of curved backs, outstretched arms, and protruding shoulder blades. Seen from an airplane it must resemble a colossal heaving jigsaw puzzle. Some on prayer mats and some on torn sheets of cardboard, the bodies spill out from the Great Mosque, bending and unbending in a great wave to the muezzin's deafening call. Vivian and I stand frozen at a street corner, afraid that moving an inch would show disrespect. Planted there, we are jostled by non-praying Jordanians simply going about their business, proceeding confidently across this human carpet. "I think it's okay to walk," I whisper, and we skitter into a shop to admire a wall strung with prayer beads. I want to buy some as gifts and ask to see a few. In the proprietor's path is a man prostrate on his prayer mat. The shopkeeper steps right over him.

Khabbaez, bakeries, are tucked throughout the souk, filling the narrow streets and alleys with their yeasty aroma. Carts are piled high with stacks of pita or shoppers place orders at windows beside the bakery; no need for anyone to venture inside. I wouldn't barge in, instead I poke my head in the window and announce sweetly, *"Ana sahaffeeya,"* I am a journalist. I follow up as best I can with some remedial verbless Arabic about my *ketab,* the book. *"Ah, sahaffeeya!"* the man cries, smiling, and motions us inside.

It's become cliché that citizens of certain countries (okay, France) are language snobs who react to amateur pronunciation with impatience, even contempt. Make any attempt at Arabic, though, and you make a friend. Arabic is a difficult but direct language. If you can master the pronunciations of some useful nouns it's not hard to make oneself understood. Because Arabic has only two tenses — what has happened and what will happen — you're less likely to flounder in verb purgatory as you would with French or Italian. Arabic has a few all-purpose words that serve as soothing refrains to everyday discourse. It's worth learning them: *bismalla*, in the name of God, *Insha'allah*, God-willing, or *ahlan wa sahlan*, which means hello and welcome. *Salaam*, peace. You can't go wrong with these. Arabs are famously hospitable and the language reflects this with a variety of ways to express "you are welcome." Vivian once insisted an old Imam of whom we'd asked directions told her to "have fun." What he said was *afwahn*, you are welcome. Beyond the everyday essentials, however, Arabic is a nightmare. For example, in his entertaining memoir *Yemen: The Unknown Arabia*, the British expatriate and Arabic scholar Tim Mackintosh-Smith points out that *firash* can mean either a wife or a mat, and *qarurah* could be interpreted as either "the apple of one's eye" or a urinal. Writes Mackintosh-Smith, "Somebody once said that every Arabic word means itself, its opposite or a camel."

One after another the bakery doors open and the men stuffed inside back toward the cement walls to let us inch through. Nothing seems to enchant the muscular young apprentices more than watching us watch them labor shirtless at the gaping mouth of a coal-fired hearth. The Egyptian bakers like to proclaim themselves. "Egyptian! This Egyptian bakery!" These bakeries make nothing but pita, which they churn out from dawn until night. Some of the bakeries do all the mixing, kneading, and rolling by hand and others have a simple machine, a system of rollers, that separates the dough and flattens it into small plate-sized circles. We poke our heads into a fragrant cubbyhole in the village of Mouta and encounter a Bedouin boy named Baha, who spends the day tossing rounds of a flax-hued whole-wheat dough in the air and draping it over a *tannur,* a kind of upside-down wok with a flame underneath. In the small city of M'aan, a popular pilgrims' stopover on the route to Mecca, we watch a boy go through the same process, but first he stretches the dough by draping it over a plump round pillow. In Wādi Mū-sá, near Petra, we pay a visit to the Sanobel Mechanical Bakery and watch flat breads march *Modern Times*–style along a groaning conveyor belt. Moyad Abdulla, the pale, blue-eyed owner, was trained in his native Iraq as an agricultural engineer. His exuberance is contagious: "Now see where it comes!" The parade of fresh pita zigs and zags its way from the third-floor oven down to the second level, where it bucks forward like the cars on a decrepit roller coaster, until the conveyor dumps the breads into a hole gouged into the floor. "Come, come!" Down the stairs we trot, to witness the breads raining from the hole onto a counter where the bemused customers queue up. "This is a very modern bakery! In Yemen and Iraq, no machines," Moyad tells us. "Everything by hand." "You are welcome," says Moyad as he fills a plastic sack for us with breads, sweets, and a doughnut-shaped *baygalah* crusted with sesame seeds.

Why is everyone so *nice* to us? In Al Azraq, about thirty miles from the Saudi border, Vivian and I are the only customers at a roadside café that obviously comes alive at night. In addition to the tables arranged outside is an immense garishly appointed dining room reminiscent of the Bar Mitzvah catering halls of my suburban youth. The walls are lined with an assortment of fantastical hookah pipes called *nargileh* (Do they sing "Have a *nargileh?*"). Exhausted from driving, we loaf all afternoon waiting for the sun to sink, while the proprietor and his cook re-fill our tea and bring us chips and Coke. They offer us a novice puff of the hubbly bubbly, its pan filled with a *sheesha,* or fragrant paste of tobacco and dried apples. It's nice, smoother than ordinary pipe smoke, with a fruity aftertaste. When we stand up to leave the men refuse our dinars. They are adamant, pressing their palms to their hearts and waving away our protests. *"Mish Mushkele,"* no problem. "You are welcome."

Vivian and I aren't so hard on the eyes but we're not exactly babes. In any case our attributes are lost under roomy shirts and baggy khakis. Vivian wears a floppy sun hat and I don an oh-so-alluring flow-ered babushka. Programmed to second-guess male attention, we ask ourselves once again, "Why is everyone so nice to us?" A bracelet peddler at a Petra café offers one possibility. "You have the good chemicals," he tells me. Finally it hits us. "They like us!" we decide. "They really like us!"

Omar likes us. Omar likes us a lot. He presides over the Hisham. Small and unassuming as an apartment house, the hotel sits on the corner of a quiet residential street lined with terraced villas, lush gardens, and flowering trees. A column of shiny BMWs stretches from one end of the road to the other. Inside, the first face one sees is Omar's, all-around fixer and right-hand man to Mr. Hisham. Omar is the Sultan of *Mish Mushkele*. Is it safe to walk to Farq-al-Din, Amman's most elegant Lebanese restaurant, at night? *Mish Mushkele,* Omar will drive us there. Where can we buy plane tickets to Tel Aviv? *Mish Mushkele,* Omar will take care of it, no need to pay until later. An elegantly dressed body builder with sad eyes, mottled skin, and hair pomaded close to his balding head, Omar is married only to his job. We assume Omar will stop looking after us once we leave Amman. We are wrong. All over Jordan Omar makes his concern for us known, his presence descending near and far like the bubble of the Good Witch of the North.

One evening Omar takes me to the roof to "view Amman at night." The hotel is only three stories tall so there isn't much to see, but Omar points there to "the rich people," and there, to the poor. He doesn't "try anything," as we used to say in high school. As a fresh arrival I was a little nervous, but I had at least one weapon, the word *imshi,* which is Arabic for "get lost."

It was one of the words I studied to repel unwanted advances. "*Imshi* should do the trick," according to the Lonely Planet guide to Jordan and Syria. "A few women have also found that laughing at the importunate individual," the guide continues, "or staring at his shoes, as if to say, 'What kind of a cheap scumbag are you?' to be equally effective."

I never have to resort to staring at Omar's shoes. He and the whole cast of suitors to follow are polite and respectful. That said, Omar seems to know a little too much about us. We suspect he is in our room sniffing our underwear while we're off scaling ruins or mired in traffic. So cozy do we all become that one evening when I set off for dinner with my hair down instead of the usual ponytail Mr. Hisham remarks, "Oh, Miss Susie, there's a salon next door where they can do something about your hair." One evening Omar and Mr. Hisham somberly inform us that Farq-al-Din, our new favorite restaurant and one vast enough to house the entire Arab League and its entourages was "fully booked." You will take dinner at the hotel, Mr. Hisham tells us. That's that. He'd had the staff prepare a lone table in the garden specially for us. It is a lovely night. Vivian,

Mr. Hisham, and I dine under a full moon and hear tales of Mr. Hisham's childhood in East Jerusalem before he and most of his Palestinian relatives fled to Jordan. We discuss the "situation" and Mr. Hisham, whose grown children live in Boston and Los Angeles, conveys no anger, only weariness. Vivian and I develop fast crushes on the courtly, white-haired Mr. Hisham. He makes us promise to call him from anywhere in Jordan if we need anything, "even SOS." Mr. Hisham likes us.

Omar and Mr. Hisham present us with gifts: a bouquet of roses, a bar of Dead Sea mineral soap, Hisham-logo duffel bags, sealed carafes of Jordan River holy water. I still correspond with Omar by e-mail. He always calls me *"Habebti,"* Arabic for sweetheart. And we still joke about the phone. Here is what happened: Vivian and I planned a day's excursion to several desert castles north of Amman. Built by the Omayyad caliphs, the first Islamic dynasty, in the seventh and eighth centuries, the now-crumbling castles were pleasure palaces used for hunting, debauchery, or retreat from advancing armies and epidemics. Poking incongruously from the bone-dry earth, the castles were as hot as the inside of a hibachi but we had them pretty much to ourselves. Back in Amman, though we could not have been more than two miles from our hotel, we got lost — for more than two hours. It got dark. We stopped again and again and Vivian set out in search of English speakers — shopkeepers, businessmen, students. I watched her converse with these people. On and on they spoke and gestured, arms orbiting, hands patting the air. Finally Vivian would climb back into the car. "Well?" I'd ask. "He doesn't know," she'd reply. This was funny the first six times. If our respective husbands were with us they would be hissing at us by now. But Vivian and I worked gallantly to maintain our senses of humor as we spun, jerked, and lurched our way along Mohammed Boulevard and Hussein highway attracting small earnest crowds with our increasingly panicked inquiries. Though several declared: "Third circle! It is so easy!" none could elaborate. We found the hotel by lucky accident. As we angled the car into the last parking space we practically ululated with glee.

I hug the beefy Omar. "We were so worried about you," he says. "It was growing dark and I kept saying, where is my Susie? Tomorrow you will take my mobile phone," he said, "and I will ring you and conduct you home."

The next day, with equal parts determination and luck, we get ourselves to the Roman ruins at Jerash. Before we reach its colonnaded entrance the mobile phone rings. (The phone is set for incoming calls only.)

"Hello, it is Omar."

"No shit."

"What are you doing?"

I describe my surroundings. Omar seems satisfied. He calls us about every half hour, getting on our nerves in a big way. The phone rings as we scale the poppy-studded ruin of an ancient courthouse. The phone rings during the afternoon call to prayer. But when we're back in Amman traffic hell searching for the elusive Third Circle, the phone is silent. I haven't a clue where we are, and drive with no purpose beyond keeping us alive. "C'mon, Omar," Vivian and I chant as if we are rooting for a sluggish horse. And then the phone rings. Vivian answers.

"It is Omar."

"Right."

"Where are you?"

"We have no idea!"

"Do not worry, I will conduct you. Now

please, where are you? What is the place you see?"

"We're, um, approaching a big hotel!" cries Vivian, "the . . . Hotel Jerusalem! There's um, a mosque . . . and a Safeway . . . and . . . a tunnel!"

A tunnel! We are yards away from its sinister mouth. I drive as slowly and ambiguously as possible in light of the roar of BMWs on either side of us. "He has to tell us *now!*" I scream.

"Do not proceed into the tunnel," commands Omar. "Do *not*."

"Whooooooooa!" Screech. A few turns and many palpitations later we are headed in the right direction. We recognize the turnoff! When we pull up in front of the Hisham I am beeping the horn ecstatically. The entire Hisham staff is outside, cheering and applauding.

The next morning we check out and head south on the Old Kings Highway, a narrow but decent road riding the banks of the Jordan River down to the Dead Sea, the lowest point on earth. The southern end of the Dead Sea Valley is actually below sea level. We drive over and around the hills and huge rock slabs or *jabals* running the length of Jordan. These form the continuation of Africa's Rift Valley. Looking at a relief map of Jordan it's as if a backbone runs the length of the country and we are working our way down to the lumbar portion. Jordan is not one of those locales where every drive is a death race and every driver a ticking testosterone bomb. "Slowly, slowly," is the prevailing sentiment. Even the lorry drivers are for the most part cautious and polite. When we break free of Amman, the driving feels more low-key and saner than, say, tooling around Boston. We stop at small villages and sniff out bakeries, whose proprietors welcome us and bring us orange sodas. It's odd to think of how everyone back home is worried about us at this very moment. Everyone likes us, and we could survive on these gifts of steaming fresh bread and sweet tea. We feel more than safe. We feel protected.

Approaching Kerak, the barren landscape swells into sculpted sandstone towers and lumpy hills shaped like beach sand patted down by a child. Bedouin tents with sloped sides of woven goat hair poke up from the most unlikely spots, miles away, or so it seems, from anything useful to men or animals. Some tents are plopped beside the highway, rubbish snagged in their supports, pickups parked outside. Many of these are the Bedouin equivalent of hunting cabins or *pieds-à-terre*. Those who fall into the category of that oxymoron, the semi-nomad, use the tents as stopovers when trading or moving herds.

Kerak itself is a disappointment but just beyond it we stumble upon the best bread I tasted in Jordan, perhaps the best bread I've tasted anywhere. Escaping the disgruntled hoodlums of Kerak, we pull over at the Al Tafileh Rest House along the Old Kings Highway. Lone guests in search of a late lunch, we sit out in the sun drinking Coke as a pale, freckled young man named Fouad turns marinated chicken pieces on an outdoor grill. We strike up a conversation with the only other customer, an English speaker in an oxford-cloth shirt and sport jacket. I don't warm to him at first. He reminds me of the many men in my life — past bosses, for example — who speak with authority on all subjects, and don't so much converse with women as lecture them. A health care administrator and former Royal Intelligence official, Ali Mahasneh has seen a lot of the world but he grew up here, in dusty Tafileh. He had driven south from Amman, leaving his wife and two children, for a reunion of his parents and ten grown siblings. "I had to escape the family house — there are a hundred people! So I'm here at my cousin's café," Ali told us as he dragged on a Rothman's cigarette. We laugh; this brand of exasperation is universal. When I tell him about my research Ali gives the table a decisive pat and rises to consult with Fouad. He returns looking pleased with himself. "It is settled," he says. Ali likes us. When we finish eating Fouad closes the café and we all pile into the rental car for the short drive to Fouad's cousin's farm not far from the Dead Sea.

The family home is an unassuming poured concrete rectangle. Like so many houses throughout the developing world, its roof sprouts metal poles supporting nothing but air. Who knows, a future windfall might pay for the addition of a second floor. On his forehead, Mohammed, our host, bears a faint "raisin," the imprint of countless hours spent bowed in prayer. Muslims who embrace *salat,* the second pillar of Islam, pray five times a day for about ten minutes. We catch Mohammed between afternoon and late afternoon prayers. As a praying man he cannot take our hands but he nods to us gently and touches his heart. He is stunning, a Hashemite incarnation of Paul Newman, and we can't stop staring at him. ("I'm in love," whispers Vivian.) We can't help noticing that almost without exception the smiles of Jordanian men reveal the most beautiful teeth. I later read in Akbar S. Ahmed's *Living Islam* that Muslims, in keeping with the teachings of the Prophet, who called for prayers to "purify your mouths," pay meticulous attention to cleaning their teeth. Mohammed himself used a medicinal twig called *siwak*, precursor to the toothbrush.

Mohammed's older sons set out mats in the shade of a circle of peach trees and pour glasses of sweet tea while we wait for the baking to begin. In Arab households guests are guided to the thickest cushions and given extra pillows for armrests. We sit there along with Ali, Fuoad, and Mohammed and soon men in keffiyeh materialize from the fields to join us. The men on the mats move in close to accommodate newcomers and I see one man unselfconsciously rest his head on the other's shoulder, another lay an arm on his neighbor's back. The littlest children summon us, and Vivian and I crouch down inside the bake house where everything, even animal carcasses, is fed to the fire. The clay oven is hot but contains no fire itself. In the stifling heat we watch Mohammed's pregnant wife Lila set the rounds of dough, each about a half-inch thick and the size of a dessert plate, onto the hot stones. She is wearing a brown flour-stained shift and her headscarf is emblazoned with Disney cartoon characters. Like all the bakers we meet, she works with her bare hands, tough and tanned as leather. Called a *taboon,* the covered pit oven resembles a broader, flatter tandoor. Jet-black, each about the size of a walnut, the *radf* or hot stones leave their imprint on the breads in the form of crispy-domed air bubbles. When the breads are ready our hosts cheerfully herd us back to our mats, where we wash down the hot doughy rounds with pot after pot of tea. The crunchy bubbles release little puffs of steam and the dough is salty and chewy: delicious. " 'He is not a believer,' the Prophet said, 'who eats his fill while his neighbor remains hungry by his side.' " I reach in my bag and find some colorful hair ties for Mohammed's four-year-old daughter Sayeeda. We give his wife a few bars of wild bayberry soap made on Cape Cod. "From my home," I say. She turns the soaps around slowly in her callused hand, and looks at us as if we'd beamed down from Venus.

It is hard to leave this place, but Fuoad has to get back to his rest house. Viv and I are anxious to reach Petra, a least an hour's drive south. They all insist we take a few breads for the road. Ali gives us his mobile phone number. "If you need anything at all, from anywhere in Jordan, you may call me," he says. "Anything at all." *"Ahalan wa sahlan . . . Jella,"* I say, Let's get going. There is no lighting on Jordan's highways and we want to reach Petra before dark.

We're about to announce ourselves to the clerk at Petra Palace, but he seems to know us. "You must be Miss Susie," declares the serious-looking young man in spectacles. His name tag identifies him as "Hardan." "Mr. Omar has been calling many times from Amman. He is very worried for you."

"My name is Hard-on," adds Hardan, as if delivering news of great import. "Do you know what it means?" Vivian and I are uncharacteristically speechless. Hard-on lifts up his specs and glares at us, then flashes a naughty grin. "Angry! Hard-on means angry!" Vivian lets out a sigh. "Ah!" is all we can think to say. We head to our room, which happens to be deluxe and poolside, because "Mr. Omar insisted we give you the best room."

As we unpack the phone rings. "Hello, it is Omar." Omar is very upset with us. Omar is getting to be worse than our mothers. "You didn't tell me you were staying one night in Kerak. Why you do not tell me this? I call for you in Petra, you never arrive there. I do not sleep for worrying. I have been trying to locate you all over Jordan." I tell Omar he is a very silly man, say good night, and hang up.

Petra. No amount of clicking flashing rewinding Japanese tourists strutting their brand-new Yasser Arafat headgear, no amount of pushy "donkey-taxi" drivers, no inundation of desert safari conscripts in head-to-toe breathable khaki, no hollering tour guides — nothing can detract from the giddy surprise of seeing Petra open before you for the first time. We pass through the soaring two hundred-meter-high rock walls of the *siq* — a deep narrow crack in the rock that flash floods transform into a river. It is cool and dark in the *siq,* which was formed when the force of an earthquake split the earth like a hatchet to a log. At points it is nearly narrow enough to touch both sides with your extended arms. The *siq* meanders for about a half-mile then extrudes you to a clearing. There you stand face-to-face with the impossibly immense facade of Al Khazneh, otherwise known as the Treasury, popularly known as the real-life version of Indiana Jones's Temple of Doom. What I would give to be in the shoes of Petra's "discoverer," Johann Ludwig Burckhardt, the Swiss explorer and convert to Islam who in 1812 was the first European to see what we see. To Burckhardt the tales seemed hard to believe — an ancient city half buried in the inhospitable Shara Mountains? How did they do it, those Nabataeans? They were a wealthy, ruthless tribe of nomadic silver and spice traders who plundered and taxed their way from the sixth century B.C. on until they fell to the Romans a century after the birth of Christ. What made them gaze at the Petra Basin and say, okay, guys, let's get to work with our little pickaxes and carve an entire city out of that solid pink rock, so handily situated in a quake-prone bowl that's alternately drowned or dry as a bone? What today's snap-happy throngs see is only a third of the city. The rest remains buried, and the world's finest archaeological teams are digging as fast as they can. Here and there a monument or tomb gropes for air like one of Michelangelo's prisoners, elsewhere dimpled surfaces catch the light and reveal themselves to be the shadows of ancient bas-relief, or perhaps an entire building worn smooth by wind, water, and time. Most visitors to Petra spend a day, maybe two, roaming the basin with its amphitheater, temples, and colonnaded street. Some slog or ride donkeys up to the monastery, a building nearly as impressive as the Treasury. But that's it. Alyce Abdallah has hiked Petra at least ten times and longs to return to see more. At her suggestion we hire a guide to lead us to Jabal Arun, which may or may not be the tomb of Aaron, but is magical in any case. It is crowned with a mosque set like a tiny diamond atop one of Petra's highest peaks. The way is at least a three-hour rugged hike from the Treasury.

Our guide Samir leads us up and out of the basin, away from the tour groups. Suddenly there is only silence, interrupted here and there by goat bells or child goatherds calling to their kin. The Bedouin remain in Petra with the government's permission and at its pleasure, a sore point echoing similar ancestral land conflicts around the world. Like Native Americans in the Southwest, many Bedouin peddle soda pop and trinkets to tourists at licensed stands among the ruins. Visitors are happy to buy keepsake "Bedouin crafts," which happen to be imported from India. The Bedouin themselves still weave goat-hair blankets, make knives, and sculpt earthen pots, none of which are on display here. They live simply and subsist on tea, sugar, wheat bread, goat, goat's milk yogurt, rice, and chicken. Our hike takes us past several tents where we are offered tea and, if someone is baking, hot flat bread peeled off a *tannur* heated by a wood fire. Samir is quiet. A sullen type to begin with, he confesses a very un-Islamic hangover and asks us for aspirin. He does offer to carry my overloaded waist pack (I'd recently undergone spinal surgery) and waits politely while we dash behind boulders to pee. We rest on the roof of the white-washed Jabal Arun mosque, a point so high that from here the basin's majestic temples and tombs resemble a Romanesque ant farm. The mosque caretaker climbs the ladder to the roof with a pot of tea. In Jordan one is never far from a cup of tea.

In these few days we've managed to become regulars at Hissam's café, which faces the amphitheater. The Hissam in question is young, irresistible, buff, and twinkly-eyed. Splayed out somewhere near

Hissam's feet at all times is his chocolate-colored hound, a pointer with sad eyes and flopping jowls caked with desert clay. As if Hissam needed any help, the dog is a *habebti* (sweetheart) magnet. Each day as the chilly Petra morning grows brighter and hotter the hiking crowd gathers at Hissam's to drink tea and Cokes. Hissam likes us. We sit there every morning and a few afternoons, but Hissam refuses our money every time. On our last morning in Petra I'm told he has the day off but I can't help keeping an eye out for him. As I walk the long dusty path back to the main gate (Vivian and I had decided to go our separate ways this morning) I'm feeling sad that I didn't get a chance to say good-bye. Suddenly he's in front of me, bounding down the path toward the café, his hound loping behind. "I'm so glad I see you!" cries Hissam, his ravishing eyes ablaze. "I come today because I don't want to miss you!" He takes my hand, kisses me on both cheeks, and we exchange *salaams* and best wishes. Hissam likes me and the world is *jamila*, so beautiful.

I agree when Samir asks me to remove my babushka and drape it around my face like a veil. I assent when Samir rubs my sore back on the roof of the Arun mosque.

And I agree when the lugubrious Samir, who has taken to gazing at me like a beggar child, invites us to the Wādi Mū-sá home of his father, a well-respected Bedouin sheik. "My mother will be baking bread," he tells us. Sitting at Hissam's, Samir looks so depressed I give him my Yankee cap. "Are you okay?" I ask him. "My silence is my happiness," says Samir, who speaks as if he learned English from a translation of *The Prophet*. Samir likes me.

Vivian and I groom ourselves to meet the sheik. In pressed khakis, blouses, and makeup we follow Samir into the sheik's home, part of a drab boxy complex on a dead-end turnoff from Wādi Mū-sá's main street. The small, immaculate L-shaped room consists of two small couches, a coffee table, easy chair, bookshelf, television, and cassette player. Bedouin rugs cover a gleaming linoleum floor. On the shelves and coffee table is a sparse arrangement of unlikely knickknacks: a miniature silk flower arrangement, a set of miniature Delft porcelain clogs tied with ribbon. Compared to what we'd seen of Bedouin homes this is palatial. The sheik has two wives (Samir's mother is the older) and all his grown children are tour guides, teachers, or health professionals. Samir makes a decent living but between his siblings and the demands of his sixty-five nieces and nephews he is constantly parting with his earnings. Like eating from a communal bowl, it is the Bedouin way. Samir does not expect to marry. He laments that he is not a good Muslim — he drinks beer and has affairs. And besides, he tells me, he expects to die young in a car accident. As bizarre a declaration as this is, by the time we leave Jordan I'd heard it many times, always from intelligent young men who, it would seem, have everything to hope for.

Wearing a faded flowered shift and loose headscarf, his kindly faced mother, who speaks no English, takes our hands. Behind her two girls of eight or nine cower shyly at first but meet our smiles with their own. Sam's half-sister, a child in a young woman's body, plops down on an easy chair and grins at us. Typical of children with Down's syndrome she is unself-consciously warm and gentle and we are glad for her company. The other sister serves us tea and thick sour-tasting soup called *rashoof*, made from wheat, yogurt, and shredded lamb. While Samir digests the fact that I'm unavailable for marriage we tromp out to the courtyard to watch his mother bake the bread. "She used to bake every day but now she's so tired all the time," Samir had told us. "She is my father's first wife, and now he has a second wife and more children (there are twenty in all) and my mother does most of the chores, cooking for about eleven people every day." She's gone from being the wife to being the maid. She never leaves the compound.

Samir's mother does her baking in a garage-like enclosure off a small bare courtyard. She places the simple round wholewheat loaves into an ancient, industrial-looking gas-fired oven on legs. She uses commercial yeast and lets the dough rise twice. First dipping her fingers in a bowl of olive oil, she presses the bread down, making depressions with her fingers. She places the breads, three rounds at a time, into the oven where they bake for five to seven minutes, after which she browns them under the broiler flames. "My mother's breads are very light," says Samir as we return to the living room. The bread is very good, similar to Lila's but less crusty. "My dad always complains about the market bread because it's so heavy," Samir remarks. And in a most American way Vivian and I grumble, "Then let him do the baking."

The sheik never shows, and Vivian is perturbed. "We got all dressed up for the sheik!" she cries. According to Samir, the sheik has come down with a headache. "He's resting." Samir's mother, bent with fatigue, gives us some bread to take home. We give Samir, his sisters, and a neighbor a ride down the road. Jordanians abhor a vehicle vacuum; no matter where or how far you're going at least four people pile in for a ride. When we say good-bye Samir looks more miserable than usual. Does Jordan have Prozac?

Mazen likes us. Mazen and his brother manage one of a string of rug and souvenir shops on the main road to Petra gate. With his long, straight, combed-back hair, Brad Pitt stubble, and tight lanky body, Mazen could model jeans in *GQ*. My Arabic dissolves the pout on his perfect features. Mazen is twenty-five, smokes five packs of cigarettes a day, and complains incessantly about working too hard. His favorite line with frugal tourists is "Don't worry be happy." He knows how to say "good price" in six languages. But the off-duty Mazen is gentle and bright with a well-honed sense of irony. I take to sitting with him on the steps to his shop before dinner, which gives Vivian some time to herself and gives me the opportunity to get to know a Bedouin man suspended between two worlds. When Mazen sees me coming he marches to the café next door and orders us a tray of tea. We sip and watch the passing tourists, all sunburned and charley-horsed from their day chasing Nabataean ghosts. I feel at ease with Mazen, so I accept when he offers to take us to the desert to meet his Bedouin cousins and watch the women bake. I figure Viv and I will spend the day there, wherever "there" is, return to Petra Palace for our bags, and leave in the afternoon for Wādi Rum, the Arabian desert to the south.

Vivian and I leave our luggage with Hard-on and tell him about our adventure. His Muppet-esque brow furrows. "What shall I tell Mr. Omar?" he asks. Is he joking? We haven't a clue.

Mazen hops in the backseat of the car and directs us out of the village in a new direction, past the sterile Movenpick Hotel and a succession of equally dreary European-financed hotels in various stages of completion. We swerve around a bend and onto a narrow straightaway slicing through a seemingly endless moonscape. It reminds me of desolate roads I've traveled in Nevada and southern Utah, but to Mazen it's the old neighborhood. "Turn left," he says, and soon we are bouncing and scraping our way to a cluster of goats. "My cousins' camp was here but they moved it," explains Mazen and after maneuvering the car around some immense boulders we drive on to Little Petra. Little Petra is Brooklyn to Petra's Manhattan. Tourists are either unaware of it or avoid it. We have the place to ourselves except for a lone Bedouin slumped against the wall of an ancient tomb picking out a mournful tune on a banjo-like *tsambouna*. Then we file into the men's side of the simple tent of Mazen's cousins Hussein and Fatima. She is dark and beautiful, has three gold teeth and a belly swollen with what will be her fourth child. These people eat, worry, and dream on a rocky patch of earth under a goat-hair blanket.

Bedouin have an expression for what constitutes a household: "They eat from one bowl." As we drink the first of many cups of tea Sayeed, the family patriarch who lives down the road, stares at us intently and smokes cigarette after cigarette, flicking the butts onto the ground between us. Fatima is busy preparing more tea on the "women's" side, separated only by a thin blanket. Through Mazen Sayeed tells us that, true to his name, which is also that of one of the Prophet's sons, he is "every day happy." Though the significance is lost on us, he assures us with a wink that he drinks only camel milk. Through Mazen he wants to know, what country are we from? Mazen explains that the family survives on the milk, yogurt, oil, and meat from their goats. The women earn a little doing embroidery. Fatima's husband Hussein, a slight, limpid-eyed man with perfect teeth, doesn't work because he is ill, Mazen said, not elaborating. A plump, wild-haired child of about two toddles toward me and I reach for her. But the moment the girl settles into my embrace her mother scurries over to grab her. It was insulting but later I read that outsiders and infidels are considered unclean. It's a sobering thought. We Americans tromp across six continents flashing our platinum cards and spreading our smug good will, squatting to pat the heads of native children. It never occurs to us that to many cultures we are the dirty ones. No one sees us wash before eating or praying. We immodestly display our legs and shoulders. We wear shoes indoors.

We are joined by a man in his twenties named Hussein, another cousin, who works as a guide and caretaker at Little Petra. Tall, friendly, and intelligent with a circa 1978 mullet haircut, Hussein speaks nearly fluent English and spends his spare time surfing the Internet at a Wādi Mū-sá café. "She says you American women have an easy life," Hussein translates as Fatima beckons me to help her with the bread. This side of the tent is Fatima's domain. On jerry-rigged shelves sit the accoutrements of Bedouin life: teapot, teacups, mixing bowls, a saucepan, matches, sacks of tea, rice, dried chamomile, sugar, and flour. On the ground sits a pile of dried desert herbs that look like thyme or sage. "For the belly," said Hussein. (Point to any herb in Jordan and you get the same response: for the belly.) Stacked up at the tent's edge are mats, pillows, and blankets. Swept several times a day, the "floor" is simply earth. The men stub out their cigarettes on it. Fatima's stove is a simple wood fire like that of a backpacker or castaway. Fatima, twenty-nine, spends a good part of her day crouched over this fire, boiling water for tea, making bread and rice. Her face is weary and lined under a print headscarf; ornate hammered gold and ruby earrings dangle from her ears.

Though fewer and fewer Bedouin live

nomadic lives, their unleavened round bread suits a traditional existence in which everything is either portable or improvised on the spot. For thousands of years nomads across the Middle East, North Africa, Persia, and Central Europe prepared bread as Fatima does now, with nothing but a wood or brush fire and a flat or concave metal sheet. These makeshift ovens are depicted in the tomb carvings of the ancient Egyptians, before barley and millet were preempted by cultivated wheat. As Fatima pats a ball of dough I notice a large rock protruding from the center of the fire pit and I wonder why Fatima leaves it there. But as I soon discover, the rock, crude as it is, reflects a technological innovation, making Fatima's work a little easier. As a gaggle of children watch in amusement I help Fatima press down the bread dough, a round about the size of a small pizza. Onto the hot coals she sets a lumpy metal slab that looks like a flattened manhole cover. Sweat begins to snake down Fatima's face as she pours water on the hot metal, then whacks it with a stick. Motioning for me to pass her the flattened dough, she sets it onto the metal and tilts the slab into the fire so she can scoop hot ashes with which to cover the bread. The rock supports the metal as Fatima maneuvers the slab around the heat like the head of a big spinning top. I can't see what is happening to the bread under the heap of ash and embers, but when Fatima begins to smack it with an empty flour sack a dense-looking, slightly ash-colored bread emerges. I expect her to point us to the men's side of the tent for bread and tea, but Fatima is not finished. With her husband squatting to help, the two proceed to rip the bread to shreds over a deep plastic bowl. It now resembles something they're planning to feed the birds, but Fatima adds a small pitcher of fresh goat's milk and some water, and with their two pairs of hands the couple works the bread and liquid into a mush. Into this slop Fatima bores a well with her small fist and fills it with about a half cup of olive oil. Our mysterious snack ready, we settle ourselves on the cushions with Mazen, Sayeed, and the two Husseins and take turns washing our hands in a stream of water Fatima pours from a pitcher. Sayeed eats first. We watch him plunge his hand into the mush, extract a blob, work it into a ball, dunk it into the olive oil and pop it into his mouth. What is this stuff called? We can't get an answer, and I begin to suspect it is some kind of good-natured joke. We would politely eat anything they give us, what the hell do we know? Vivian and I reach in, trying to stifle our bourgeois Western paranoia about all those hands, the water, and the unpasteurized milk. And what exactly is Hussein's illness, anyway?

Sayeed enjoys watching us eat. He never takes his eyes off us. There is something so compelling about this skinny man whose face radiates kindness and good humor. At one point he motions for me to eat the bread balls whole, not in wimpy little bites. When I follow his silent instructions the men, the children, and even the wary Fatima share a raucous laugh.

Through Mazen, Sayeed asks if we would be his guests for dinner this evening at his house in the government enclave. We accept. Before we leave we slip Fatima about ten dollars' worth of dinars. Suddenly Hussein, her husband, rises, says something to Mazen and hops into our car for a lift to town. "He needs to go to his car," says Mazen. I leave Mazen at his shop and Viv at the hotel and find myself driving Hussein first to his dead truck, where he collects an empty petrol can, and then to the petrol station for fuel, then back to the car. Everyone stares in amusement at this Western woman in khakis and shades driving around with a Bedouin man in headdress. From Hussein's show of gratitude I realize what has happened: with our money he is able to put fuel in his truck. He had run out days ago.

Hard-on actually looks happy to see us. "You are having fun?" he asks. "You missed a call from Mr. Omar."

Just after dusk we collect Mazen and drive along the Little Petra road to the compound where Sayeed and his family live. The road is pitch dark and the turnoff unsigned, but Sayeed has been waiting in his pickup at the turnoff to signal us with his lights. The long bumpy road leads to a cluster of small characterless concrete blockhouses, the antithesis of the Bedouin tent. "I had . . . expected tent-dwelling pastoral nomads who lived quietly with their herds," writes anthropologist Lila Abu-Lughod, whose book *Veiled Sentiments* is an account of her years with a Bedouin clan. "But [I] found instead that these same people who touted the joys of the desert lived in houses (even if they continued to pitch tents next to them and spent most of their days in the tents), wore shiny wristwatches and plastic shoes . . . and traveled in Toyota pickup trucks. They did not regard these as alarming signs that they were . . . no longer Bedouins, because they define themselves not primarily by a way of life . . . but by . . . a code of morality, that of honor and modesty."

But when we get inside we realize it *is* a tent. A cooking fire smolders in an open courtyard. Off it are two rooms, bare of any furniture except stacks of cushions and blankets. There's a small pantry off the courtyard, and the bathroom, or *hamam,* is a squat toilet out near the chicken coop. At first I think I hear a radio, but when Vivian and I slip off our shoes and join the men and children in the main room we find them riveted to the immense screen of a television set which, thanks to a satellite dish, beams images of Ferraris, rock videos, and half-naked supermodels into this home where supper is cooked on an open fire and eaten on the floor. Sayeed plunks down, motions his wife and daughters to bring tea, and, like patriarchs the world over, hogs the remote. He will flip channels incessantly all evening long.

Already the mother of six, Sayeed's wife is about six months pregnant. Through Mazen, Sayeed told us he wants at least ten children. His wife and daughters had obviously been slaving over the food since

Sayeed sprang the news of our visit that afternoon. Bedouin hospitality is legendary, and traditionally an animal is slaughtered to honor guests. We'd heard that the traditional Bedouin dish called *mensaf*, a mixture of lamb, lamb fat, steamed rice, and pine nuts, was served with the lamb's head poking out of it and guests of honor were presented with the eyes. Thankfully there is no lamb here. We sit down instead to *maghlubah*, or upside-down. A plateau of steamed rice, eggplant, tomato, and chicken with the circumference of a hula hoop, this simple dish must have cost the lives of three or more chickens. Seated in a circle around it, Vivian and I and the men each scoop away at our section — the men with their hands, Viv and I with tablespoons, until the upside-down begins to implode. It's delicious, mushy and oniony. Upside-down is the comfort food of the Arabian Desert. We each have small dishes of salad and yogurt, and Sayeed's wife and children peek in periodically to see if we need tea ("Bedouin whiskey") or soft drinks. If Vivian or I rest for too long Sayeed flashes us a stern look, then stares at the food and back at us. Thus humbled, we pick up our spoons and resume digging away at the platter, which could easily feed fifty people. As they grow full and sleepy the men lean on or into each other and I watch Mazen giggling and humming, settled in contentedly with his cousins. Later he tells me that until he took us to Hussein's tent he hadn't seen these people in many years.

The younger Hussein calls for tea and presents us with riddles. What belongs to you but is used mainly by other people? What is between the land and the sky? Sayeed flips channels. His exhausted wife stares at us from the doorway. We yawn conspicuously. "Bedtime," announces Hussein. He asks if we could please move our car to the back of the house. This is the first we learn of the fact that our visit here might arouse suspicion by the police, who make the rounds in routine night patrols. Whether the vigilance is related to smuggling, drugs, or the burden of foreigners' safety we don't know and can't get a straight answer. Even Mazen is at a loss. We must look nervous, though because Sayeed gets a serious look on his face and says something to us. Mazen translates: "He says, if anyone tries to harm you while you are in his house, he will kill them." Sayeed likes us.

Soon a troop of Sayeed's sons appears

bearing sleeping mats and pillows. We watch them march out the door and up a narrow ladder to the roof. When we are summoned, four mats have been laid out on the rooftop head to toe in a square (for Vivian and me along with Hussein and Mazen, our bodyguards). The men bring a teapot and cups. Soon Sayeed, the older Hussein, and the boys join us under a full moon. They pour our tea, and then they sing to us, mournful Arabic tunes. "I write poems," Hussein tells us. "Would you like to hear one?" His long head sways as he speaks the lilting Arabic lines. We ask Mazen to translate. "I have no idea what that was about," he says. Then Mazen sings a sweet song. "Now you," says Hussein. The men sat still and silent as Vivian and I go through the verses of "Michael, Row Your Boat Ashore." "The River of Jordan is deep and wide, Hallelujah, milk and honey on the other side . . ." I sing with my eyes closed but when I open them I see this tableau of Arabs gazing at us, charmed and perplexed. I know better than to think that bridging the cultural divide is as easy as exchanging songs on a moonlit rooftop. But tonight I want so badly to believe it.

The family descends the ladder and

leaves us to sleep. Soon Hussein is snoring loudly, Vivian is dead to the world, and Mazen has dragged his mat to the other side of the roof. Only I lie awake, staring at the stars and the moon and listening to the baying of wild dogs and the sounds of un-identifiable creatures crunching along the gravelly earth. A hideous dog fight erupts and ends just as abruptly. I'm still hoping to fall off to sleep when the morning prayers pierce the chilly air and roosters follow suit with their own raucous version. There is No God but God. In the first light I notice that the rooftop is adorned here and there with piles of turds. We listen to Sayeed's family coming to life below us. When we climb down to the courtyard the children are all dressed for school and the older ones have laid out a breakfast of fried eggs and flat bread. Arranged like a Bed-ouin incarnation of the Von Trapp family, they watch us eat and allow Vivian to snap a few photographs.

"*Jella* Wādi Rum?" says Hussein. It's time to go but before we leave Vivian places a small bundle of dinars into the hand of Sayeed's wife, who nods her head shyly in thanks. "To place it in the hand — that is the Bedouin way," Hussein says ap-provingly. Sayeed and Hussein join us for the ride to the main road and the children run beside the car, waving and laughing, their book bags swinging wildly. I keep one hand on the wheel and reach back with the other, find Mazen's hand, and clasp it. *Salaam habibi.*

We spend a night and a day in the slow cooker known as Wādi Rum. Settled into our tent in a tourist camp resembling a MASH unit, Viv and I sit in the stupefying heat hydrating ourselves until it is cool enough to walk into the open desert just a quarter mile beyond. The heat sucks the energy out of every living thing. For example, at one point Vivian flops down on some lumpy cushions in the main tent and quickly sinks into a heat-induced coma. An hour later when she wakes, so does one of the "cushions"; she'd been asleep on top of a puppy, also too hot to care. In the setting sun we walk in this, Lawrence's Arabia (they filmed the movie here) toward the seven pillars of wisdom. There we collide with a group of tourists tumbling out of Land Rovers and amassing before their guide: Samir. *"Oy,"* says Vivian. Samir gazes at me, wanting something I can't give or even fathom. *Salaam* and good luck.

The thermometer reads 110 degrees and

we cut short our stay in Wādī Rum. At the military checkpoint charged with nabbing terrorists and smugglers a soldier presents a hapless-looking middle-aged man with a briefcase and beseeches us to drive him to M'aan, a trading center about two hours north on the Desert Highway. The man speaks no English. Vivian and I begin to connive. What excuse can we make to get this strange man out of our car? Why did we allow ourselves to get stuck with him? But it suddenly occurs to me that this man is polite and harmless. Why are we so indignant? "They would never treat us this way," I say, and Vivian sighs. "You're so right." "We'll take him to M'aan," I say. "It's the Bedouin way."

To Omar's delight, we wind up our visit to Jordan with a few nights at the Hisham. We shop in the gold souk, eat hummus and *fool,* pay one last visit to Farq-al-Din, and drink tea at the Eco-Tourism café. Omar arranges for our car to the airport. We say our good-byes. As we reach the city's outskirts the driver's mobile phone rings. "It's for you," he says, handing me the phone.

"Hi, Omar."

"You have a nice trip, Miss Susie. Already I am missing you."

Bedouin Flat Bread

INGREDIENTS:
Three cups unbleached white flour or
  wheat flour
Two teaspoons salt
About two cups warm water

You will need a wok.

Place flour and salt in bowl. Make a well in the center and pour in warm water. Stir water into flour mixture and continue stirring until dough forms, adding water if dough appears too dry.

Knead dough for five to ten minutes, adding flour as necessary.

Divide dough into eight pieces. Roll out each piece as thinly as possible, ten inches or more in diameter. Keep pieces covered before cooking.

Turn wok upside down over gas flame or hot coals of pit fire. When the wok is hot (throw some water on if unsure) oil it lightly using a cloth or paper towel.

Gently lay out bread and press on to cooking surface. (Bedouin use their bare fingers but you can protect yours with a paper or cloth towel.) After about two minutes turn the bread over and press it to hot wok for another minute or so.

Cover cooked breads with a towel to keep them warm.

The World's Largest Bakery:
Biddeford, Maine

Today, in various sections of the country, girls hired by Continental and "preferably starry-eyed" are setting up their little stands in grocery stores, holding out to curious customers a black tray with six or more slices of bread on it, smiling sweetly, and launching into: "Do you think you can pick out the best bread?" To date, almost 90 percent of the 450,000 who have taken the test have picked — you guessed it — Wonder Bread.
— FROM "WONDER BREAD AND CIRCUSES," AN ARTICLE IN A 1938 ISSUE OF FORTUNE

Ninety miles north of Boston, between the Maine Turnpike and the dingy center of Biddeford sits the largest bakery in the world. Opened two years ago by Interstate Brands, the Missouri-based parent company of Nissen and Wonder Bread, the 240,000-

square-foot structure towers over a vast parking lot with a vintage Wonder Bread delivery truck parked permanently by the entrance. This nod to simpler times is dwarfed before the metallic-hued monster beyond, glowing ominously in the sunlight. Its facade looks like that of a high-tech research facility, the type requiring security clearance. It emits no familiar smell. But don't go calling it a factory.

"I'm working on a book and I'd like to visit a Wonder Bread factory," I told George Lampros, vice president of Marketing at Wonder Bread's St. Louis-based parent corporation, Interstate Brands. "And what's your interest in seeing one of our *bakeries?*" he asked. I gave a quick description of my project. Lampros suggested I drive up to the Biddeford *bakery,* the company's biggest and newest. I agreed to send a fax with some possible dates. Lampros was friendly and encouraging. I must have been his last business call before he disappeared on a month-long vacation.

I started from scratch with Mark Dirkes, senior vice president. In contrast to Lampros, his tone was suspicious. "And what exactly is your interest in the *bakery?*" Dirkes wanted to know. Thus began a lengthy screening process. Before I was allowed entry to the inner sanctum of sliced bread I was required to send a proposal outlining my intentions. Dirkes would present it to the other corporate higher-ups, who would mull it over for a few weeks and arrive at a "decision." I pictured a *New Yorker* cartoon conference table assembled with Suits, all harrumphing as they rifle through photocopies of my upbeat paragraphs, heavily edited for their benefit. I knew the company had some widely publicized labor disputes, including a recently settled class-action discrimination suit with black employees of the San Francisco plant. Or maybe they were worried I'd pack the chapter with unflattering if minor facts, such as: for many years Wonder Bread cost less to make than it did to ship. But Dirkes finally spelled out his chief concern. The bigwigs feared I would write that Wonder Bread *isn't good for you.* "It's very nutritious. That's our message and we want to make it clear," said Dirkes, noting that some influential people are unfairly fixated on the virtues of whole grains. Did I know that Wonder Bread is a rich source of calcium? Later, I would see irrefutable evidence to that effect. I would watch a technician dissolve that calcium, in the form of pills the size of yo-yos, in water and dump it directly into a seething vat of Wonder dough.

I come in peace, I assured Dirkes. "I was raised on Wonder Bread," I told him. "I grew all twelve ways, ha ha." A few weeks later I got the go-ahead, and soon I was heading north to Biddeford.

In hand bakeries from Paris to St. Petersburg the daily bounty of puffy loaves or flat rounds are tended by bakers with the focus and intimacy of a midwife. How does a loaf of Wonder Bread come into the world? How do ingredients not much different than those found in the simplest village bakery mingle and morph into something with the uniformity — and, some insist — the taste of drywall? Where are the holes? If possible, assuming it emerges from something so quaint as an oven, I wanted to sample a hunk of Wonder Bread fresh from that oven.

The factor— I mean bakery is the best thing that's happened to latter-day Biddeford, a blue-collar town along a dejected chunk of Maine's southern coast. A conglomeration of mostly defunct textile and brick mills along the Saco River, Biddeford is one of Maine's coastal communities that goes beyond not attracting tourists. These places seem to repel them.

It's not hard to see why.

I inch along Biddeford's main drag looking for coffee early on a Tuesday in October. My dog Louie and I had spent the night in the picturesque village of Ogunquit, about a half-hour south on Route 1. We stayed at the only dog-friendly bed-and-breakfast in a room so cold I clung to Louie's flanks all night to soak up a little of his canine heat. Hours of shivering deformed my posture and everything hurt. Instead of taking breakfast there, I backed out of the B&B's kitchen offering regrets when I decided I'd rather not watch the owners, two paunchy men, padding around with bed-heads and flimsy robes.

Even in the crisp morning light Biddeford's main street looks surreally dark, like a Magritte painting. I cruise all the way up and then back again, past vacant storefronts and consignment shops, and pull up smack in front of an interesting-looking "coffeehouse" over which waved a huge OPEN flag. The colorful sign over the window is framed by steaming cups 'a Joe. In the window is a Goth Halloween diorama, a grinning vampire relaxing in his coffin. Someone had obviously spent a lot of time crafting it. It is eight-thirty in the morning, and I'm applauding my espresso radar, which rarely fails me. The place is vast — I could picture rock bands performing here — but absolutely still and empty. Behind the L-shaped counter heaps of napkins and paper cups lay in disarray. Along the wall stand two Bunn coffee machines, not much bigger than domestic Mr. Coffees. Both are shut off, half-filled with yesterday's congealing brew.

"You looking for coffee?" A pale, pasty-looking man in his thirties appears from the depths of the place. He looks as if he'd been asleep in a coffin, too. He stops to switch on the radio, which spews forth a heart-stopping blast of gansta rap. "Darn cleaning crew," the man says, ambling ever so slowly behind the counter. "What can I get ya?" "Um, I'll have a small hazelnut." "Hmm. No problem. I'll just make a pot, it won't be long." I watch him rummage through the mess for the coffee. "You ought to get an espresso machine in here, do cappuccinos and lattes," I suggest. What a yuppie; I silently scold myself for sounding like a typical jerky tourist. "Oh, I tried that," he replies mournfully, measuring the hazelnut into the filter. "But Biddeford folks don't like anything new or different. We're stuck in the fifties here, in case you didn't notice." So what was the deal with this place? A "coffeehouse" with a huge OPEN sign, and inside, two filthy coffeepots and not so much as a stale doughnut. "I've got this place up for sale," he tells me. "Been two years. Soon as I unload it I'm going to try to work for the bakery." Several industrial parks in the region are thriving with plants manufacturing electronics, machinery, and plastics. But the bakery, he tells me, is "the best deal in town." Everyone wants to work at the bakery.

At the edge of a sea of cars I find myself a spot in the visitors' section of the exalted bakery. A gleaming hulk, it beckons to Biddeford's citizens like a holy shrine. I get Louie settled and head for the entrance. Inside, security is curiously tight. The receptionist sits in a space set back, above and apart like a Supreme Court justice. And something else is odd. This "bakery" doesn't smell. How can that be? For the moment I blame my stuffy allergic nose. I approach the receptionist and her invisible radar field, and after a few minutes of hushed communication she buzzes me in through a broad glass partition. Right there to greet me with a hearty handshake is Jeff Jordan, the forty-five-year-old di-

156

rector of operations. A small but beefy man with a thick head of silver hair and pleasant, boyish features, Jordan has been with the company for twenty-three years. He was relocated from Natick, Massachusetts, to head operations at Biddeford, which replaced several older bakeries, now all defunct. Like many Wonder Bread line supervisors and managers, Jordan graduated from the American Institute of Baking in Manhattan, Kansas. It's the Princeton of industrial baking. Here a baker learns not just the math of the baker's percentage, sponges, or the chemistry of fermentation; he or she studies the science of uniformity in consistency and flavor. The best Parisian hearth bakers will tell you the bread may differ slightly from day to day. But like Big Macs and Coke, Wonder Bread comes with the implied promise that wherever and whenever someone partakes of it he or she will know exactly what to expect.

Actually I grew up on two kinds of bread: onion rye from Bambi, the neighborhood bakery, and Wonder Bread. Like most of my contemporaries, my memories of the bread draw more on feel than on taste. One of the things we loved about Wonder Bread was the way we could smush it into little hard pellets. My neighbor Michael used to come out to play carrying a Baggie containing three or four slices of Wonder Bread. It was the same bread we all ate at home, but somehow we'd all lust after the contents of that bag, in which the familiar cottony slices were upgraded to the status of snack. Michael was stingy with the bread and made a point of fondling it tantalizingly before popping it in his mouth. I stopped playing with Michael in the wake of a misguided deal we'd made, namely that I "would show him mine if he showed me his." He led me behind a spruce tree on neutral ground — the Cohens' backyard — where he abruptly dropped his pants. I shrieked and ran home, reneging on my part of the deal. I avoided him after that, and soon we were grown up and the incident was a distant memory, like the notion of Wonder Bread as a playground treat.

My friend Vivian, an artist, uses Wonder Bread to work pastels into paper. I almost blurt this out to Jordan but I catch myself, assuming he'll find it insulting. Maybe not. Later I notice that on its Web site menu Wonder Bread invites nostalgic memories. One woman's contribution is to recall her beloved childhood game of "Wonder Bread basketball." You took the insides of the bread, squashed and rounded them into pellets, then you chucked the "balls" into the "hoop" left by the denuded crust, explains the woman, now a mother herself. She's basically telling us she preferred playing with Wonder Bread to ingesting it, but the company loves this stuff. The important thing is, Wonder was the bread her parents bought.

Originally conceived by Taggart Baking Company of Indianapolis, Wonder Bread was born in the spring of 1921. At the time it was a very big deal. Wonder's debut was afforded the kind of fanfare more suited to that of a luxury car or newfangled aircraft. For weeks the company offered teasers in the form of blind advertisements and billboards hinting at the coming "Wonder." The label for the new "slo-baked," unsliced (the commercial slicer wasn't invented until six years later), 1.5-pound loaf was the inspiration of Elmer Cline, a vice president for merchandising who was spellbound by a sky blooming in primary colors at an international balloon race.

Times were ripe for Wonder Bread's rise, so to speak. In 1919 the Fleischmann Company, largely a supplier of yeast to commercial bakers, launched a national advertising campaign exhorting housewives to buy bakery bread instead of slaving over homemade loaves. The following year a Kansas City chemist named C. J. Patterson and his associates developed an additive called Paniplus. A mixture of calcium peroxide and buffering salts, it increased commercial bread's dryness, making it far more amenable to large-scale high-speed manufacturing.

Three days before the big balloon race the following ditty appeared in the *Indianapolis News and Star*:

So now the mystery will end,
And to every home a message send,
A message that brings joy to you,
to mother, father and grandma too,
to Mary, Betty, Jack and Joe
For all the family will learn to know,
The meaning of this wonder word,
That everyone has read and heard.
A new delight with every bite,
both morning, noon and every night,
For Mary knows, you know her well,
And many a truth she's had to tell,
And now the best she ever knew,
she gives in this new loaf to you,
For as the bakery leads, they're still
    ahead,
And now it's Delicious WONDER BREAD.

If Wonder Bread, The Movie existed it would have starred Donna Reed and Jimmy Stewart. Judging by the company literature, all America was giddy with anticipation. At last, on May 24, Taggart trucks arrived at markets bearing helium balloons for the children. The newfangled loaves flew out of the stores at the introductory price, a penny a loaf.

Etching Wonder Bread in the American lexicon was a marketing success story akin to Ford and the automobile, DeBeers and the diamond. But unlike cars and gems, bread had been a ubiquitous staple since biblical times. In most parts of the world humans are content to eat the bread of their ethnic ancestors, prepared in much the same way. To seduce "housewives," as the company literature put it, into buying Wonder Bread the company had to convince them to switch to Wonder from whatever bread, homemade or store-bought, they were accustomed to eating. Its marketers bestowed this ordinary white bread with an almost mythical status, a necessary trapping of wholesome family life. The crusade went over the top with the acquisition of the Indianapolis Bakery by Continental Baking Company in 1925, after which American radio listeners were routinely subjected to the cloying jingles of the Happy Wonder Bakers. In their bleached and starched uniforms the quartet sang, "Yo Ho! Yo Ho! We are the bakers who mix the dough, And bake the bread in an oven slow . . . We are the bakers in spotless white, Whose pans are polished and shining bright, Who bake the bread that is always right, Hurrah for the Wonder Bakers!" Wonder sponsored hit daytime dramas like *The Great McCoy*, *Pretty Kitty Kelly*, and *Bachelor's Children*.

As a very young child in the dawn of the media age I was a fount of predigested wisdom. I knew, for example, that Winston tasted good Like a Cigarette Should, that when the bargains go up up up, the prices go down down down. I could tell you who put the "ooh" in shampoo. And though I could not explain why, I knew that Wonder Bread Built Strong Bodies 12 Ways. That campaign was unveiled in the thirties, and somehow the original eight ways burgeoned to twelve. At the 1939 New York World's Fair a balloon-festooned state-of-the-art bakery hosted a constant stream of visitors, who were instructed in the wonders of Wonder. Those were the free-wheeling days before the government concerned itself with advertising claims, so

Wonder could trumpet its nutrients' ability to build muscle, body cells, appetite, brain, blood, energy, growth, bones, and teeth. It was nonsense, of course. The same could be said for just about any food in existence.

Today Jeff Jordan laughs about the "twelve ways" Wonder Bread promises. He is also painfully aware that white bread, long synonymous with blandness and lack of imagination, has had its image pummeled since the late seventies. That's when our generation — his and mine — became enamored of whole wheat, cracked wheat, oats, bran, anything but the gluten-packed, highly processed high-protein flour that finds its way into Wonder Bread. It's a fact: the whiter the flour, the lower the fiber, protein, vitamin and mineral content, all of which decline with increased processing. Of course, today's food industry is adept at putting all this stuff back in the form of additives or "enrichment." But to adult foodies Wonder Bread is a joke, anathema, and a euphemism for all things cheesy and fake.

Kids adore the stuff. "The kids — that's our main market," says Jordan. A preschooler wouldn't express it in these words, but kids love Wonder Bread because of its even, seamless crumb. Wonder Bread is soothing to that segment of the population that is put off by food exhibiting any irregularities, however innocuous. What this means to a child is that Mom and Dad dependably cart home from the supermarket a sliced bread with no holes, a bread from which the jelly half of classic peanut butter and jelly doesn't deteriorate into a sodden purple mess while nesting in junior's lunchbox. It's bread that easily lends itself to gleeful mutilation, bread the misnamed "crust" of which is easily peeled and discarded by finicky toddlers. To kids, denuding a slice of white bread is as instinctive as separating the halves of an Oreo.

"You know, it's a lot easier to make bread with holes than without holes," says Jordan, handing me a paper cap to wear before we enter the factor— oops, the bakery floor. I'm reminded of a passionate treatise by evangelical baker Dan Wing, a Vermont physician who's rigged a masonry oven to a small trailer so he is never, ever reduced to eating anything less than naturally fermented hearth bread. In his book, *The Bread Builders*, cowritten with Alan Scott, Wing launches into a vitriolic deconstruction of supermarket bread, tinged with pity and contempt for the rubes who actually consume it. "The supermarket bread taste is vapid, neutral," Wing writes. "There is not really a taste of wheat, and only a little of caramel (unless caramel was added to the dough as in commercial "wheat" bread)." Wing goes on to dismiss supermarket loaves as being "like insipid students passed from grade to grade and then out into the world — unable to read or figure, ignorant and showing no signs of how they spent the last twelve years." Attempts to solve what he calls the "supermarket bread problem" by baking yeast bread at home, adding some whole grain or forming the loaves into "French" bread, don't work well because, he writes, "you are sending dull students to vocational school where they will fail to learn welding as they have previously failed to learn the history of colonial America."

To Wing, an operation like the Biddeford "bakery" might prove more torturous than the sulfur stench of hell itself. Here Bakery Institute graduates like Jordan — the bread maven's anti-Christ — have perfected a bread that is bleach-white, chemically altered to make it taste moister than it actually is, spongy as a genuine sponge, fortified with sweeteners, and so uniform it allows no light to shine through anywhere. Or as Wing would put it: "The crumb is soft because the walls of the gas cells are thin and flexible — squeeze it a little too much between your fingers and it collapses, never to spring back. Put it in a bowl of soup and it instantly dissolves. Bite it and you can see a little rim of collapse in the crumb where your teeth have . . . crushed it. Chew it and it is gone — a moist plug of paste that slides down the throat on its own moisture, having failed to stimulate a flow of saliva in its short stay in your mouth." One wonders if Dr. Wing would stoop to eat this "moist plug of paste" as an alternative to starvation.

Jordan likes hearth-baked bread, too. He urges me to visit When Pigs Fly, an artisan bakery one exit south of here on the Maine Turnpike. But Jordan loves his job. Even as we relax on upholstered swivel chairs, bread loaves and doughnuts and hamburger rolls and English muffins and Susie Qs are marching in formation to their cellophane and plastic destiny on the aisles of Stop & Shop, Shaw's, Cumberland Farms, the A&P, and thousands of other outlets. Jordan would not be so silly as to call Wonder Bread a gourmet sensation any more than he would compare Susie Qs to *pain au chocolat* from the local patisserie. But when slow-food, whole-food, designer-food types maintain, as Wing does, that the nutritional value of supermarket breads approximates that of water, the folks at Wonder Bread get rather testy.

Though nearly completely automated, the baking of Wonder Bread "isn't a whole lot different from thirty years ago," says Jordan as we stride down what feels like a hospital corridor. "Mind tucking in those earrings?" We enter a cool storage area so deep and wide I cannot make out where it ends. Each week the bakery uses about 1.8 million pounds of flour, which arrive by rail from Cargill Mills in the rustic village of Ayer, Massachusetts. Pressurized and stuffed with two hundred thousand pounds of flour each, the rail cars divert to the bakery's spur off the main line and come to rest in the yard outside where we stand now, dwarfed by bins marked EDIBLE, VEGETABLE PRODUCT, or TROUGH GREASE. Pumping air pressure into the rail cars "fluidizes" the wheat flour into a dust that's easily air-blown into the building, explains Jordan above the din as a succession of flour tornadoes rage in the pipes clustered overhead. Here too are towering tanks of soy and sunflower oil, also pumped in, untouched by human hands.

We all read *The Jungle*. What rodents and random body parts lurk in the soybean oil? If there were cat carcasses in the flour how would we know? There are ways, however. Every flour shipment passes through a series of magnets that remove even tiny scraps of metal and elaborate sifters to root out most insects and anything larger.

Advancing into the "processing area," Jordan directs me to a pungent tank of frothing yeast, maintained at forty degrees. With a straight face Jordan tells me that Wonder Bread is made "the old-fashioned way." By this he means the bread begins with a sponge of flour, water, yeast, and shortening and the ensuing goo is allowed to ferment for four hours just like a bread you'd make in your kitchen at home. Well, not exactly. The mixers handle three thousand pounds ("you won't see anything bigger anywhere") says Jordan, and each batch of fermented sponge is automatically hitched onto a track, lowered, and dumped into the immense mixing vats like rubbish from the back of a garbage truck. The "bakery" can store up to twenty-five vats of fermenting sponge at a time. "The entire process is computerized," says Jordan, handing me a prune-sized blob of unfermented sponge, and another of fermented sponge. The first feels like Play-Doh and the second feels like whipped cream cheese. I hand the samples back to Jordan, who absentmindedly continues to play with them as we move on. We collide with a human, a man named Tom. Like Jordan himself, Tom is a graduate of the American Institute of Baking in Kansas City and he's been trained in the relatively young science of food additives. After the sponge demonstration we find him busy with a tray of giant pills in varying shades of yellow. Tom dissolves the nutrient pills — ascorbic acid, for example — in a plastic bowl full of water and waits for the computer to announce: "READY TO DISCHARGE." Plop comes the sponge, untouched by human hands, and Tom dumps the yellowish additive broth into it. Here I see that another additive is a calcium-packed dust of chalk or gypsum, the "great source of calcium" for which Wonder is touted. Tom types away at the computer keyboard and at his instructions the snakes of stainless steel writhe and rumble to life: flour, molasses, soybean oil, water. He dumps in a bucketful of salt. The rounded door groans shut while its contents fold and churn like those of a cement mixer.

When Jordan leads me across a kind of catwalk to the other side I find myself gazing upon a massive panorama of stainless steel. Like a cross between a Rube Goldberg creation and a roller coaster the tracks climb and curve, disappear and reappear in a chaos of vats, tubes, and tunnels. To my right a procession of empty loaf pans advances in neat columns while on a nearby conveyor a machine spits identical dough balls. "Now the dough gets sheeted out — pressed to get out the gas bubbles," says Jordan, reaching over to fix a logjam. The dough momentarily disappears under a roller and like an immortal cartoon character, emerges flat. Another gizmo folds each circle into a loaf-sized roll just as the pans are entering stage left, each freshly spritzed with a shot of oil from a pipe organ of nozzles. Six pans abreast, they proceed to a junction where they're snatched away to a proof box to bask in 115 degree heat, 70 percent humidity, for fifty minutes. Out they come and onward they march, right into a small city of gas-fired ovens. After nineteen minutes at 400 degrees, it's on to the de-panner, essentially a cluster of vacuums, which literally suck each loaf out of its pan. The bakery's output is 210 loaves a minute.

So dazzled am I by this bread version of *Triumph of the Will*, that I fail at first to note, again, that this place doesn't smell. Legions of bread loaves are baking, and there is almost no smell. "It's the new ovens," says Jordan with a sweeping gesture. "They burn off the ethanol, which is what you're smelling when you smell bread baking. All this bread would produce more than fifty tons of ethanol, enough to pollute the atmosphere. Our ovens are more environmentally sound." I'd heard of bakers getting drunk on fermentation fumes. I suppose without those newfangled ovens Jordan and I would be putting lampshades on our heads.

I'd like to taste the bread fresh from the de-panner, but when Jordan plucks a hot loaf off the assembly line and rips it open it's only to illustrate just how hot and steamy the bread is before its circuitous cooling route above our heads. We pass a Dumpster marked INEDIBLE and Jordan chucks the fresh loaf into it. The Dumpster is half full of damaged or imperfect loaves. "We call them the cripples," says Jordan. After about an hour the cooled loaves feed into a slicer and bagger, and this is the point where Jordan grabs a bread, hands me a slice, and takes one for himself. We both take a bite. "That's the real thing, huh?" says Jordan, giving the bread the thumbs-up. To me the bread tastes no different at all than it would after a week on the A&P shelf. Jordan chucks the rest of the loaf into another reject bin and we watch as a computerized inkjet brands each packaged loaf with an expiration date. Next the wrapped and dated loaves will be hoisted into the bellies of a fleet of delivery trucks. But that's boring, so Jordan guides me to the dessert portion of the bakery. Soon we are watching a million doughnuts march and witnessing a chorus line of mini-piecrusts being dosed — splat! — with a shot of bright red, blue, or beige goo.

Back in his office I thank Jordan profusely. I really did enjoy myself. And apparently he did, too. He ducks out of the room and is all smiles when he returns with a sack of Susie Qs, fruit pies, and a few packages of those cream — I mean "crème" — filled cupcakes with the chocolate icing and the white squiggle. He's included a loaf of classic Wonder bread. I can't bear to dispose of it so I stick it in the freezer and promptly forget about it. That was almost a year ago, and still it remains. Apparently I attach some sort of significance to it, something having to do with the past, with simpler times. It's as if I were stashing a Shirley Temple doll or an original hula hoop. For someone of my vintage that squishy bread has a lot of connotations. Not one, however, has anything remotely to do with calcium content.

Wonder Bread Basketball Set

Take slice of Wonder Bread and with your fingers, remove center of bread from crust, leaving crust intact.

Press removed center of bread into several small, hard balls.

Have opponent hold intact crust "basket" aloft; toss balls into basket.

Switch roles and repeat.

Simple Gifts:

Shanagarry, Ireland

*So, her hands scuffled
over the bakeboard,
the reddening stove
sent its plaque of heat
against her where she stood
in a floury apron
by the window . . .*

*And here is love
like a tinsmith's scoop
sunk past its gleam
in the meal-bin.*
— FROM "MOSSBAWN:
I. SUNLIGHT,"
SEAMUS HEANEY

In chilly November I flew the red-eye from
Boston to Ireland's Shannon Airport, where
I rented a car and drove south to County
Cork. Big mistake — the driving part, I

mean. I believe I may be wanted in Ireland as a terrorist, the kind who wantonly shears off side mirrors and tramples hedges.

I stumble off the plane, exhausted from lack of sleep and emotionally drained from weeping through a mawkish in-flight film, *Autumn in New York*. Soon, still in a stupor, I find myself at the controls of a rental car from SixtSixtSixt. Doesn't that have something to do with Satan? It was one of those tuna cans on wheels existing only for rental and possessing, God help me, a standard transmission. In it I lurch ambivalently along the construction-choked streets of Limerick. I am sick with fear and fatigue. I must be insane — driving on no sleep, on the wrong side of the road, reaching into thin air for the clutch, mauling the local flora and trying to make sense of a map that may as well have been of Tajikistan. I can't sense where the car is on the road or even *if* the car is in fact on the road. It occurs to me only after an hour or so it might be wise to adjust the rearview mirror. In it I see only a swatch of the backseat upholstery. Hungry and dispirited, I eat my first hunk of real Irish soda bread at a workingman's café chosen only because I manage to pull up there without causing a multivehicle pileup. The bread lingers unnaturally in my esophagus and tastes as appealing as a sulfa pill. A burly farmer seated beside me scarfs down ham steak and beans mired in a bog of grease. He never looks up from his plate. I finish my tea and step out into the cold rain, feeling lost and lonely. In the few hours I've been here Ireland seems a punishing place: sad cafés, sad farmers inhaling sad ham, sad dry bread.

It's a long way to Shanagarry and Ballymaloe House, my destination there. The harrowing trip will be well worth it.

Why do the Irish alone eat soda bread? Despite its recent, unprecedented prosperity Ireland has always been an austere place, the modest needs of its citizens honed by centuries of deprivation. Before bread there were potatoes, so abundant bread was an afterthought to the Irish table. Wheat was precious and bread was a treat. Until the 1840s Irish tenant farmers raised grain and cattle to pay their rents, they subsisted on potatoes. By 1845 Ireland's entire potato crop had succumbed to a fungus that rots potatoes not just in the ground but where they are stored. This set into motion events leading to the deaths of at least a million Irish from starvation and typhus. What happened to the wheat? The British absentee landlords continued to export it, and changes in the tax laws make it more profitable for farmers to switch from growing wheat to raising cattle, a change that resulted in the eviction of small Irish farmers. America's gestures of aid turned disastrous. Emergency grain arrived but the Irish lacked horses and carts to transport it. There were few ovens and no bakers. The Irish way was to steam the bread in a covered kettle under a layer of embers. When the U.S. exported cornmeal, or "yellow meal," to ease the famine the Irish used it for porridge and only slowly and reluctantly blended it with rationed wheat flour for soda bread. In fact, Ireland's proverbial obsession with "the drink" is said to date back to the days when whiskey was cheaper than bread. During my time spent in the stony embrace of Irish country kitchens I saw wheat flour still handled as if the loss of even a teaspoon to the countertop or floor would be a sin.

The notion of yellow meal bread never really caught on, but otherwise the recipe for soda bread hasn't changed. A loaf of the ubiquitous brown soda bread is a thing of rough-hewn beauty that tells a story as poignant as that of an octogenarian's face.

The bread is crusty and unyielding. Its patina is earthy and coarse enough so that if you laid the bread on the earth one might confuse it with a rock. Throw in an egg, raisins, and a bit of sugar and you've got Irish "wedding cake." Traditional soda bread isn't even tainted by the pretensions of a mixing spoon — the dough is churned with a stiffened hand. Ingredients vary ever so slightly from family to family but the bread is born always from flour, buttermilk (or sour milk), and sodium bicarbonate, better known as baking soda.

A hunk of warm, crusty soda bread effectively fills the stomach. But aside from the protein in the wheat and milk, its nutrients are actually sabotaged by the sodium bicarbonate, the poor man's leaven. Soda bread is "good for you" only as an alternative to starving.

With the confounding roundabouts, traffic jams, and road construction in Limerick my progress southward toward Cork is horrifyingly slow. I am headed to the tiny farming village of Shanagarry, near the Irish Sea in southeast Cork. There I will spend a few days in the company of the Allen family, who run a guesthouse, farm, and cookery school. Both matriarch and son are famous for their soda bread and Irish brown bread.

I have been in a bus crash in India. I have rappelled off a towering rockface, hugged the ocean in an ultralight plane, and nearly collided with a hulking black bear in the Olympic Wilderness. But nothing I've done is scarier than driving alone in Ireland. At one point I am so thirsty I abandon all reason and make a grab for the water bottle on the seat beside me. I nearly nosedive into the bloody hedge. Maneuvering the Fiat in the narrow chaotic streets of downtown Cork City I hear the ugly sound of metal on metal, the sound of the Fiat dismembering its first side mirror, that of a double-parked pickup truck. "No problem, love," says the cheerful driver, who could just as easily have lost an arm. The truck was already battered and covered with rust. "These things happen. But could you do me a favor, love? Could you fetch it for me?" Leaving the idling Fiat where it has the greatest capability of pissing everyone off, I sprint up the street to where the mirror lay, scoop it up, and breathlessly hand the mangled metal to the pickup driver, who actually smiles and thanks me. I drive off trying to appear nonchalant while the Fiat bucks like a mechanical bull. At least I know I'm not the first foreigner to wreak this brand of havoc. As the couple argued, my friend's husband once barreled down a residential street in North London with a disorienting rat-tat-tat, shearing off mirror after mirror on a line of cars.

Though the actual roads bear no resemblance to the neatly arranged routes on my map, I find my way to the seaside village of Kinsale in East Cork, and check into the Long Quay bed-and-breakfast. The sun had long disappeared and the Fiat had hydroplaned its way past a string of inviting lodgings. But I choose Long Quay for the following reason: it is the first building along Kinsale's main street that possesses several legitimate parking spaces. I slide into one, manage to silence the odious little vehicle, and first push, then fall, through Long Quay's tall double doors: "I hope you have a room," I announce, "because I cannot, I will not, get back in that car."

I sleep right through breakfast, waking to the signature soundtrack of the Emerald Isle — rain hammering the windowpanes. Wrapped in scarves and a parka, I head out to Kinsale's main street, a pleasing jumble of pastel-colored storefronts, cafés, and pubs. In a river of umbrellas I march to the first bakery I can find and sit down at one of several tables inside, watching the drenched locals come in for their morning scones and soda breads. As in America, fewer and fewer Irish bake bread at home, though as bread baking goes there is little labor involved. The Cork grandmothers I'll meet can whip up soda bread in minutes and baked bread for their families daily, as their mothers and grandmothers had. At this particular bakery the soda breads are squarish lumpy pillows the color of beach sand. Once claimed, each loaf falls into its crinkly plastic bag with a thud. My stomach is still a little queasy from yesterday's ordeal, and all I can manage is a few bites of a dry wheaty scone.

Imagine my reluctance to embark on the round of Russian roulette the ride to Shanagarry promises to be. If someone were willing to chauffeur me there in the Fiat I would've paid an obscene amount for the service. But this isn't the third world, one of those countries with an eternal supply of jack-of-all-trade freelancers with wide-open schedules. This is the new Ireland, its streets lively with young professionals, its antiquated roads screaming with BMWs, its blossoming consumer economy inching toward the crass materialism of its friend across the Atlantic.

After many harrowing miles and another side-mirror amputation (this time my victim was a parked Mercedes) I am indescribably relieved to be veering at last onto the narrow lane to Ballymaloe House. A four hundred-year-old stone farmhouse cloaked in wisteria, the inn sits at the end of a narrow lane at a hairpin — and hair-raising — turn off the road from Shanagarry. A large pool slumbers in the autumn chill along with its adjoining carriage house and thirty-six guest rooms. Ballymaloe struts the kind of understated, slightly tattered beauty that attracts the confident rich and the unflashy famous. Hillary Rodham Clinton and her daughter Chelsea came here for a rest after a state visit to Ireland. Waiting to be escorted to my room in the carriage house, I find other guests huddled in easy chairs by the fireplace, handsome couples in sturdy walking shoes and cashmere, sipping tea from delicate English porcelain. Ballymaloe is one of those places where staff are so unfailingly warm and good-humored one isn't sure whether the management treats them exceptionally well or programs them with electrodes. As the Fiat slumbers in a mud puddle in the gravel parking lot I could hug them all.

My room is simple and cheerful, pale yellow with a small couch and tea table. After soaking in the clawfoot tub I dial Tim Allen, the "bread man," to tell him I've arrived, nearly in one piece. "Oh good, good," he replies. "Then I'll come 'round at seven and join you for dinner." The bay windows of my room look out across a cobbled path to the Ballymaloe kitchen. Resting on my elbows I drink in a scene out of Dickens. Young rosy-cheeked maidens in gray and white pinafores carry baskets of fruit, greens, and fresh herbs. Soon the kitchen windows are fogged opaque from the steam of a row of simmering pans and cauldrons. I expect to see a boy in knickers come to deliver a goose. My stomach makes pleading noises: two hours until dinner. I climb under the covers and sleep until six-thirty.

An assortment of handsome, tweedy middle-aged couples fans out from the heat of the grand fireplace in Ballymaloe's main drawing room. Those rosy-cheeked girls appear periodically with trays of wine and cocktails as I park myself in a wing-backed chair — the only person without a companion — and await Tim Allen, who is late. He is habitually late, but I've no way of knowing this as I fidget and sip soda water. At about half-past seven a rumpled, ponytailed man in sagging trousers enters the room as gracelessly as if someone on the other side of the door had pushed him. Squinting through his small round specs, he gives me a dismissive once-over and goes on to scrutinize everyone in the room. This is entertaining. He has decided I can't be me, and, frankly, I wasn't expecting someone like him either. I watch him make inquisitive eye contact here and there before pivoting back to me and asking, "You're not Susie, are you?"

With his perpetually furrowed brow, billowing trousers, pilled sweater, and general lack of vanity Allen seems a behind-the-scenes sort of guy. I take to him instantly. His wife, Darina, is the confident, photogenic force — and I mean force — driving the cookery school, having spun her gift into a series of glossy cookbooks and a popular television cooking show. Allen is accustomed to baby-sitting journalists while Darina is away on one of her frequent culinary excursions. She's on the road now, at a Thai food conference in Napa, California. She won't return until the night before my departure so I have

Tim to myself. After just a few minutes of his gentle company I'm glad for that.

The Irish do not strike the visitor as a frivolous people. I accompany Tim to the seaside village of Ballycotton to deliver birthday presents to his one-year-old grandson Joshua, who lives in a tiny cottage with his mother, Rachel, and father, Isaac, Tim and Darina's oldest child. Each simple timeless present — a wooden train, a wooden wagon — is wrapped in newspaper. Rachel's effusive, even giddy thanks could not be anything but genuine. Both Rachel and Isaac do well at the farm and cookery school but the trappings of their life in this tiny cottage near the sea seem far tamer than that of an American couple of equal means. The Irish haven't yet unlearned the habit of making do with very little.

"I'm sorry I'm late," Tim says when he comes to collect me the next morning, an hour later than we'd planned. I just sigh. He's one of these people who are always late, and always sorry. But his excuse is disarming and unexpected: "I volunteer for a suicide prevention hotline, and I had a fellow this morning in very, very bad shape." Two days in the country and I can sense how difficult it would be to be alone or lonely or both, in this place. Already I can empathize with the siren call of the sleeping pill. The days are so short. The weather is bleak, soggy, downright punishing. Long daunting miles lay between home and the nearest café or grocery store. The cattle and sheep outnumber the people. Listen to me. I may have to call that hotline myself.

Though he has a cast of Irish melancholy, Tim feels blessed in his life here. His children are bright, cheerful, and productive. He is a new grandfather. Cultivated slowly and casually as a way of pulling in extra income, the cookery school is wildly successful, with an international reputation, a waiting list, and celebrity chef instructors. Thanks to Ballymaloe, "Irish Cuisine" is no longer an oxymoron.

"In my life I am eternally grateful for two things: I can cook. And I can make bread." So begins Tim as he commandeers his Volvo like a submersible through the downpour en route to Cork City, where he will take me through the main food market. As the narrow road spills into the city limits both lanes seize up with traffic. Tim remains calm and chatty as he careers around front-end loaders and roadblocks and threads through the chaos so that be-

186

fore too long we are one of a line of cars headed into the gaping mouth of downtown Cork's main parking lot. Like the laid back, chronically delayed Tim, the Irish don't appear to be in a rush.

The car finally parked, Tim leads me along a network of malls into the farmers market, a chilly succession of stalls hawking meat, poultry, produce, cheese, coffee, bread, and sweets. But the smell of raw meat overwhelms, and many of the stalls appear to specialize in profoundly unappetizing organ meats. At least to me the stuff looks disgusting, and it's hard to imagine anyone gazing upon these vats of slimy body parts and saying, as one might in reference to a thick filet mignon, Yum! Resembling a Cold War propaganda photo, a sullen matron in a stained apron presides over a pale coiled heap of . . . what? Intestine? Pancreas? And whose? "Lots of the local dishes are made from offal," explains Tim, on his way to collect a sack of defleshed chicken carcasses for cooking stock. Before Irish independence the British overlords hogged, so to speak, the choicest meat cuts, leaving the peasantry to make do with discarded organs, bones, and fat. In the same way that the Irish cling to a bread tradition born of extreme shortages and hardship, they continue to dine on offal, which remains Cork's "specialty." If I so much as had to look at that grisly slop every day, I'd weigh ninety pounds.

Tim meanders among the stalls procuring odds and ends for the cookery school and some treats for us, including a few varieties of spicy oil-cured olives. As far as fruit, vegetables, and herbs go, Tim and Darina rely almost completely on the harvest of their organic farm, including an acre of greenhouses and an idyllically landscaped Victorian garden whose stone-edged walking paths meander past riots of flowers and herbs. The farm is as lovely as it is productive. On their twenty-fifth anniversary Tim commissioned for Darina a tiny cupola-crowned cottage, covered ceiling, walls, and floor with mosaics crafted entirely of seashells. It's stunning. When the sun shines, light reflects off swirling nebula of mother-of-pearl, oyster, conch, cowrie, and abalone, and illuminates inlaid necklaces of nautilus and conch. A young British woman who lived with the Allens while she worked crafted the shell house over six months. It was her first big commission. *HG* magazine ran a spread on the shrine-like house, and, presto, now she's busy inlaying shells on the bathroom walls of Beverly Hills celebrities.

"We started the school in 1983 as a way of making some money, actually," says Tim as we drive through a bleak, endless tunnel of rain. "We were struggling with four small kids and a farm." Darina's unbounding energy and business smarts were crucial; she holds a degree in hotel management. The two met when Ballymaloe House hired Darina. By all accounts Darina is a typhoon wrapped in a woman's body. In the school's colorful corridors I encounter Darina's long square face beaming from a succession of cookbook covers, newspaper and magazine spreads. With brightly colorful decor inspired by the family's annual visits to Oaxaca, Mexico, the school has expanded to include a café with a sweeping view of the hills and a hint of the sea beyond. But the Allens closed the café, both defeated and incensed by the local licensing and health requirements. "The inspectors would be in here grousing about how our pans are dull and stained, saying they should be shiny! Can you believe that? We are *cooks*. Our pans don't stay shiny for long." Fortunately the rules for the cooking school are less stringent. The place is immaculate, though, and doesn't feel the slightest bit institutional despite the rows of regulation sinks and mixers and butcher blocks. The floors are tiled in terra-cotta stone, the whitewashed walls are hung with milagros and tapestries, and bowls crafted by local potters line the shelves.

I know a man who took courses at Ballymaloe and decided to return again and again. The school's twelve-week professional course accommodates fifty-six students, about forty of whom live in converted stables and former servant quarters on the farm. They come from everywhere — Britain, the U.S., Canada, New Zealand, Belgium, South Africa, and lately, Japan. There's a waiting list to get in, which isn't surprising. In these days of food celebrity cults Ballymaloe is a big draw with ladle-bearing luminaries for instructors such as Chez Panisse's Alice Waters, Madhur Jaffrey, Nina Simonds, and, of course, Darina Allen herself.

Darina rules the roost. She is the muse, the enforcer, and the den mother. But when it comes to bread Tim is The Man. Pastry is for the fastidious and the fussy, bread is the messier passion, one of free spirits and poets. I have no idea if this is true. I just made it up. But spending time with Tim I hatch a theory about bread people. The student chefs at Ballymaloe painstakingly craft the most photogenic layered pâtés, things glacé, and things *en croûte*. "But I never see them so excited as when they bake their first bread," says Tim. "Perhaps because bread dough is actually alive, people don't feel worthy of the task." Unless they grew up with homemade bread people attribute something mystical to the process; surely they as mere mortals will fail at it. "There's something about their faces when they take that bread out of the oven." Steeped as they may be in the alchemy of the kitchen — sugar melting into syrup or gluey egg whites morphing into snowy white froth — they are struck by the magic of bread. "Once they understand that all you really need is flour and water, they're just amazed," says Tim. "It's a revelation."

Tim joins me for late dinners at Ballymaloe, famed for its homegrown organic free-range gourmet feasts served up with orgiastic flair. At Ballymaloe House, where Tim and his five brothers and sisters grew up, every evening is a rerun of *Tom Jones*. Tim's late father Ivan first came here as a farmhand at the age of seventeen. It was during World War II that Myrtle learned how to cook wholesome food with surplus tomatoes, mushrooms, cucumbers, apples, cream, butter, and eggs. In the fifties the family began renting a few of the mansion's more far-flung rooms, and his mother Myrtle began cooking for the guests, testing her recipes. Word spread fast; this is, after all, Ireland, where even the well-heeled are known to sup on boiled meat and potatoes and pepper is considered an exotic spice. By 1964 the restaurant was open five days a week.

It's understandable that Myrtle shares a deep professional bond with her friend Alice Waters across the ocean. Like Waters at her famed Chez Panisse, Myrtle and kitchen manager Rory O'Connell, Darina's brother, begin conjuring the day's menu by asking what's fresh. It's as if a dressmaker were handed ostensibly mismatched remnants of silk, linen, velvet, and burlap and commanded to fashion an evening gown. Their suppliers read like the cast of a children's tale. There's Mr. Cuddigan, the butcher who "watches over his cattle and sheep down to the last sprig of burnet in his old pastures and the sweet meadow grasses in his hay." There's Patty Walshe, who brings in shellfish from Kenmare Bay and fresh organic vegetables and greens from the gardeners at the cookery school. And there is Fingal Ferguson's bacon from free-range pork smoked with wild herbs. I have never tasted anything like this bacon, and find myself lying awake at five in the morning thinking: only three more hours until the bacon. Fingal Ferguson, you have made this non-kosher Jewish girl very happy.

Dressed smartly in dark tailored suits and soft printed blouses, Myrtle cuts an impressive figure as she moves from table to table to chat, resting a hand on a guest's back and leaning in close to greet his children. Framed by a neatly styled mane of white hair, her face radiates intelligence and the faintest hint of impatience. She is Miss Marple with a commanding edge. I could tell that somewhere offstage this woman can really raise hell. Since her husband passed away two years earlier she is wedded to Ballymaloe. The union seems harmonious and satisfying to all concerned. Myrtle has twenty-two grandchildren and two great-grandchildren. She works harder than anyone else does at Ballymaloe, which may be one of the reasons her staff seems to respect more than fear her. Myrtle has class, and her invisible touches explain the international allure of this understated old house. Of Ballymaloe's many soothing qualities is the fact that, with the exception of the shop, you never see money changing hands. After a day the staff seems to have divined your special needs: the wine you drink, when you take tea, whether you prefer biscuits or cake.

I get the feeling Myrtle isn't crazy about me. Mainly, I feel my presence at the A-list table cuts into her time communing with Susie and Betsey, American visitors who are close friends of the exalted Alice Waters. For better or worse, I'm a pretty transparent person. I am unsuccessful in masking my irritation with Susie, a fundraiser and close personal friend of Hillary Rodham Clinton, who drops names like "Elton [John]" and "Drew [Barrymore]" and "The President [the President]" and Alice, Alice, Alice. We hear, ad nauseum, about Susie and spouse's private audiences with the luminary chef, how she whipped up a crimini mushroom-dingleberry this and a grilled jalapeño huckleberry guinea hen that, and on and on. Tim is mostly silent, but Myrtle seems enchanted by everything Susie says, and not at all amused by this Susie's meager contribution to the dinner conversation. That Susie: "It's so exciting! Alice raised all this money to start a program in the Berkeley schools and now all the kids are learning organic gardening!" This Susie: "Terrific. Maybe now someone will donate money for textbooks."

It doesn't help that I blurt out how I thought making soda bread was easy. This is no way to score points with Myrtle. "It is *nawt* easy!" Myrtle says, her reply punctuated with a gasp. Humbled, I try to recover by adding that by easy, I meant "simple." But the damage is done.

There's nothing you can tell Myrtle about Irish bread. Like all matriarchs of her generation, she baked for her large family every day, usually more than once. Her brown wheat bread is famous. Immortalized in James Beard's classic *Beard on Bread*, it is at once dense and airy, like the finest hand-woven Irish scarves. It's got the kind of wholesome wheaty aroma that makes you want to rub your nose in it like a dog. Howie and I once stayed at a bed and breakfast in Galway. The proprietress was beautiful — she resembled Liv Ullman — and she had strong, elegant hands. She didn't seem to mind us lingering in the kitchen to watch her work the dough for the brown bread. I remember waking up to that bread and thinking it was just about perfect. Myrtle's breads have that effect on people, so much so that she's packaged the dry ingredients for sale in the Ballymaloe Shop. The store is constantly selling out, and departing guests can be seen pacing in wait for a promised shipment.

On a frigid Sunday morning I drive two miles along the narrow Shanagarry road to Darina and Tim's farmhouse for a day of baking. The Fiat and I have arrived at a truce, though I know better than to take my hand off the gearshift for even a second. I pull up to the cookery school parking lot and follow a friendly terrier through a gang of free-range chickens to a succession of locked doorways until I arrive at the main entrance of Tim and Darina's home, a stone manor house with a grandly framed doorway. A striking white-haired woman in a thick button-down sweater greets me: Elizabeth O'Connell, Darina's mother. The house is deadly still as I stand in the living room, all squishy armchairs and throw rugs and smelling of damp. Elizabeth bundles up in her parka and I follow her out past the garden to the school, where we find Tim in the office, fiddling with his nemesis, the computer.

"Ah, so you're here," he says, spectacles askew. "Come, then. Let's collect some flour." As he fiddles with canisters and scales in one of the school's many pantries, Tim explains that the method of using soda as a rising agent in bread began in the nineteenth century. In these worst of times, the only staples in the poor peasant's kitchen were sour milk and very low gluten, soft flour. It performed poorly, but when baking soda was added the bread rose beautifully. And a family could make soda bread on top of the fire; they didn't even need an oven.

It's the oven that dominates Tim and Darina's rugged kitchen. A massive Aga stove, it stays hot and ready for cooking as long as the fuel holds out. All the Aga's simple controls and burner protectors are nonconductors, cool enough for the cook to lay his hand right on them. "The Aga was designed by a Swedish doctor whose wife was blind," explains Tim. "He wanted to create an oven she never had to light, with burners she could maneuver without burning herself." You can't regulate the temperature on the Aga. "You just say, okay, it's hot enough," says Tim. I concede that the Aga is a brilliant invention. But the lout should've given his poor wife a break and sprung for a cook.

As I sit at the long wooden table watching Tim crash around with various implements and mixing bowls, the low-ceilinged kitchen reminds me of an illustration for a fairy tale. The Three Little Bears, perhaps. On exposed shelves with scalloped trim sit squadrons of teas, herbs and spices, and sturdy hand-fired Irish crockery forms shelves full of colorful lilting towers. The cabinets are painted the candy blue of a child's bedroom. One side of the kitchen opens to a stone courtyard with the Victorian gardens and working farm beyond, on the other the terra-cotta floor climbs a few steps to a set of French doors that open to a patio reminiscent of a Tuscan villa. I so much prefer this place to the stainless-steel test-kitchen look of my most serious foodie pals back home, but I knew its earthy charms were far from haphazard and the designer's fingerprints are all over the place. Still, Tim seems as if he could make do with a mess kit and a campfire.

Tim has devised an agenda: "We'll make some brown soda bread, white soda bread, white scones, some Ballymaloe brown bread, and some spotted dog." Spotted dog? That would be white soda bread with sultanas, the traditional Irish wedding "cake." When it is all over we'll sit down to a lunch of bread, scones, more bread, butter, sharp cheese, and strong French press coffee. Staring at the random canisters of flour and the strange hulk called the Aga, I feared our snack is a long, long way off. Luckily I binged on Fingal's Nobel-worthy bacon this morning. I also ate a basket full of Myrtle's bread.

"When the kids were small we used to take a houseboat on the Shannon and I made bread every day," says Tim as he weighs flour for spotted dog, the first round of soda bread. "The first time I was left alone after our son was born I made my mother's brown bread. I did it from memory, from watching her all those years. When I was little she'd tell me to mind the dough. That's the one thing I miss when we're traveling — the brown bread. I went to Italy with the girls for two weeks and brought the brown bread flour with us. The trouble was, we stayed with a family that had no butter."

What Tim has trouble conveying to his students is that baking the same type of bread is different every time. "I compare it to developing film," he says. Conditions always vary slightly so you must feel, smell, taste. Into the cream flour Tim adds some coarse salt and a level teaspoon of baking soda, which he's put through a sieve. He adds a few spoonfuls of sugar and works the dry ingredients with his hands, to aerate and lighten it. "Soda bread is more of an art than a science," says Tim. "It's your hands, it's how you handle the flour. The first thing I tell my students is, get rid of the mixing spoon."

Tim cracks two free-range eggs into some buttermilk. The eggs and dried fruit were what made spotted dog such a rare treat. "Poor farmers always sold eggs for cash, so they were a real treat for the family," says Tim. "And dried fruit was so expensive they'd only use a tiny bit, for weddings and special occasions." Some people call spotted dog "railway cake." "On the slow train from Dublin to Cork you'd eat a raisin at every station." (There were thirty stations and, perhaps, thirty raisins.) When Tim pours the egg and buttermilk mixture into the flour bowl his expression turns intently serious. Like Jekyll's body yielding to Hyde's, his arm and hand stiffen. He plunges the scary-looking extremity into the bowl and lectures: "You *don't* want to use a relaxed hand. You *must* use a stiff hand, and go just a few times around." His hand circles three or four times, just enough to wet all ingredients. "That's it!"

Because it requires no kneading, soda bread poses a challenge to the dilettante, the weekend baker. (Kneading would build up the gluten level and toughen the dough.) It's this practiced light touch — a few turns with a rigor mortis arm and that's that — that leaves a fidgety amateur like me itching for more. But there isn't much more to do. I watch Tim lift the dough onto a baking tray and gently pat it around the edges to approximate a circle. Grabbing a knife, he cuts a deep cross into the bread to "let the fairies out." The bread won't rise without the cuts, which in the baking form deep furrows dividing the bread into four fat triangles.

Into the Aga goes the spotted dog, and with a single pirouette Tim is back at his workstation mixing coarse ground flour with soda put through a sieve. He buys the flour in bulk from a miller in Kilkenny who produces only organically grown custom blends. "You can also add pinhead oatmeal, bran, or wheat germ, and I think I'll put in an egg," says Tim. Elizabeth looks up from her Sunday *Irish Times* and gasps. "I would never put an egg in brown soda bread," she declares. "Though growing up on the farm we'd put in leftover sour cream or butter, if the fresh buttermilk was too watery."

"Would you like to have a go?" Tim's dumped the buttermilk into the flour. Now it's my turn to tense my hand into a claw. I plunge it into the bowl but instead of my arm doubling as a utensil my entire body seizes up. Even my jaw is frozen, and I fight a cramp as I turn my wrist once, twice, three times. "Enough." (Myrtle is correct, this is *nawt* easy.) Tim fashions another soggy mound and allows me to let the fairies out. About ten minutes later the spotted dog is ready. You can tell because it makes a hollow sound when you rap it with your hand. "It was traditional for the groom to break the spotted dog over the bride's head," says Tim, wielding the boulder-like loaf in my direction. "But you are not my bride." That is a relief. He sets the loaf down to cool on the steps leading out to the garden, and we move on.

Along with soda bread, the whole-grain yeast bread is the national loaf of Ireland. In America whole-grain bread is synonymous with healthful living. When we unfold our cold cuts onto whole-grain bread, even the ersatz mass-produced variety, we feel virtuous — it's jam-packed with meta-mita-vegimens, and a potent laxative to boot. But in the early part of this century when the Irish lived on little else, consumption of brown bread led to an epidemic of rickets in Dublin that peaked during World War II. The bread contains phytic acid, plentiful in wheat bran, which blocks absorption of calcium. It wasn't that the bread was harmful by itself, but the typical Irish diet was already poor in calcium.

But there is no shortage of calcium in the well-fed Allen clan, and Myrtle's brown yeast bread, extolled by Beard, is the bread that helped launch Ballymaloe's international reputation. After turning the school upside-down in search of active yeast, Tim puts his hands on the last little chunk and now has it growing in warm water and molasses. To the stone-ground wheat flour he adds salt, which draws out flavor and slows down the rising activity of the yeast. "I'm using molasses because I don't have treacle," says Tim. "Uh-huh," I reply, and then it hits me that even though I've been hearing the word forever I have no idea what treacle is. I wouldn't know it if you rubbed my nose in it. Turns out it's similar to molasses only slightly more refined, one step closer to being sugar.

Now the kitchen is a cacophony of smells — the drunken fumes of the yeast, the aromas of fresh-baked spotted dog and baking brown soda bread, and a tray of white soda-bread scones. My stomach is talking. Specifically, it is saying, let's get on with this bread party, shall we? I expect the yeast bread to involve hours of rigmarole. But Tim works the yeast liquid into the flour fleetingly and with that same stiff hand pours it into a loaf tin, covers it with a towel for one rising. It seems so easy — I mean simple.

"With my students, I want to take the mystery out of breadmaking," says Tim. "But I want them to be aware of the bread and what's happening with it. I watch them when they first make bread. They look at their watches, not at the bread." I was reminded of the ABC news anchor who once cracked that the weather room was packed with every conceivable high-tech monitor, but what it really needed was a window.

When the wheat bread dough rises over the sides of the pan it's ready for baking. In the meantime Tim makes us some excellent coffee and he, Elizabeth, and I sit down to a mélange of hot sliced soda bread, spotted dog, and scones with lots of butter lopped on top. The sky outside the window is teal-colored, rain pounds on the roof. This and the morning's whole starchy marathon, pleasurable as it was, combine to make me long for my room. Tim promises to bring the wheat bread to dinner at Ballymaloe that evening.

I decide to nap for an hour or two and then brave the roads for the short trip to Ballycotton for a walk on the cliffs. When I wake up something seems terribly off kilter. It is that peculiar light coming through the windows. I squint in the direction of the apparition and realize what is happening. The sun is shining.

I'd been to Ballycotton once before. About fifteen years ago Howie and I spent the summer traveling around England, Scotland, and Wales, where we decided on impulse to ride the ferry to Ireland. After a few days in the constant crossfire of the video recorders of package tourists (will they really go home and look at videos of the Cliffs of Moher?) we escaped to County Cork. We drove the most direct route to the sea and when we got to Ballycotton checked into a motel whose only other guests were nuns and priests. They were a welcome relief from the Blarney-stone kissing hordes. The motel sat right on the rugged beach at the edge of the fishing pier. With one pub and one sandwich shop, the town was so quiet its dogs slumbered in the middle of the road. Our first day there I walked the soggy bluffs for miles and promptly came down with a rotten cold. We ended up staying for a week, long enough for Howie to offer a confident rendition of "Foggy Foggy Dew" at the pub's singsong, and long enough for an old-timer to track us down and ask us to mail him a Red Sox cap when we got back to Boston.

Wrapped in woolies and polar fleece with just enough face exposed to see my way, I follow a spongy dirt track along the cliffs of Ballycotton Bay. The tide hammers away at the jagged rocks below. Above me couples bundled in sensible coats move slowly along the road as it curves higher and higher. I consider the apparent simplicity — not ease — of middle-class life in Ireland. Of course, Dublin must have its contingents of cuppies — Celtic urban professionals — who are spending the Lord's day roaming the malls. But Tim Allen and his family seem as earthy and unpretentious as a hunk of brown bread. They vacation in France and Italy and Mexico and employ artisans to labor over frivolities such as

Victorian garden sculpture and that fantasy shell house. But Tim seems most in his element when cradling a big lumpy spotted dog fresh from the Aga. This place is growing on me. When I head back to Ballycotton's blink-and-you-miss-it main street I feel as if my nose is about to fall off, I've been too long in this raw biting wind. Could I live here? Either you're out being lashed by the wind or you're curled up fireside with a blanket over your legs. In *Mother Ireland*, Edna O'Brien writes of something "secretly catastrophic" about the country: "The visitors talk and are talked at, they fish, they fowl, they eat brown bread, dip into holy wells, kiss wishing stones, are bowled over but have no desire to stay."

My flash of homesickness fades at dinner that evening. Everyone's in a jolly mood. Myrtle joins us and we all eat Tim's and my spotted dog and brown bread. Tim makes a big fuss over my contribution, which is sweet of him, because I didn't really help at all. Susie Namedropper was in rare form at dinner, saying stuff like, "They don't know me yet in New York, but *everyone* knows me in San Francisco," and referring to Drew (Barrymore) as her surrogate daughter. Again she drones on and on about Alice, Alice, Alice: Alice the virtuous, Alice the wise, Alice, who certainly could and just may yet change the world. And I'm sitting there slurping hazelnut soup and thinking, "Get a grip, guys. We're talking about a *chef.*" I ask Namedropper how she met her friend and traveling companion, to whom I've taken a liking. "Through the President," she replied. "You met Betsey through the President?" I am confused. "Oh," sighs Namedropper. "I thought you meant how did I meet *Hillary.*"

One of the secrets of Ballymaloe bread is the high quality of the flour, custom ground from a mix of local and Canadian wheat by a purist who left a highly successful international career as a food technologist to revive the small family mill. The man's name is Bill Mosse and Tim could not say enough about his dedication and integrity. A visit to the mill would be both a journey back in time as well as a glimpse of what the new artisan bakers are trying to do. It would also be a long, hair-raising stint in the Fiat. I decide to pay Bill a visit anyway.

Kells Wheatmeal Mill sits on the banks of the river Nore, which courses through the tiny hamlet of Bennets Bridge in

County Kilkenny, a few hours' drive east from Cork. The mill itself dates back to 1750, and owner Bill Mosse grew up in this photogenic village of potters and artisans. The most successful is Bill's cousin Nicholas, whose vast pottery, shop, and snack bar operate out of one of the family mills. Even with the pouring rain, endless construction, and a few harrowing encounters with the hedge, I arrive in Bennets Bridge about an hour early and end up taking refuge at Nicholas Mosse pottery. It appears to be the only establishment here that's open. Water courses down my parka forming puddles on the floor. I eat a scone at the teashop, leaving just enough time to grab a beautiful floral-patterned fruit bowl, a sugar bowl, and a creamer. In my absence the puddles in the gravel parking lot have been upgraded to kettle ponds. Wet and freezing, I drive down the road to Kells Wheatmeal where a secretary wearing three sweaters greets me. "Cold out there, eh?" she says. I sit shivering in a bare-walled boardroom while she fetches me tea.

After what seems like a very long time Bill Mosse bursts into the room as if he'd been shot out of a cannon. A hulk of a man with a ruddy complexion, a pursed Albert

Finney–type expression, frameless specs, and an unkempt shelf of graying hair, Mosse wears a white laboratory coat that tugs across his belly. He is panting. He knows why I am here, and launches into his story.

"I'm trained as an engineer and for about five years I went all over England, the Middle East, and Ireland teaching people how to build flour mills," says Mosse. "Then I ran another mill, then I moved on to commercial baking, running production in a big factory." After a while that didn't feel right. With all Mosse's technical and industrial expertise he remains a man attached to the old, simple ways, and when he got involved in a small company making mixes for high-end bakeries he decided it suited him. Meanwhile back in Kilkenny, Mosse's father planned to shut the mill he'd operated all his working life. "I told him don't close it," says Mosse. "I said I'll run it, which I did, but I couldn't run it on a commercial basis, the output just wasn't enough. So I moved the whole operation back here to Bennets Bridge. That was twelve years ago. My milling operation is as small as it can be and I sell only to a special market — people like Tim Allen. Let's have a look at the mill."

Mosse and I charge coatless through the downpour into his Subaru station wagon, which smells like a stable. He drives over the bridge — that would be Bennets Bridge — and pulls up to a lopsided stone building which, if not for the small KELLS WHEATMEAL sign, would appear long defunct. "Some of these mills have been revived for the tourists," says Mosse. But this one drones on in relative obscurity. Mosse's operation is strictly wholesale, his clients few and discerning.

Inside the old picturesque mill Mosse creates low- and high-gluten flour blends ground specifically for soda breads or brown yeast breads. I follow him as he ducks beneath whining conveyor belts and around vats of wheat in various stages of gleaning. Mosse stops to scoop a few kernels so I can see the wheat slowly progress to flour. "Nobody in the country is doing what I'm doing," says Mosse, who handles wheat the way an Antwerp dealer palms diamonds. "Nobody's crazy enough." After each show and tell session Mosse carefully empties the contents of his cupped hand — every last grain — back into the mouth of the machinery.

"Bread is declining," Mosse remarks with a sigh. "On one hand you've got the new organic craft bakeries, but commercially bread is declining. I went to San Francisco to research sourdoughs and learned that a lot of people are using chemical sourdough. If you're aware of what's happening you can taste the chemical as soon as you bite into the bread." Mosse places a handful of soft wheat in one of my hands, hard wheat in the other so I can feel the difference. The by-products of the gleaning process (a succession of spinners and air separators) are cracked wheat, immature wheat, wild oats, and hedge seeds, which are used for animal feed. After gleaning the grain is left in a moist tank to soften. "Dry grain shatters," says Mosse. "It will bruise. You want to open it without shattering it, like hitting stone with a hammer." Mosse walks me through the process, pausing at each of the millstones, crafted of flint and emery fused with magnesium. The grain passes between two stones, the top one fixed and the bottom one turning. Stone grinding generates a lot of heat, which lends a toasty flavor not found in flours ground from steel blades. Every few years the stones wear away enough to be replaced. Mosse is on his third set.

An ocean away from the streamlined

computerized quality control of the world's biggest bakery and its flagship Wonder Bread, when it comes to assessing the consistency of his blends Mosse relies almost exclusively on three tools: his eyes, nose, and hands. In a rugged loft stacked with sacks of flour Mosse implores me to feel this coarse blend or that fine one, to plant my nose in an open sack and smell its earthy perfume.

On my last morning at Ballymaloe I shamelessly devour about a pound of Fingal's bacon, then climb into the Fiat for our last jaunt. "You were really quite clever to find your way here on your own," says Tim. After five days it has just occurred to him that having to navigate the Fiat from a microscopic road map all the way from Shannon to Shanagarry was as impressive as it was idiotic. Back at the airport, when I returned the Fiat I had to stifle the urge to kick it.

I return home a week before Thanksgiving. My friend Madeline has invited us for dinner and I offer to bring salad and bread. I experience a rare compulsion to bake and Tim's demonstration is fresh in mind, so I go out and buy a sifter, and get to work. My brown soda bread is a bit out of scale. It emerges from the oven looking like a giant cow pie. But when I thump it the bread sounds as hollow as Tim's did. I think Madeline, her family, and her friends are frightened of it at first but, once sliced, the bread looks irrefutably appetizing. When they sink their teeth into the dense slabs the guests — a few of them genuine Irish — actually swoon. They finish every last crumb, and these honorary Irish eyes are smiling. I also write Myrtle a letter telling her how knocked out I was by Ballymaloe House. A few days later I received a really sweet note back, telling me how much she enjoyed meeting me. I guess all is forgiven.

Ballymaloe Brown Yeast Bread

INGREDIENTS:
Four and a half cups whole-meal flour
One teaspoon salt
One teaspoon black treacle or molasses
Two cups warm water
One-quarter cup baker's yeast or dry yeast
  equivalent

Preheat oven to 450 degrees.

Mix flour with salt and warm it slightly in oven just beginning to heat.

In a small bowl mix the treacle with some of the water and crumble in the yeast. Put the bowl in a warm place (e.g., stove top). Grease a loaf tin and put it in the oven to warm, also warm a clean tea towel.

Let yeast grow for about five minutes or until the mixture is creamy and slightly frothy on top.

Stir yeast mixture well and pour it, with most of the remaining water, into the flour to make a wettish dough. The mixture should be too wet to knead. Put mixture into the greased, warmed tin. Put the tin in a warm place and cover it with the tea towel.

Let the loaf rise for about twenty minutes or so, until it rises to twice its original size. Remove the tea towel and bake the loaf for 45 to 50 minutes, or until it appears nicely browned and sounds hollow when tapped. At Ballymaloe the loaves are removed from their tins about ten minutes before the end of cooking and immediately placed back in the oven to crisp all around. If you prefer a softer crust leave bread to finish baking in the pan.

Bread of Affliction:
Brooklyn, New York

*This is the bread of affliction that our fathers
ate in the land of Egypt. Whoever is hungry,
let him come and eat; whoever is in need, let
him come and conduct the Seder of Pesach.
This year [we are] here; next year in the land
of Israel. This year [we are] slaves; next year
[we will be] free people.*
— PASSOVER HAGGADAH

*Baruch atoh adonoy elohenu m'elech a'oholom,
a motzi l'echem Minnie Horowitz.*
— MODIFIED BLESSING
OVER THE BREAD,
JEWISH SUMMER CAMP

We weren't a religious family when I was
growing up. My mother liked to joke that
our synagogue was "so reformed it's closed
for the holidays." I guess you could say we
were strong in the culture if weak in the

faith. Each spring we sat down to a Passover seder, chugging sickly sweet wine and racing through the pre-meal readings like Bar Mitzvah boys on speed.

Things only deteriorated as I got older. One year my friends and I recounted the nine plagues — frogs, lice, boils, et cetera — to the tune of the "Twelve Days of Christmas." Still, with all the infantile heckling and stupid puns ("Thank you for not smiting") my lapsed relatives and friends have managed to tell the story in a kind of condensed abstract. Three thousand years ago we, the Jews, were slaves in the Pharaoh's Egypt. We were forced to build the king's cities and roads and toil in his quarries, but these indignities did not stop us from being fruitful and multiplying. *"Dayanu,"* we moaned, Enough. And the aging Moses faced down Pharaoh and said "Let my people go." When Pharaoh refused God got really, really angry and turned the waters to blood, covered the land with lice, killed the domestic animals, and ultimately slew all the gentile firstborn males in the land of Egypt, including those of the cattle. Led by Moses, the newly liberated Jews eluded Pharaoh's army. And when the children of Israel came right smack up against the shores of

218

the Red Sea Moses said, "Now what?" and God said, not to worry, and the waters parted, just long enough to let the Jews through and stop Pharaoh's army in its tracks.

This is the story as I understood it. Everything consumed at the seder table recalls part of the saga. *Charoseth* — a mixture of chopped apples, nuts, and wine — symbolizes the mortar with which the enslaved Jews layered the Pharaoh's bricks. Bitter herbs recall the bitterness of those years, salt water the tears shed, into which we dip boiled eggs, symbol of enduring fertility. And the bread of affliction, the matzo, an incarnation of the unleavened bread baked in haste as the Jews fled across the desert.

I always adored rituals, preferably those of other, exotic, faiths. But with each recounting of the Passover story I secretly felt that God overreacted. I thought it was really mean and unnecessary to kill all those baby boys. In my opinion He made his point well enough with the frogs, lice, and boils. Jews weren't murderers, we all knew that. When David "Son of Sam" Berkowitz went on his killing spree my grandmother could not stop reminding anyone who'd listen that he was born a

gentile and adopted. And why the wholesale slaying of all the Egyptians' innocent
animals that, if anything, were slaves themselves? But at our seders we didn't debate
the finer points. Once the rapid-fire
reading was done, and the now tipsy adults
raised their glasses and droned, "Next year
in Jerusalem!" we didn't debate or discuss
much of anything. Our mouths were full.
We weren't accustomed to postponing
gratification, and by the time we allowed
ourselves to begin the meal we scarfed
down everything in sight. I come from a
family of magicians. We make brisket disappear without a trace.

On seder nights we'd break open boxed
decks of matzo. Perfect, hankie-sized
squares reminiscent of corrugated cardboard, they tasted best with cream cheese
and salt, our Passover breakfast of choice.
Though we didn't refrain from eating leavened bread we munched on matzo for the
eight days of the Passover festival and in
the weeks to follow, until our supply ran
out. This was the only matzo I knew, and
part of what I loved about it was that it
only showed up once a year, in incarnations ranging from matzo and butter to
fried matzo brei, the unleavened version of
French toast. Sometimes, in other seasons,

my mother brought home egg-and-onion matzo "crackers" but they never tasted as light and crunchy as the Passover variety, prepared only from flour, water, salt, and sometimes egg and cider. Years later, in my last year of college, I was a guest at the seder of the family of my boyfriend Mark. His parents were Orthodox and lived in what I called a "grandma house" in Brooklyn's Flatbush. It was a narrow brick Tudor with a sliver of yard and barely a bicycle length between neighbors. Day and night an oniony, boiled-meat smell permeated the house, the fumes born mysteriously out of a tiny kitchen as sterile and Spartan as a surgical suite. Mark's mother was a whip-smart schoolteacher with a wig and bifocals, the kind of woman who finished the Sunday *Times* crossword puzzle in about eight minutes. Her son worshiped her, and I avoided her beady-eyed gaze. The kitchen was her domain and we tred there cautiously. Mrs. Brown wore a pinafore apron when she cooked. In the days before Passover she just left the apron on all day long.

The day before the first seder Mark's father came home with what looked like two pizza boxes. They were lettered in Hebrew and Mark's father set them down carefully.

"Oh, boy, the holy matzo!" Mark said, and opened the box to reveal a lopsided stack of rough-hewn rounds with undulating surfaces and charred edges. Mark and I tore into one and I was surprised at its toughness. Handmade matzo is hearty and thick. I imagined it to be like the hard tack that sustained the Arctic explorers, whalers, and sealers in the sagas I loved to read. Spreading cream cheese on this matzo would be just plain weird.

In the last few years I've come to enjoy matzo as a year-round snack. As nourishment goes, it's just this side of nothing, and I say that to recommend it. "Simplicity is precisely the point," says the Lubavitch guide to Pesach. "Matzo is the humblest of foods — flat and unpretentious, unadulterated, and unadorned. Eating matzo on Passover actually helps us to cultivate the trait of humility . . . and humility is the beginning of liberation." I'd rather dwell on virtues like humility than on the notion of the entire non-Hebrew population of Egypt covered with seething boils and lice. And for me it rings true. All year long I eat matzo when I can't think of what to eat, when my appetite is dulled by grief, depression, stress, or indifference but I know I must eat. At these times matzo is the only thing my palate will embrace, the purest and most fundamental sustenance.

Baking matzo in strict accordance with the body of Jewish law, the Torah, is considered an ennobling act. It's what Jews call a *mitzvah*. Other mitzvahs include helping the needy, your kid getting into medical school, and sexual intercourse between a man and his ovulating wife. The genuine kosher article is called *schmurah* matzo. *Schmurah* means "guarded," because its bakers are so meticulous about preventing the matzo's contamination with even the slightest trace of leaven — the dreaded *chametz* — that the entire procedure, from the harvesting of the grain until the rolled-out rounds of dough are slid into the fire, is guarded to keep the matzo kosher. Orthodox believe this holiest matzo should be round because a circle, like the creator of the universe, has no beginning and no end.

I'd heard that some seasonal *schmurah* matzo bakeries welcome visitors. At the suggestion of Cape Cod's Lubavitchers I telephoned a Rabbi Dubrovsky in New York City's Chasidic enclave of Crown Heights, Brooklyn.

"Yes, yes, you can come watch," the

rabbi said wearily. He spoke over a strange, not quite human-sounding din. As I asked questions his voice grew more impatient and mean. "You take no pictures!" he growled, and I envisioned an arthritic finger shaking in my direction. He hung up without saying good-bye. I could hardly wait to meet the man.

Dubrovsky's *schmurah* matzo bakery comes to life every year a few months before Passover in the basement of a rundown building on Albany Avenue. I visited there on a dreary damp Sunday in March. The address, 460, appears handwritten on a ripped slab of matzo box tacked to the door. It looks like a warning, or a ransom note. To step inside was to cross a vast cultural barrier, and even before I reached the place I realized why: with only the East River between us the rabbi and I existed in two different worlds. How strange to board the subway near the ruckus of Twenty-third Street, Starbucks double-latte in hand, and emerge a half hour later in what looked like pre-war Cracow, Poland.

Before he hung up on me the rabbi had barked some rudimentary directions but once I surface on Eastern Parkway I am disoriented. Chasidic Jews populate this tranquil neighborhood almost exclusively.

Ragged at the edges but still beautiful, Eastern Parkway is a wide tree-lined boulevard bisected by a broad esplanade. An army of upscale gay guys could do wonders with this neglected crabgrass, these quirky row houses. Is this the same New York City in which pierced, shaven, post-apocalyptic-looking adolescents clomp up Broadway in pursuit of Ecstasy and platform sneakers? The black-suited men marching face down along the paved median make my octogenarian aunts look as if they hang with a fast crowd. In their almost ingrained refusal to make eye contact I read a rebuke, a sneer at the immodesty of my clinging sweater, my eye makeup and untamed hair. In the company of Chasidim I have always felt defensive. My secular Jewish friends feel the same way.

"You'll see the boxes. Look for the boxes." Aside from the street address this was all the direction Dubrovsky had offered. Outside there is little to distinguish the bakery from any other of the drab doorways and stoops along treeless Albany Avenue. From the subway stop I walk along a battered promenade populated by Chasidim bundled in black wool and the black and Hispanic laborers who commute from Bedford-Stuyvesant or Brownsville. I turn onto Albany Avenue to encounter a few expensively dressed matrons in scarves or hats moving along the sidewalk with their broods. From the windows of a yeshiva comes the warbling sound of boys reciting from the Torah. With the exception of computers, popular culture seems nonexistent here. There is no Gap; there are no Starbucks, movie houses, cafés, or pet shops. There is nothing but hardware stores, kosher markets, and no-frills pharmacies with signs advertising wigs made from human hair.

I spot the boxes. They are balanced in the arms of local patriarchs and their wives busy preparing their homes for the eight-day holiday, during which Orthodox Jewish law forbids the eating, and in fact the mere presence, of leavening, or *chametz*. That includes a Milk-Bone dog biscuit, or the dregs of an Oreo in a jacket pocket. At the Seder table they will recite that "On other nights we eat both leavened and unleavened bread. On this night we eat only matzo." Scholars have written that Jehovah, God himself, would eat nothing but matzo. And to hear the Lubavitchers tell it, the only matzo worth presenting to Him would be their own *schmurah* matzo. Coals to Newcastle, you'd assume, but I'd heard that people living in Jerusalem order their Passover matzo from Dubrovsky's.

Even the minutest granule of *chametz* can contaminate the sanctum of the *schmurah* matzo bakery, and so I respectfully shake the flecks of this morning's croissant from my sweater. I rid my coat pockets of wayward dog biscuits. In truth, though we never practiced the ritual in our house, I always loved the notion of "getting rid of the *chametz*." I warmed to its metaphorical power. It is really a cleansing, inside and out, timed with the rebirth embodied by spring. Getting rid of the *chametz* to me meant getting rid of petty grudges and the lingering stings of persecutions real and imagined. After sunset on the eve of Passover religious Jews conduct a ritual, candle-lit search for any wayward *chametz*. We're not talking about a stray Yodel or Fig Newton. The devout are meant to search cracks in the floorboards and the netherworld behind dressers and couches. No microscopic fleck of leaven should escape them. Just for good measure the sages advise people to plant a little baggie of *chametz* — bread crumbs, say — and pretend to "find" it, thereby fulfilling the Passover commandment. Next morning they must take the *chametz* outside and burn it and recite the following, or something close to it: "I hereby relinquish any association with or ownership of all and any leaven or leavening agents in my possession that I did not see or did not find, and that I have not destroyed, or that I do not know about. They are null and ownerless, just like dust on the ground." Furthermore, those who wish to be reunited with their *chametz* at some later date can sell it, with a contract, to a gentile and buy it back. As a kid, when I first heard about this little wrinkle I took it literally and thought, how incredibly dumb. *Sell* our half-eaten box of Mallomars to the Bridgens family across the street, our neighborhood's token gentiles? But these days I do try, in my own secular humanist way, to greet spring by ridding my life of *chametz*, even if for me that means schlepping a few loads of clothing to the Goodwill.

When I step down into Dubrovsky's matzo den, the air itself seems older and heavier than it did on the street. The front room is a chaos of boxes stacked to the ceiling. I collide with several black-suited men in long unkempt beards and curly forelocks. A man behind a counter dips and twirls as he constructs box after box, plunks in a pound of matzo rounds and secures the covers. I try to make out the delivery slips on stacks of finished orders. One stack of boxes is on its way to Chicago, another to Johannesburg. As it is with Chasidim from Brooklyn to Jerusalem's Me'a She'arim, it's hard to assess the men's ages. There seem to be only two categories of such men: old and older. A customer nods toward Rabbi Dubrovsky and the oldest-looking of the men casts a chilling glance in my direction. I'm on the verge of turning and fleeing when Rabbi Eli Cohen, a blessing on his pleasant red head, steps forward and greets me with a warm smile. I follow Cohen and the wizened, still silent Dubrovsky into the baking area. I'm only five two but I feel the need to duck as I snake through the narrow, dimly lit room, as crowded as a rush hour subway car. Lots of the men look like rabbis. That's due in part to the proliferation of beards and the sepia lighting, which lends the scene the air of a Roman Vishniac tableau. In H. E. Jacob's book *Six Thousand Years of Bread* I came across a reproduction of a 1726 German woodcarving depicting matzo bakers at work rolling dough and extracting rounds of unleavened bread from a fiery stone oven. Add wristwatches and athletic shoes and the scene before me is no different.

Cohen confirms that there are least seven rabbis on the premises. There's enough going on to keep them all busy, guarding the flour, the water, supervising the mixing, the rolling, the perforating and the baking, and keeping time to make sure the journey from dough to matzo takes well under eighteen minutes. Eighteen minutes is the length of time in which a mixture of flour and water will automatically begin to leaven and rise, and that would spell disaster. Disaster has a name: *chametz*.

The place only appears to be a madhouse. In fact, the operation is choreographed down to the last detail. The rules are very strict, says Cohen, a father of ten, and I now see, probably younger than I am. The basic process is this: Under the rabbi's watchful eye the designated water pourer is careful not to stir even a grain of flour dust as he adds the water to the flour. A kneader steps in to work the dough for thirty seconds or less, after which the dough is divided among the rollers. These are the drones of the operation, whose task it is to roll the dough into rounds of matzo.

After being perforated to release any trapped air bubbles (hiding places for *chametz*), the matzo is placed in a brick or stone oven heated to 2,500 degrees Fahrenheit. The baked matzos are scrutinized one last time for more suspicious bubbles or craters that might contain holdouts of uncooked dough — again, the specter of *chametz*. From start to finish the process takes less than five minutes.

How can something so simple seem so hopelessly complicated? The almost raucous chanting of prayers makes it hard to hear oneself think. Add an admonition against using any wooden utensil more than once unless it's thoroughly re-sanded. Fill the narrow, dungeon-like space with men whose sole purpose is to observe, and make certain those doing the work will have to run an obstacle course around them. Throw in a language barrier or two, and the occasional out-of-control toddler.

I notice the flour and water are kept separate in their own little cubicles, and the water is handed out through a small window. My fears of tripping and flying into the guarded water and sending it cascading into the guarded flour are unfounded. Clueless heathen that I am, planted awkwardly in the middle of this tornado of activity I decide I'm the least of these people's worries.

Percolating in the Orthodox community is a debate over whether it might be more kosher to prepare the matzo by machine. On one hand there would be far less chance of human error, though there would be the chance that *chametz*-tainted matzos advancing along an assembly line might elude detection. On the other hand authentic *schmurah* matzo is prepared the way it was under the gaze of Moses himself. On the other hand — well, as Tevye would say, there is no other hand.

These lumpy rounds are the result of a formula as specific and delicate as the one for enriched uranium. Serious business, this. Close on the heels of a kindly Chasid named Moshe, I thread my way through the operation, step by step. A dreary catacomb fogged with flour, the room is crammed with what looks like a hundred people, all of them alarmingly overdressed in the infernal heat. The ceiling is so low that the tallest men hunch, and the blotchy walls are unadorned except for a photo portrait of Lubavitcher Menachem Schneerson, the late grand rebbe who some believe to be the *Moschiah*, the messiah. Like those garish images of Krishna adorning the walls of baking stalls all over India, the rebbe hangs askew beside a torn slab of cardboard upon which something has been scrawled in . . . what? "It's Russian," says Moshe. That would explain the long table crammed with monobreasted matrons from Uzbekistan by way of Brighton Beach. It's quite a sight. Every day different groups of observant Jews from all over the city rent the bakery in four-hour slots. For the privilege of a morning spent rolling matzo dough each person gets to take home about four pounds of the matzo, which usually sells for $13 dollars a pound, and that as my father would say, ain't cheap, especially if you've got a large family.

For the mitzvah of rolling their own matzo, these women in babushkas have, they announce to me, schlepped *"von hower!"* (one hour!) on the bus. Stuffed into woolen sweaters, whose colors collide with loud jersey shifts, the mamas are good-natured and giddy. Their mischief provides a welcome counterpoint to the lugubrious presence of Dubrovsky and the other rabbis. "Vee are twenty-two of us — all family!" They want to know my story: "You speak zee Russia? You marry? You children?" The most rambunctious among them, a bottle brunette with a constellation of moles on her heavily jowled face, points to my breasts and then with a wicked grin plants her hands under her own and works the heaving orbs up and down. This draws hysterical laughter from the Uzbeks and makes me fold my arms in helpless embarrassment. "What journal you write? You give me your phone number now!" booms their lone male compatriot, Yakov, an immigrant from Samarkand. The women hoot and howl. Their bawdiness strikes me as unorthodox, to say the least. Gesticulating around the long wooden table, they look like tavern revelers from *Oliver Twist*. I love them all.

To make their visit more cost-effective the women have been urged to go as fast as possible. So, what begins to look like an Uzbek version of the assembly line episode from *I Love Lucy* is soon punctuated by admonitions from the matzo police. "No, no, no, not like zat!" "It's much quieter here during the week," Rabbi Cohen tells me with a sigh.

Before each cycle every surface in the bakery is covered with fresh sheets of brown wrapping paper. "Do you know what you have when even one speck of dough sticks to the rolling pin?" asks my new best friend Moshe, an ebullient Czech. I open my mouth to answer. Moshe is already shaking a finger at me. *"Chametz!"* This is why the yeshiva boys replace each woman's rolling pin — sanded, rounded lengths of pine, actually — for each new matzo. Somewhere way in the back of the building a lathe grinds out new roller sticks. The women cry out "Matzo!" each time they roll one out. In response a helper, rabbi, or yeshiva boy, will rush to trade a new rolling pin for the used one, the plate-sized round of matzo dough draped over it. "You cannot allow the two sides of the matzo to touch," says Moshe. "If they do. . . . *chametz!*" From the crowded dais-like table where the rollers labor, the matzo is carried to a narrow work surface where one of the bakery's few paid employees works a manual machine that perforates each matzo with a series of tiny grooved wheels. I'd always taken the perforations for granted, like the ridges on a Ritz cracker. But now I realize that this is no cosmetic touch. "What is the point of that?" I ask Moshe. "To get rid of any air bubbles," he replies. "Because if you have even one little air bubble . . ." *"Chametz!"* I say. Moshe nods his head and smiles. He is very proud of his student.

Moshe is a gentle soul, I can tell. He immigrated first to Canada, alone, at nineteen and didn't embrace orthodoxy until he became a yeshiva student at twenty-six. He's married and admits sheepishly he has only two children, a "very, very small family." "Torah is the inner food," says Moshe, apropos of nothing. Or, "The Bible says you can only be satiated if you're blessed, and you can only bless the lord when you're full." How's that again? He is full of such pronouncements and pauses with a fixed, kind stare to assess their effect on me. I giggle. He giggles. The rabbis' eyes cast little daggers in our direction.

Carefully draped over eleven-foot poles in groups of six, the matzos are marched to the mouth of an immense brick coal-fired hearth. With *chametz* always one doughy fleck or air bubble away, the rabbis are understandably unamused by the Uzbek women's antics. Assisted by a platoon of black-suited yeshiva boys as dour as their elders, the human assembly line is punctuated by frantic bursts of activity and expectant lulls. Everyone is sweating.

Only with *schmurah* matzo does the vigilance begin with the harvest itself. The unremarkable-looking flour I see in a bucket is ground of grain harvested from a kosher wheat field in Spain, a harvest that has never come into contact with moisture. Because, as any rabbi or yeshiva boy here will tell you with a weary sigh, grain and moisture lead to fermentation or leaven.

If my new friends at Dubrovsky's bakery seem obsessed with *chametz* it's because the weeks ahead will be marked by a tedious purging of blatant *chametz*, stealth *chametz*, or anything that has touched or contained them. Hence the frantic eating or burning of the last perishable *chametz*, the stashing in a locked or taped-shut storage area of *chametz*-tainted dishes and utensils, and the selling of whatever *chametz* remains to a non-Jew. Handled with the utmost seriousness and gravity by the rabbi, the Lubavitch *chametz* contract, for example, stipulates that the undersigned empower Rabbi X to "sell all *chametz* possessed by me, knowingly or unknowingly as defined by the Torah and rabbinical law (e.g., *chametz, possible chametz,* and all kinds of *chametz* mixtures). And the contract also refers to the sale of "all kinds of live animals and pets that have been eating *chametz* and mixtures thereof." Do the Orthodox have *chametz* kennels?

I'm here watching the watching and it's making me dizzy. With all its ritualized footwork, though, as it is with all bread, the process is about flour, water, and heat — simplicity itself, though a person would be excused for drawing the opposite conclusion. From where I stand near the kneading bowls I see everything and find myself alert to any breach in procedure that might spell *chametz*. I myself feel like *chametz* incarnate, a Gomorrah-esque pillar of *chametz*. Whatever curiosity these men express about me wilts instantly when they discover I am childless. This is an anathema to most Orthodox religions except the Shakers, who took vows of celibacy and proceeded to dwindle right out of existence. In Judaism "be fruitful and multiply" isn't a blessing, it's a command. At one point during my visit a neighborhood woman who looks about eleven months pregnant waddles in with a baby in her arms and a vibrating orbit of toddlers whose heights increase like the shadows on a bar graph. I find myself thinking that it's okay. It all works out. For every kid I don't have, women like her will have three. I'm shaken out of my little flash of wisdom by Rabbi Dubrovsky, who is staring at me so hatefully I wonder if he is endowed with

238

X-ray vision into my mind, my soul, my sexual history. But the bakers assure me the man is rude to everyone, the devout and heathens alike. "Don't you worry about him," whispers Moshe.

In spite of myself, Dubrovsky's ferocious glances make me feel a sense of vague, free-floating guilt. More pregnant women drop in with their broods and I'm starting to feel as if I'm wearing out my welcome. If they only knew. The Chinese takeout I ate on Yom Kippur. My preference for roast beef, Swiss, and mayonnaise sandwiches.

In fact, Dubrovsky reserves his sternest expression not for me, but for the water man. Though his function is basically that of a carefully programmed robotic arm, the water man is the one who can really screw things up, *chametz*-wise. His is one of two jobs too important to be left in the hands of volunteers. The other is the kneader. From a Bible-sized window cut in a makeshift plywood cubicle comes a dis-embodied-gloved arm clasping a large cup full of water. This isn't tap water. It is drawn from a well and left overnight to come to room temperature. Pouring the water is a delicate operation, because any resulting flour dust might float around the room and attach itself to a surface, later coming into contact with water and creating leaven. At the start of each cycle, after everyone handling the matzo has washed, every sheet of brown wrapping paper has been replaced, all rubber gloves have been disposed of in place of new ones, the hand dumps the water into a mixing bowl holding three pounds of flour. The flour, too, has just been poured from within a second cubicle. Several rabbis keep watch, checking to see that the new flour is certifiably dry before contact is made. And then the clock begins ticking and the whole tableau comes to life. The Uzbeks, rabbis, and yeshiva boys chant *Matzo Mitzvat*. What I witness here is a mitzvah. A pair of paid employees knead the dough and swiftly divide it into small patties the size of dinner rolls. The Uzbek women roll the patties into Frisbee-sized rounds. Sticks change hands as in a relay race. The process is repeated until the four hours are up. By the oven there is a sign: OVEN: THIS BRICK OVEN HEATS UP TO A TEMPERATURE OF 2,500 F. IN THIS HEAT THE MATZOT BAKE TO A CRISP WITHIN ABOUT 30 SECONDS (TRY COUNTING YOURSELF AND SEE)

The emerging matzos, ovoid and crisp,

are inspected yet another time by yeshiva students. "What are you looking for?" I ask them. "Bubbles may conceal uncooked dough, which is *chametz*," said one. "Where did you learn to do this?" I ask. Everyone in hearing distance joins the chorus of disgusted groans. "It's not *hard*," spits one.

It's time to go. I'm hot, I'm getting hungry, and I've seen the whole process several times. At this point Dubrovsky is eyeing me as if he's about to order me physically removed from the joint. The Uzbeks are getting restless. I would like to be well across the river when the *chametz* hits the fan. Accepting the warped reject matzo the yeshiva boys sullenly hand me, I snake my way toward the door, stopping to buy a box full. Moshe waves good-bye and Rabbi Cohen offers his office phone number if I come up with more questions. I thank Rabbi Dubrovsky, who responds with a weary nod. The air out on Albany Avenue feels oddly invigorating.

Not long after my visit to Crown Heights I sit in the century-old offices of Streit's matzo factory, which remains at its original address, 148 Rivington Street, on New York's increasingly gentrified Lower East Side. My father grew up near this place, and the Streit's factory is among the few holdovers from those times. Its first factory, on Pitt Street, opened in 1916. In 1925 the bakery moved to Rivington Street, where it remains today, long after the Lower East Side's Jewish immigrants' exodus to the suburbs of Long Island, Westchester, and New Jersey. The *flanken* and chicken soup aromas of my father's childhood have long since given way to the scents of jasmine, sandalwood, and empanadas. The pâté and sun-dried tomato crowd is closing in fast. One immigrant family's crowded tenement is the first floor of another man's roomy duplex.

An Austro-Hungarian immigrant, matzo baker Aron Streit went into business with fellow immigrant Rabbi Weinberger, making all their matzo by hand. When Streit died in 1937 business was thriving. Though he ran the business with his brother, son Jack Streit carried on his father's tradition as the baker of the family, the one who kept the rudimentary conveyor belts in working order and resisted the urge to adulterate the basic flour-and-water recipe. He died in 1998 at the age of eighty-nine, leaving the country's last family-run matzo company. The company promotes its image as an enduring icon, an

Old World institution dedicated to maintaining Jewish values in America. My family ate it because it tasted better than the others did. It was, and still is, crispier. Streit's was the matzo of my childhood, and Jack's late-life nod to contemporary tastes, the Egg/Onion variety, was my mother's carbohydrate of choice.

Today Streit's offers a line of eighty products from matzo meal to Passover sponge cake mix. The company showcases its quaint history in a snazzy Web site. "But we're still the little guy," says grandson Mel Gross, a lawyer who joined the company only three years ago. The company's main competitor is Manishewitz, which gobbled up the kosher product lines of Goodman and Horowitz-Margareten. In Florida several years ago Manishewitz was fined in a quite unkosher price-fixing scheme that jacked up the price of a box of Passover matzo to as high as ten dollars and gave new meaning to the term "bread of affliction."

Gross is an attractive, personable man with curly hair, a golfer's tan, and well-cut suit. All the Streit grandchildren live in Long Island's wealthy enclaves of Hewlett, Lawrence, and Manhasset. On a tour of the assembly line Gross tells me the plant is closed, completely scoured, and retooled for the Passover line. *Chametz* is not taken lightly here, either. Streit's follows the kosher laws down to the letter, but *schmurah* matzo aficionados would just as soon consume a bacon cheeseburger. Streit doesn't want or expect to please the purists. He shrugs his shoulders in a classic Jewish gesture, the one that says, "So what are ya gonna do?"

That shrug; at one point at Albany Avenue I'd asked Moshe, friend to friend, "What if?" You know, the unspeakable. An undetected gob of *chametz* beats the system? And Moshe does one of those shrugs, topping it off with a faint wink. What are ya gonna do? I'm relieved that when it comes right down to it, there appears to be a tiny bit of wiggle room on the *chametz* issue. The reason I am relieved is that, on the train back to Manhattan I discover, embedded in the folds of my purse, a half-eaten chocolate chip cookie.

Homemade Matzo

Adapted from A Treasury of Jewish Holiday Baking *by Marcy Goldman*

INGREDIENTS:
Two cups all-purpose flour
One cup whole-wheat flour
Spring water

Preheat oven to 450 degrees. Line two large baking sheets with parchment paper.

Mix flour with spoon and add water until dough is soft. Knead dough for about five minutes, and let it rest about three minutes.

Break off palm-sized portions of dough and roll them into very thin oval slabs. Prick each slab with a fork.

Place ovals on baking sheets and bake until crisp, about three minutes.

No Trespassing:
Pueblo Country, New Mexico

*For five centuries, our people have suffered
from narrow attitudes and outside influences.
I don't foresee the attitudes changing . . . our
sovereignty will again be under attack during
the millennium. . . . So, for me, I foresee more
struggle before we may truly live the way we
choose to live.*
— JACOB VIARRIAL, GOVERNOR,
POJOAQUE PUEBLO

The first time I saw a photograph of an
horno oven I was smitten. Can a bread oven
be described as adorable? Simple, wood-
fired domes of adobe and flagstone, hornos,
are fixtures in the Pueblo villages of the
American Southwest. To me they looked like
they belonged in Pooh Corner. In the
searing heat of early September, season of
the harvest festivals, I laced up my hiking
boots and rambled among the New Mexico

Pueblos, checking out the hornos, running my hands over their sun-warmed roofs, poking my head inside. I saw tiny hornos, towering hornos, and hornos pointy as warheads. I circled plump, squat-looking hornos, hornos deep and wide enough for a child's playhouse, petite hornos that looked like the buds or offspring of their neighbors, and twin hornos rising skyward like the breasts of a colossus. In Sandia Pueblo I saw a deluxe, sleekly detailed horno that looked as if someone had ordered it recently from Hammacher Schlemmer.

In fact, hornos are as abundant in Pueblo country as mushrooms in a soggy wood. Unfortunately, ovens cannot speak. And so I set out to chat about bread baking with the proprietors of these ovens. I may as well have been pursuing the engagement codes for Strategic Air Command. Even if her scribbling pertains to nothing less innocent than the recipe for oven bread, around here an inquisitive Anglo with a notebook can expect replies in cold monosyllables, if not stony silence. There is one word for the curious who venture beyond the tourist-clogged perimeters of the Indian reservation: trespassers. I wasn't warned of this. It took a while to sink in.

Indispensable for centuries, hornos might seem anachronistic in today's landscape, pocked as it is with satellite dishes and billboards. But these beehive ovens are to Pueblo communities what the Weber is to Anglo suburbia. The surviving ovens are backyard fixtures and protected historical landmarks. Many are used only sporadically or left to crumble. Some sit shrouded in tarps held down by a circle of bricks. In good repair a horno looks almost livable, a cob house for an elf. Some are more than three centuries old. They rise from the hard desert clay and lava mesas like terracotta gumdrops. On baking day, typically once a week for those who still do their own baking, Indians feed the horno's fire with cedar wood for several hours then sweep away the embers to make way for the bread, and later for pumpkins, squash, or corn. No need for temperature settings; hornos bake beautifully because the process relies on radiant heat. Whether the oven is at five hundred degrees or cooled to half that temperature, their densely packed earth gives off the heat it has stored at a steady rate. Like the three little bears, the hornos are Papas, Mamas, or Babies. The "Papa" hornos are as high as four feet and can turn out up to three or four dozen loaves at a time. Mama ovens hold only two loaves. Babies are a foot high or smaller and are used just for burning incense.

Though I was as welcome as Goldilocks, I could not resist poking around the yards where the ovens stand. What is it about them? It isn't just their beauty, soundness, and simplicity that draws me to these ovens. Set against blue sky in courtyards smelling of smoke, earth, and dung, the ovens embody what I've seen and inhaled in North Africa and the Middle East. Due to some blood memory or perhaps an ancestral dip or two into a forbidden gene pool, Arabia and the Sahara are my dream landscapes. Hallucinate a burst of date palms, a camel or two, and a modest Pueblo settlement like Picuris, "those who paint," could be a village of Tuareg or Bedouin.

Beholding the Sahara while my feet are planted somewhere between Santa Fe and Albuquerque is more than my own quirky vision. Moorish influence, filtered through the empire-hungry Spanish, lurks throughout the Pueblo lands. The word adobe is, after all, a corruption of the Arabic *affub,* which means "brick of clay or mud." We all know Spain expelled the Moors in 1492

— public school history had me envisioning the Moors departing abruptly en masse with the entire Spanish population jeering in their wake. But the Moors' purging came after three hundred years in which Arabic influence percolated throughout the Iberian Peninsula. When the Spanish conquered Mexico and were seduced farther north by fantastical tales of cities and their rulers all swathed in gold, they found themselves in a New Spain that looked a lot more like North Africa than Andalusia. The gilded fortresses were an illusion, viewed in the light of the setting sun, which cast a golden glow. Perched on a sun-baked butte, Acoma Pueblo could pass for a Saharan casbah.

Year after year the hornos smart in the heat and hibernate under the winter snow. If the resulting fissures aren't repaired with mud and straw the horno will eventually implode, a Taos baker named Geronimo Romero told me. These days hornos are also reinforced with cement. The hornos suffer mainly from neglect but occasionally one meets a more violent end. An incompetent, distracted, or impaired driver, a lone horno, and, slam, bam, three centuries are smashed to rubble. For the surviving ovens, with each successive face-lift what was once a beehive of stone, sand, and clay morphs into a portly earthen igloo. The smoke hole near the top gets deeper and more chimney-like. Often blocked by nothing more elaborate than a slab of wood, the horno's door resembles the mouth of a cave. Into this mouth go fifty or sixty round loaves for each day of baking, followed by cakes and cinnamon cookies and sometimes freshly harvested corn. As long as a horno retains its heat, someone will think of something to pop inside. I met one woman who slow-cooks whole pumpkins in them, and others who take advantage of the lingering heat by warming meats and stews. "How old is this horno?" I ask, and after the third time resign myself to the stock answer. "This one? Oh, about three hundred years old."

My plan was to drive back in time, from Pueblo to Pueblo, to villages that existed as long as five centuries before the arrival of the first Pilgrims. By the time the Spanish "found" them, as most accounts quaintly put it, there were as many as a hundred Pueblo villages in New Mexico with clusters west of Albuquerque and north of Santa Fe near the Rio Grande River. Their only domesticated animal was the dog. They were farmers and artisans who had cultivated and irrigated 25,000 acres and lived in multifamily houses, which the Spanish named Pueblos.

It's amazing how far away a person can feel in her own country. As I tick them off on the map their names alone feed my incessant craving for exotica: Nambe, Tesuque, Pojoaque, Santa Ana, Picuris, Sandia, Alcade, Acoma, Jemez, Taos. Indian names battle it out with Spanish ones in the same way my own Cape Cod has Sandwich spilling into Cotuit and Priscilla Bradfords and Goody Hallets colliding with Nausets and Wampanoags. No matter how many generations of schoolchildren parrot the historic prominence of Plymouth "rock," it is my little barrier spit, Provincetown, Massachusetts, where the first Pilgrims landed. (They didn't hang around at first and locals like to joke it's because they couldn't find a parking space.) But unlike the American Southwest, any physical traces of Outer Cape Cod's Native American heritage have been all but obliterated. In the partly reforested Province Lands that the settlers decimated to build their ships and feed their fires, the occasional National Seashore marker pays tribute to the Nauset Indians who lived here for centuries in harmony with the land. I walk these woods and dunes every day yet I've little conscious awareness or abiding respect for their ancient past. I'm far too distracted by the still evident flotsam of what was once one of the world's great shore-whaling ports: the battered foundation of a lifesaving station, the skeleton of a rotted wharf poking up from eroded sand flats, the crude numbered posts marking the graves of the nameless victims of a nineteenth-century smallpox epidemic. In North Truro's Pilgrim Heights recreation area, a plaque commemorating the Outer Cape's Indians refers to nothing less fleeting than "footprints in the sand."

Despite frequent tenacious efforts to the contrary, New Mexico's Native American past refuses to be buried or trivialized. Its Native American present resists being turned into some bite-sized living diorama to indulge the popular culture. With their lands decimated the reservations draw crucial tax-free income from their casinos out on the interstate. Devoid of charm or architectural inspiration, these buildings are institutional-looking, self-contained, and way out of scale, as if they took flight somewhere in New Jersey and plopped down in the Pajarito Plateau. It is easy to say, "Tsk, tsk, so it's come to this." I said it. The casinos are tacky and in my experience gambling is an industry that produces nothing except grief. But as I pass a succession of them — one for each tribe — the casinos begin to strike me as necessary eyesores, like public works garages or hospitals. With federal money for health, education, and environmental programs shrinking fast, the Pueblos rely on casino dollars to keep the villages livable and inspire a new generation to live, work, and raise families in the community and embrace tribal culture. Even with the revived interest in their unusual pottery and other crafts, many Pueblos are forced to commute off the reservation to earn their livings. "Some people would enslave us as living museums," says Jacob Viarrial, governor of Pojoaque, "Water-Drinking Place," Pueblo. "For instance, as soon as a tribe begins an industry to better itself, many politicians do everything in their power to keep the industry from advancing."

Away from the casinos' looming presence, though, the scene is pastoral and timeless, the kind of setting that can make even a satellite dish look organic. Adobe hamlets and high desert were an antidote to the Victorian excesses of the Bottger-Koch mansion, an Albuquerque bed-and-breakfast I'd booked on a recommendation from the cheerful woman who answered the phone at the New Mexico Bed and Breakfast Association. "It's a little expensive but for sure that's where I'd stay if I had my choice of anywhere in Albuquerque," she told me. I took the bait, forgetting, as we all tend to do under such circumstances, that this nice woman and I could harbor violently opposing tastes. The Bottger-Koch Mansion, built in 1912 of brick in the American foursquare style, sits on an oddly angled plot near the corner where Albuquerque's Old Town bumps up against the generic urban sprawl of Lomas Boulevard. The place was a private home until the arrival of Route 66, when it began offering lodging to such colorful travelers as Machine Gun Kelly and his gang. Or so the brochure boasts; historic bed-and-breakfasts love to lay claim to long-dead luminaries. When I walked the Katy Trail across the Missouri bottomlands I rarely occupied a bed that didn't allegedly bear a trace of the DNA of Daniel Boone.

A small cluster of low, Spanish-style adobe buildings and tiled courtyards, Old

Town radiates from a sleepy central plaza, a welcoming patch of green with benches, flower gardens, and a gazebo. Much of the park's activity, particularly the delightful profusion of little girls in yellow or white frocks, stems from its status as photo-opportunity of choice for the wedding and confirmation parties that spill out of San Felipe de Neri church, which has existed in some form since 1706. I've always loved gawking at wedding parties because each one packs so much drama and intrigue of the family kind. Also it's okay to behave like a voyeur. It's expected, and you're pretty much invisible to these preoccupied people anyway.

I thought staying at the mansion for three nights would give me at least one entire day to poke around Old Town. The B&B's brochure touts Old Town Plaza "and its 200 shops Restaurants and galleries [sic]." The day I allotted was a hot, suffocating Sunday. I moseyed, I strolled, I wove, and otherwise investigated every nook, side street, mews, and back alley. All of an hour passed. (Sadly, the rattlesnake museum was closed.) I stopped at a tiny café tucked behind a souvenir shop selling salt shakers, tote bags, and earrings in the shape of chile peppers. Collapsing into a plastic chair feeling hot, pale, and fat, I nonetheless ordered a platter of tamales. Stuffed into a flowered shift, the waitress, who is also the owner and chef, complained to me in a good-natured way about her heel spurs and good-for-nothing husband. The tamales tasted like potting soil but it was fun to make a friend. I emerged in the soporific heat and dragged myself, belly distended with tamales and lemonade, back to the mansion for a nap. Let's face it, I told myself, I've done Old Town.

On the way back, hopscotching lazily past blankets laden with the wares of Pueblo and Hopi traders, I ask myself: Where does all this jewelry come from? I envision a distant planet populated by crafter slaves who carve, hammer, and solder day and night to meet earthlings' apparently insatiable demand for dreamcatcher earrings, fetish beads, and turquoise-studded belt buckles the size of hubcaps. Here I am cooking up scenarios of intergalactic sweatshops and I have yet to work my way to Santa Fe and Taos. I ain't seen nothing yet. Sooner or later I will break down and buy, knowing that Dick and Jane Paleface may be able to carry off this look in the shadow of the Jemez Mountains but when they get home to Sarasota or Secaucus they look over-loaded and goofy, like WASP children playing Tiger Lily. Besides, a lady sculptor I know who lives in a vast Manhattan loft with a dog and about eight tons of Hopi jewelry, told me the real stuff is found only in New York City.

Back at Baader-Meinhoff — why do I keep calling it that? — a different kind of kitsch reigns. If there were a legal limit placed on Victoriana, proprietress Yvonne Koch, a dainty stylish blonde, would be in serious violation. The woman is irrepressible.

Propped up on my king-sized bed in a room named "Savannah" after one of Yvonne and Ron Koch's daughters is a seemingly impenetrable nest of roll pillows and poofy cushions with ruffled shams, all in colliding floral prints. Over the bed hangs an unfurled boa wrap with flowers and birds poking out of it. In this abode no lampshade goes unfringed, no surface un-draped, no molding unstenciled. Every-thing that can be feasibly tied with a bow, is. Feeling like the princess thrashing to accommodate the concealed pea I sleep poorly. There is something ghoulish about all these pillows, as creepy as the Charlie-McCarthy-in-drag dolls that monopolize the furniture in the mansion's drawing rooms. I dream I am being strangled by a heather-and-tea-rose wreath. I awake choking on the scent of lavender, which is infused in the bedding.

I want to smell the earth, the desert air, to tear into the simplest fresh bread. I escape to the freeway in search of a soothing collage of adobe, mesa, and sky. My destination is Acoma, oldest of New Mexico's Pueblos. This is the day of Acoma's annual harvest dance, one of the few feast days open to outsiders. Acoma sits sixty-five miles west of Albuquerque but for all its resemblance to an American town it may as well be in Peru. I'd seen photographs of Acoma's Sky City, a densely constructed adobe settlement that sits nearly camouflaged on the mauve table of a sandstone butte rising nearly 360 feet from the surrounding desert. Accustomed to living within reach, if not in the middle of places with the prefix "New," Americans cross oceans in search of antiquity. Yet Acoma has been continuously occupied since A.D. 1075. Like the surviving Anasazi glyphs in Utah's red rock country, Acoma forces us to contemplate a thriving culture centuries before the arrival of Columbus, or Leif Eriksson, or anyone with milky skin and tender feet.

I'm excited about joining the celebrated Feast of San Estevan. So, apparently, is every other sentient human in the Southwest. I arrive at about nine-thirty in the morning and the parking lot already seems stuffed to Woodstockian proportions. But my panic soon subsides. Never mind the belching tour buses, the redundantly dubbed "Tourist Visitors Center," the Sky City Restaurant "meticulously designed in Pueblo-style." To the credit of its elders, Acoma Pueblo is untainted by the heavy Disney-guided hand we've come to expect. It is the real thing. Acoma children still learn the ancient Keresan language. The Pueblo's name, Aco ma, is Keresan for "people of the white rock."

Less than a hundred of the estimated 3,200 Acoma Pueblo Indians still live in Sky City. Most families moved off the butte so their children could easily attend school. But those who remain live as their people have for centuries. They drink water caught in natural cisterns. There is no electricity, and the one nod to contemporary living standards is a squadron of Porta Potti's at the settlement's edge. The dense arrangement of ceremonial chambers, or kivas, and dwellings, some four stories high, surround a small plaza where elaborately costumed festival dancers advance and retreat to ceaseless drumbeats. On the eve of traditional festivals the Pueblos burn fires in their hornos and bake bread in the heated ovens throughout the night. With the last few hours of heat they'll roast pumpkins and corn. On the 246,000 acres of reservation land the Acoma raise cattle and sheep. They also grow wheat, corn, melons, squash, and hay. And they run the hopping Sky City Casino out on the interstate.

The Acoma never saw a white man until 1540 and they've been under siege, in one way or another, ever since then. In their unwieldy conquistador regalia the army of Francisco Vásquez de Coronado dragged themselves up the nearly vertical track to the lava mesa in agony and disbelief. Catching their breath they found a community of farmers wanting for little, with maize stockpiled in dizzying abundance. Duly noting their respect for the natives' resourcefulness, the Spanish proceeded to plunder, pillage, and enslave.

Today all Anglo visitors must submit to a kind of processing and initiation reminiscent of a low-security border crossing. I'm not accustomed to the label "Anglo." Despite my complexion the fit feels all wrong

to this granddaughter of a relentlessly per-
secuted people who fled the pogroms of
Poland and Romania. Call me insensitive,
but I can't seem to muster any personal
guilt for the punishments inflicted on Native Americans at the time my people were
being tortured by the Inquisition and
blamed for the bubonic plague. So I confess that at first I find the tribal adminis-
trators on the paranoid side. But the
sketchiest reading of their history vindi-
cates their jitters about outsiders. For centuries after Cortés landed in Mexico in
1521 the Spanish thirst for land and riches
would not be extinguished in the face of
one Indian revolt after another. In the late
sixteenth century the young Juan de
Oñate, born in the New World, made an
expedition north from a Spanish settlement near the Rio Grande. When Oñate
ordered his nephew to seize food from the
Acoma Pueblo the Indians killed him and
six other men. The ensuing battle claimed
the lives of nearly eight hundred Acoma
Indians. The remaining villagers were
taken to the mission capital of Santo
Domingo, where Acoma males over
twenty-five had one foot cut off and sixty
Indian girls were sent to convents in New
Spain. Pueblo and Spanish blood spilled

over the next two centuries, with Spanish attacks and atrocities and Indian reprisals. Many Indians spared death were forced into slavery — hence all those charming mission churches built with logs hauled up the daunting mountains. Even less fortunate Indians succumbed to smallpox, a Spanish import. In retaliation Indians massacred priests and friars. In one spasm of violence the Spanish torched all the kivas, the Pueblos' ceremonial chambers. In 1860 the Pueblos plotted a great rebellion in which the Indians were to kill all Spanish sympathizers including women and children. Indians cut off the water supply to the Santa Fe Palace of the Governors where hundreds of Spanish took refuge, and the Spanish were ultimately driven south to Mexico. Twelve years later they were back. And on and on it went, with Pueblos fleeing to the Hopis and then aligning with the Spanish to fight a common enemy, the Apaches. Spanish rule officially ended in 1848 with the Treaty of Guadalupe Hidalgo, and New Mexico was transferred to the United States. Between Spanish foreclosures and American land grabs the 35 million acres once held by native New Mexicans dwindled to the size of a national park. This was before the Gold

Rush, and the Civil War, in which Texas invaded New Mexico. At one time four flags flew over Santa Fe. Then came One Nation, Indivisible and its Forest Service, which began to gobble Indian community lands. The Department of the Interior chimed in, revoking native Americans' grazing permits.

Paranoid? I'm amazed we're allowed in at all. Now I understand why, when I asked the Hopi public relations liaison, a man named Lee Mayestew, if I could visit Hopi communities to watch the women bake, he demanded an official proposal and directed me to appear before a Hopi review board. One would convene in two weeks, he said, and I was welcome to fly out for it. I replied that seemed like an outlandish expense under the circumstances. He was unmovable. "But I'm only interested in bread!" I protested. "I'm not part of any organization. I'm not an anthropologist, an apologist, or even a scholar! I'm not researching a scathing exposé on the protein content of winter wheat!" "How do we know you're not going to steal our recipes for your own purposes?" he snapped. By this point I was convinced he was teasing me and I laughed. But the man was not kidding. "The Anglos have stolen everything else from us. They come here to 'ob-serve' and go off to mass-produce Hopi-style jewelry, blankets, and pottery." Lee offered me an ultimatum: you appear before the review board or your proposal will not be considered.

I may be thick but I can take a hint. I decided not to visit the Hopis.

Most of the people spilling out of the trucks and minivans encircling Acoma are Native Americans from Acoma lands or other Pueblos. Waved right past the visitors' entrance, they lug chairs and coolers to settle in for a day of eating, dancing, and drumming. We Anglos are funneled through the Tourist Visitors Center to pay admission, a donation of our choosing, and receive a briefing on the local rules and regulations: Always stay on the pavement when descending on foot, stay within designated plaza and street areas, keep clear of dancers, restrain your children. Also: Do not interrupt non-dance participants' concentration by asking questions or talking. Do not approach dancers. No alcohol, weapons, drugs, or pets. Kivas and grave-yards are *not* to be entered by non-Pueblo people. Applause after dances is not appropriate. The Pueblo, bless them, allow no video recorders but still photographers may purchase permits, which is enough of a deterrent to humble snap-happy tourists into a day equipped only with the senses God gave them. The Pueblo provides shuttle buses to haul visitors up the mesa but I could use a walk.

It's about a mile walk up to Sky City. Even the road presents a steep climb, made more irritating by the intensifying heat and the roar of buses in low gear. In shorts and a sleeveless blouse I'm naked compared to Coronado's divisions and I'm already drenched with sweat. With the asphalt molten under my hiking boots I ignore the "stay on the pavement" rule and search for a more appealing way to slog up the mesa. I see children horsing around at the base of what looks like a narrow trail slicing through the volcanic boulders. This, I later learn, is Padre's Trail, a succession of steps carved into the sandstone by centuries of foot traffic. Time has sheared the steps to a treacherous angle. To keep my balance I grab at the surrounding wall of rocks and discover a neatly spaced succession of handholds. Smooth as soap, these too have been sculpted into the rock by the endless procession.

"My mother-in-law would bake in the horno every Friday but now we use it mostly for the festivals," a woman named Rosie tells me. With her sister June, both of whom live on Acoma land beyond Sky City, Rosie is cooking up a heap of fry bread for the feast. Covered with a plastic cloth, the table in front of Rosie and June's fryer is arranged with honey, powdered sugar, and cinnamon. Most cultures offer some variation of fry bread. Americans have doughnuts, Portuguese have malassadas and flippers, Germans have the Berliner. Like these, fry bread involves some delicious, lethal combination of flour, baking powder, milk or oil, and lard.

The Indians didn't invent fry bread. Before the onslaught of the Anglos, Native Americans knew nothing of wheat flour, their staple being cornmeal. Different Indian nations became acquainted with wheat under varying circumstances, few of them voluntary. The Navajos, for example, learned about fry bread from U.S. Army wives during the Indians' internment at Fort Sumner.

Rosie's dough combines white flour, powdered milk, and baking powder, which she kneads, forms into burger-like rounds, and fries in lard. Anglos dabbling in fry bread often flatten the dough with a rolling pin, but hands like Rosie's work the springy rounds with an expertise that seem instinctive. And unlike less authentic, high-volume incarnations of the specialty, Rosie's bread is fried in pork fat rendered from locally slaughtered pigs. She prefers nonfat dry milk to regular, which makes the dough too sticky. The oil must be really, really hot. The hotter the oil, the less greasy the bread.

"It's our festival treat," says Rosie, whose daughter is dancing in the festival. "Fry bread is the only thing you can't get ready-made." She'll fry bread all day for the visitors and the dancers, who are ravenous after hours on their feet, stomping, bowing, waving, and snaking their way around the plaza. In the plaza itself Indians crowd the rooftops to witness a spectacle worthy of Busby Berkeley. Men in eagle headdress glide in synchronized circles, their arms lost under five-foot-wide feathered wings. A line of humans with bear heads pinwheels this way and that, followed by a chain of small children in painted wooden crowns. A few dancers carry small doughnut-like oven breads strung on twine.

Everyone around me is dancing, eating,

or shopping. It appears that when people can't point their cameras or yak into cell phones they just eat more. Along the main street that spills into the plaza are tables and stalls offering corn, tamales, oven bread, and cinnamon rolls. Food stalls alternate with craft tables crammed with kachina dolls, pottery, jewelry, and more jewelry. To a constant, visceral drumbeat the dancers, hundreds of them, advance while the visitors form an impromptu conga line of their own, stopping to finger the turquoise, coral, and Acoma's signature ceramic pottery and ornaments.

Though the more rigorous local crafts nearly disappeared in the years of the Pueblos' isolation and decline, a new entrepreneurial generation has revived them. I've always found pottery collectors a tiresome bunch, but running my fingers along the cool glassy surface of a San Idelfonso onyx jug or picking out sepia birds, deer, and turtles among the arabesque designs of a signature polychrome Acoma pot makes me lust after these objects, which, if authentic, can cost hundreds or thousands of dollars. Acoma potters work with a fine, pale clay dug on the reservation. Polished first with a smooth stone, the pots are painted in lively, nature-inspired designs of orange, brown, and black on a white background. A few of the pots beckon to me, but the only ones I can afford are of a size befitting Barbie's adobe dreamhouse. I must put these pots out of my mind and move on. At a sparsely arranged table, one of the few where the local crafts haven't been augmented by chotchkes imported from Hong Kong, I select a delicate choker of, what else, turquoise and coral. I hand the cash to a heavily made-up teenage girl in a skimpy outfit who leans over to help me clasp it around my neck. She smiles, closing her hands around the money. "Great!" she announces. "Now I can go to the casino!"

It's time to take the lead of the Indian visitors and spend my cash on the real goods: the food. I wait on an unruly line to buy horno-roasted corn on a skewer. This must be some corn; people are pushing and shoving like crazy. Here is the way they prepare it: Roll corn in butter. Spread buttered corn with a layer of mayonnaise. Coat mayonnaised, buttered corn with a thick blanket of grated Parmesan cheese. Sprinkle corn, thus slathered, with salt, pepper, and paprika. I'm glad my husband isn't here; he would surely make some annoying crack about a triple bypass. The corn looks so scrumptious I sink my teeth into it immediately. And there, jammed into a crowd of distracted strangers, I nearly choke to death.

No one notices. Meanwhile I'm struggling for air, certain I'm a candidate for an al fresco Heimlich maneuver. Wheezing through what feels like a pinhole I stumble into the cool shade of a ruined cliff dwelling where I squeak and gasp until I feel normal enough to take a sip from my water bottle. It is only when I reenter the world of the breathing that I see a cluster of local children staring at me. A ragged little boy of about eight is the first to speak. He points to the corn, sitting in its wrapper on the stone beside me. "You gonna eat that?" It is my pleasure to watch the boy attack the corn holding it in his plump little hands. Heimlich-schooled myself, I keep an eye on him.

Along with the escalating heat and the choking incident, the pounding of drums is beginning to unnerve me so I decide to commit another wee act of civil disobedience. I set off to explore the back streets. The hornos I encounter are the classic beehives, with smooth flat floors and off-center smoke holes near the pinnacle. A cross section of a typical horno would reveal a layer cake base of mud, rocks, and more mud. Sculpted of clay and straw, the domes were originally shaped by a mound of sand or earth that served as a mold and was removed when the dome hardened. It's a big deal to bake in the hornos, Rosie and June had told me, so the Acoma women "try to bake as many breads as possible in one shot." Most breads bake in forty-five minutes or less, but it takes at least an hour of wood burning to heat up the horno for baking. (Right after the fire's removed the inside of the horno is about 500 degrees.) If you're not baking for a crowd, the women say, there's just no point to it.

When I slip back onto the main way the plaza is packed as tightly as a sack of worry dolls and it's so hot the fry bread ladies could save on fuel. On the hike back to the parking lot the road is wall-to-wall people on their way up. An hour and a half later I'm conked out at the Baader-Meinhoff, blessing everything in this overdecorated, over-air-conditioned room from the gargantuan pillows to the garish landscape mural.

I wake from my nap to the message that my childhood friend Andrea has called. She's flying down from Salt Lake City today to join me. Andrea and I have one of those friendships you pick up right where you left off, with little intervening correspondence. I make excuses to stop in Salt Lake for a few days when I'm headed West on an assignment, and once Andrea, her husband, and their two daughters came to visit us on Cape Cod. For years Andrea worked as a partner in a corporate law firm representing insurance companies. And for most of that time, encased in tailored navy suits and trying to sway judges and juries against ruling for claimants with canes and whiplash collars, Andrea was miserable. Her stomach was ravaged, her nights were a torment, and her girls grew feisty in her absence. Finally Andrea quit law and decided to become a landscape gardener, but she ended up filling the days with volunteer work and chauffeuring the girls everywhere this side of the Wasatch Range. Her new life makes trysts like this possible. It's a real treat for me, too.

I stop and pick up a latte for me and a nice tall one for Andrea and sit at the Albuquerque airport feeling giddy. Soon, slurping caffeine and babbling a mile a minute, we're headed to Chimayo on a roundabout route that will take us to every Pueblo we can find. I'm not exactly sure what I'm looking for, but with Andrea here I'm feeling a lot more adventurous. Together on the cusp of menopause we giggle and blab like teenagers. It's just like old times except we're middle-aged, a bit creaky in the knees, and we're usually in bed by nine. I'm reminded of something Jonji, my favorite yoga teacher, once told me: "When you're older you can do everything you've always done, except it hurts."

Where is everyone? Andrea and I navigate the rented Cirrus along lumpy roads to San Felipe Pueblo, Santa Ana, and Sandia — Tiwa for "dusty or sandy." No name could be more suitable, but it begs the question: why aren't they all named Sandia? Choking on the dust, we park the car and poke around timidly at first until our shared Hayley Mills past ("I have a scathingly brilliant idea!") gives us the shot of nerve we need to trespass with abandon. We head up a dusty deserted street past apparently vacant schools and snoozing tourist offices. The villages resemble studio backlots and our presence feels more and more illicit the deeper we explore. We bump up against dead ends, back the Cirrus out of enormous potholes, get out and hike over fields and ditches. My hopes of seeing people bake are dashed, but we'd be happy just to see even one person.

I'd read that the Pueblos' traditional social system divides them into "Summer People" and "Winter People." This is probably the only thing these Native Americans will ever have in common with New Yorkers who own property in the Hamptons. But beyond that the system passes supreme tribal authority back and forth among the two groups, called "moieties." The changing of the guard, so to speak, occurs in February and September. Have we arrived to witness some kind of Summer-Winter limbo? Is there a very quiet meeting in progress, a meeting so crucial everyone except the chickens is in attendance?

Andrea and I drink tea and confer on a porch swing at La Posada de Chimayo, a rustic bed-and-breakfast at the edge of the Sangre de Cristo Mountains. We've got half of a low adobe and log cabin hemmed in by boulders, scrub, and prickly pear. A writer who sequesters himself in this place periodically occupies the other half. He leaves his door ajar, and something about his behavior makes me think he is unpublished, perhaps even writing the same sentence over and over again. Heeeeeeere's Johnny! Andrea and I try to solve the mystery of the disappearing Indians. We flip through our guidebooks and Web site printouts to see if we missed any mention of the region's evacuation or relocation. The truth is neither sinister nor alarming. September is Pueblo party time, a whirlwind of feast days and corn dances. An Indian we meet the next day will tell us, as if we are a bit thick, when there is a feast day in the "neighborhood" everyone goes. These are the days when the community celebrates itself, and the festivities normally go from morning until dark. Very few are open to Anglos.

Before we head up to Taos for the day Andrea and I pay an early morning visit to the Santuario de Chimayo, often referred to as the Lourdes of America. A small, squat adobe building with twin bell towers shadowed by a sacred mountain peak, the *santuario* opens like a jewelry box to deliciously colorful murals, milagros, and an altar by the great *Santero*, Molleno, known as the "Chili Painter." It looks like the icing on an immense wedding cake. Built in 1814 on a site sacred to Indians — Chimayo is a Spanish corruption of the Tewa word for "good flaking stone" — the church draws thousands of Indian and Hispanic pilgrims who touch, rub themselves with, or ingest its reputed healing soil. These days the soil is accessible from a small hole in El Pozito, the "little well" room, actually an alcove off a larger room crammed with abandoned crutches, canes, eyeglasses, and body braces. These are accompanied by a collage of poignant snapshots, letters, and other testimonials. The faithful have been partaking of the dirt for nearly two centuries and lately, according to Father Roca, the *santuario*'s Portuguese-born priest, they've become downright greedy. Father Roca invites me into his office for a chat. Ancient and stooped, he bears an uncanny resemblance to old man Prizzi of the film *Prizzi's Honor*. He even sounds like Prizzi, the way he growls out of one side of his palsied mouth. "We get a lot of stupid publicity, and now they come for the dirt, always the dirt," he snarls. "They don't stop to pay their respects to Christ, they don't sit, nothing. They just ask where is the dirt. Stupid dirt."

"I'm so sorry," I say. Father Roca has reason to be in a foul temper. He's been the padre here for forty-six years, he's not getting any younger, and he's tired of schlepping thirty-pound sacks of earth from the local Agway to fill up the little hole. Keeping up with the demand for healing, holy dirt is killing the man. And it isn't just the dirt, he complains. "These people are stupid," he adds. "They ask stupid questions. They ask if I was here when the church was built. I tell them yes, yes, I've been here a hundred years. What I should tell them is they should stay home and go to Mass, not come all the way out here just for some dirt." I take Father Roca's gnarled hand in mine and promise him that I will not, either verbally or in my writing, encourage people to come and partake of the stupid dirt.

Because of the ever-swelling ranks of pilgrims to the *santuario* a little village has sprung up there, consisting mainly of flat-fee parking lots. Andrea and I stop in at one of the souvenir shops, where I buy a ceramic incense burner in the shape of an horno beside a palette and a few minuscule breads. The whole thing fits into the palm of my hand. We drive north to Taos, New Mexico's northernmost Pueblo. Taos rises like Brigadoon from a swath of high desert at the foot of Wheeler Peak, New Mexico's highest mountain. The Pueblo is a prosperous village that manages to endure as a real place while accommodating a steady stream of tourists exploring Santa Fe and the town of Taos, two miles away, with its galleries, jewelry, jewelry, and jewelry. Taos is a Tiwa Pueblo that may have been named for *tu-o-ta,* "place of the red willows," or *tuah tah,* "down at the village," or something else entirely. These days it may as well be synonymous with crafts, because Taos is packed with accomplished artisans selling drums, paintings, pottery, storyteller figures, and leatherwork out of a cluster of small shops in the plaza, with its priceless view of adobe dwellings piled high against a shimmering curtain of mountain peaks. You pay the parking fee, admire the timeless beauty of the place, stroll the plaza, buy a set of handcrafted quivers or a drum, and leave content.

But somewhere beyond this self-enclosed plaza is a Taos that doesn't exist for public consumption, where everyday life proceeds unperturbed by your naïve exclamations and feeble bargaining attempts. How does a person penetrate that other Taos, or for that matter, the real Acoma or Tesuque? One cannot, almost by definition. At least those places allow a visitor to soak up a little atmosphere before sunset. When Andrea and I pulled up to the Jemez Visitors Center for information we toured a small museum with a gift shop open for business. A clot of sweaty tourists had formed near the cash register. By the door we collided with a sign: "Jemez Pueblo Closed to Visitors." And we are left to contemplate the notion of a visitors' center for a place that forbids visitors. Did stopping at this place constitute a "visit" to Jemez Pueblo? We ignore the sign, drove into the Pueblo, and visit with a family who has a small sign reading POTTERY. Our hostess shows us her horno, shrouded in plastic. We follow her through the kitchen into a small living room where the woman sits at a child's desk and demonstrates how she works the clay with her fingers. Andrea and I each buy a small pot. So we are, in fact, "inside" — but it is a business transaction, nothing more. The whole time Andrea and I are in their small tidy home, a man and a teenage boy sit several feet from us watching television. They never even glance in our direction.

Wherever Andrea and I go, if we are not there to buy we meet only stony stares and No Trespassing signs. As a writer I'm frustrated by this lack of access. Here is a place where my interest and enthusiasm do not, as they say, cut any ice. But I remind myself that all those years when Howie and I lived in a historic house on the water in Provincetown Harbor guests at the neighboring inns and condominiums would pass the time by standing with their arms folded over on their second-story decks, staring down at us. They were unabashed, as if our existence constituted an ongoing exhibit, The People Who Really Live Here! Early in the morning I'd step outside in my nightgown to hear someone call, "Say, what kind of dog is that?" So I've had the faintest taste of how it feels to be on display. From Taos Plaza I gaze at the adobe clusters wistfully.

Andrea and I decide to go our separate ways for an hour, during which I make some feeble attempts to penetrate the inner sanctum. Where are the real people? As it turns out, you can't get there from here. The way is barred with barriers natural and manmade. But I have no trouble affixing myself to the baker Geronimo Romero. He makes a major chunk of his living off tourists. His bakery sits at the far edge of the plaza, skirting both worlds. Actually the "bakery" consists of a large, circa 1706 horno, a table arranged with oven breads in clear plastic bags, and a chair where Geronimo sits, waiting for the breads to bake. Born and raised in Taos Pueblo, he moved away to Albuquerque as a young adult but recently returned. Between the locals and a constant stream of tourists, business is brisk. "The village people come and buy my bread, especially for feast days," says Geronimo, who, to his chagrin, is usually called "Gerry." Asked his age, he offers only a platitude: "You are as old as you want to be." He looks to be in his early forties. Geronimo wears a striped shirt, well-fitted black jeans, and leather boots, and his hair hangs to his waist in a loose ponytail. "We are the only bakery inside the village and there was a real need," he says. Geronimo is articulate and attractive and the working horno fascinates people. So tourists don't flinch when he charges them five dollars for a round loaf smaller than a dinner plate. Geronimo bakes all year, even when the horno wears a blanket of snow. Every spring he lays some fresh clay on the floor and packs, then smooths a new layer of mud, clay, and straw on the horno's surface.

"My bread's flavor comes from the wood," he tells me. "I use cedar because it burns hottest and fastest and has the sweetest aroma. We use it for all our baking, cookies and pies, too." Geronimo tells me each family has its own secret oven bread recipe but they're all some variation of the basics: white flour, salt, sugar, water, commercial yeast, Crisco or lard.

Geronimo's breads are crusty and round like typical peasant loaves. But for special occasions Pueblos might bake loaves separated in roll-sized sections, and festival breads called *mandi* emerge as plump, three-fingered claws, like a bear's.

Geronimo's was one of several oven breads I sampled in my sweep of Pueblo country. And like those other breads it was unremarkable. The grain is harvested locally but the flour isn't the fussy high-grade stone-milled article found in artisan bakeries and no bakers seem to bother with sourdough cultures. Still I have the feeling there is wonderful bread lurking somewhere beyond these public plazas, even though most Indians and Hispanic people in these parts have gone the way of the rest of America — they buy processed breads at the market. Horno bread's appeal has less to do with culinary prowess and more to do with the fact that it emerged, as it has for centuries, from these rare and beautiful ovens. Still, as Andrea and I survey the passing desert on the ride from Chimayo back to Albuquerque I can't help wondering if the Pueblos' real oven bread — if everything that's authentic and true about Pueblo life — is as out of reach as the ordinary people who bake it.

Rosie's Fry Bread

With pointers from Breads of the
Southwest *by Beth Hensperger*

INGREDIENTS:
Four cups unbleached all-purpose flour
One-half cup nonfat dry milk
One and a half tablespoons baking powder
One teaspoon salt
Four tablespoons lard
One and a half cups very hot water
Flour or cornmeal for dusting
Two quarts vegetable oil for frying

In mixing bowl combine flour, dry milk,
baking powder, and salt. Using a knife, cut
in the lard until dough is crumbly.

Add hot water and mix well, using a
fork, until dough comes together in a ball.
Knead dough briefly, no more than ten
times, until soft and smooth but not sticky.
Cover with plastic wrap and let stand at
room temperature for at least a half hour.

On flour- or cornmeal-dusted surface
pull off small knobs of dough two to three
inches in diameter. Cover pieces with a
damp towel. Working with one piece at a
time overlap the dough and with a rolling

pin roll the resulting knob into a thin circle. Cover dough rounds with plastic wrap, let all rounds sit for about twenty minutes.

Heat two inches of oil in a Dutch oven, heavy kettle, or deep-fat fryer to 380 degrees. Drop dough one piece at a time into the hot oil, tapping and pushing the pieces gently with tongs until they bubble up and become golden and crisp. Pierce dough with a fork before gently turning it to cook evenly on both sides. Remove breads with a slotted spoon and drain on paper towels or clean brown paper bags.

Serve plain or with powdered sugar, cinnamon, or honey.

Brijendra's Kitchen:

India

There is a cycle that Europeans — by Europeans I mean all Westerners, including Americans — tend to pass through. It goes like this: everything Indian is marvelous; second stage, everything Indian not so marvelous; third stage, everything Indian abominable. For some people it ends there, for others the cycle renews itself and goes on.
— RUTH PRAWER JHABVALA,
OUT OF INDIA

For weeks after we left India his name echoed in my head: Brijendra. The gentle manservant of my friend Shubhadarshini, Brijendra has been indispensable to the Singh family for nearly two decades. All day long, whether she's seated at the dining table in her New Delhi home, applying kohl at her dressing table mirror, or in her chauffeur-driven BMW nuzzling a mobile phone,

Shubhi can be heard calling for Brijendra. At times the call is plaintive, like Catherine scouring the moors for Heathcliff.

Whether summoned with a shout or whimper, he is never far away. He fixes, he faxes, he tends to the dogs. Small and graceful with thick, side-parted hair and a narrow mustache, Brijendra pads around in near silence. He searches the house for Shubhi's misplaced papers and prepares her insulin injections. Chez Singh, if you alight for more than a minute in any spot he materializes with a cup of tea. Mostly, though, Brijendra cooks. India's streets and markets are punctuated with bread makers ranging from the simplest chapati vendor — a man, a pan, a plan — to the nan maker pulling puffy flat breads out of a clay tandoor. But it is Brijendra who teaches me everything I needed to know about Indian bread.

It often seems as if every American who has been to India feels moved to capture the experience in words or photographs. With professional flair or earnest ineptitude, in hometown newspapers and at Rotary Club luncheons across the U.S., those who have braved the chaos, din, and pestilence of the subcontinent return home to spread the news. They almost always focus on India's street life. The click and whir of his camera as reliable as a pacemaker, the visitor bears witness to the colorful, incessant clamor. He laughs, he cries, he gasps, he nibbles gingerly then clutches his ravaged gut and congratulates himself for his embrace of adversity and his open mind.

I certainly did my share of slogging, agape, among the masses. But thanks to Shubhi I was privy to the taste and rhythms of Indian life behind the clatter of the street. Just as it is among the markets and street stalls, bread is the mortar of the Indian kitchen. Most Indians do their eating at home. Top executives and menial clerks alike eat lunches prepared at home and delivered warm at midday. In the north, Indians scoop up their curries with clay-oven baked nan, fried chapati, roti, puri, and paratha. In the tropical south, one is more likely to encounter leavened rice pancakes called appams and their unleavened cousin the *dosa*, immense puffy crepes big as a satchel into which someone has tossed spiced potato and onion.

Bread is more than sustenance; it's the plate, the spoon, and the drumbeat that paces a meal. Retreating to Brijendra's kitchen offered me a sedate reference point, an inside-out look at the way bread is woven into the soul of Indian life. And I would see on the streets of Old Delhi or in the tiniest Rajasthani village as well as in the hysterical commerce of the Calcutta bazaar, fingers working the dough as elegantly and methodically as Brijendra's, guided by a kind of blood memory. How many millions of beedie-stained hands are at any moment, pressing, turning, and slapping?

Though monastic compared with the world outside, the kitchen of a wealthy Indian household is a very busy place. It resembles that of a monarch, a president, or Madonna. The cook must be qualified, willing, and prepared to honor absolutely any request. What mystifies me about Shubhi's — Brijendra's — kitchen is its sparseness. Where is all the stuff? In a household with drivers and servants there's no need to store perishable foods. At the very least, though, I expect something resembling the pantry of an American macrobiotic, the kind of person with eight shelves of Mason jars filled with nuts, grains, and beans, one of those unsettling kitchens in which absolutely everything edible must first be soaked overnight. Several times a day Brijendra pads out of this seemingly empty kitchen with steaming curries, soups, and pakoras for a late afternoon snack. In this kitchen Brijendra hacks up scores of chickens, grinds pepper and cardamom, makes cheese. I spy only a tiny bowl of fresh chiles. Brijendra is to the average cook what levitators are to health club yogis.

Howie, our friend Lenny Alberts, and I are spending some time with Shubhi and her husband, S.P., before we head west to explore Rajasthan. Single and in his fifties, Lenny is an old friend and tireless traveler who has been on all seven continents. Howie and I used to vacation with Lenny and his lover, David, before David died of AIDS. The three of us are accustomed to one another's faces; our highs, our lows are second nature to each other and we are able to bicker like siblings with no residual hard feelings. (Shubhi and S.P. do not grasp that Lenny is gay and commend him periodically for his "decision" not to chain himself to a spouse.) Shubhi and S.P. live in a large, chaotically designed house in Sadhana Enclave, a gated neighborhood arranged around a green that is remarkable in these parts for its lack of festering trash, cows, squatters, monkeys, or drying laundry. The Singhs employ a full-time watchman, two drivers, a maid, and a man to tend the jungle of aloe, lemon, and frangipani encircling their walled estate. In India, where the woman who sells dung patties on the street is still a considerable distance from rock bottom, this is the tippy-top of the socioeconomic scale. In Sadhana Enclave Hindus and Muslims live side by side, wealth and privilege being a more potent common denominator than faith. The amplified Muslim call to prayer floats through the neighborhood and some of the Hindus grumble about it. But Shubhi doesn't object: "I feel it's important that the minority feels comfortable," she says. "And besides, we make enough noise ourselves." She giggles when she tells the story of a Hindu employee whose tiny son recently bellowed his first word: "Allaah!"

A short drive from Shubhi's house is a sleek new American-style shopping mall with an ersatz English pub and a McDonald's offering meatless "aloo tikki" burgers. When she takes us there I'm most struck by one detail: an airless underground parking lot — the kind in which I'm reluctant to leave my dog — where each car has a waiting driver, either seated behind the wheel or polishing the exterior. Indian to the marrow, Shubhi nonetheless adores this sterile arcade and often takes her grandsons there to shop and eat McDonald's ice cream cones. When S.P., a former Indian Air Force pilot now with an international consulting firm, isn't away on business in Australia or in the U.S., he sits with Shubhi in front of their giant-screen television watching movies, the news, or the Indian version of *Who Wants to Be a Millionaire*. Shubhi's father was a pilot. Her son-in-law flies for Jet Air, one of India's two domestic airlines, and twenty-six other pilots are scattered among Shubhi's and S.P.'s families. Shubhi is a freelance film and video writer and producer with lofty ambitions. She is always leafing through books and papers, eyes scrunching behind her bifocals. Her place at the table is arranged with the accoutrements of her existence: a box of Rothmans, a lighter, a cordless phone, reading glasses, a cup of coffee with Equal. Though their two children are grown and have moved away the Singhs have several phone numbers. Between the two of them phones ring nonstop.

It's Howie first trip to India, and culture shock has yet to jolt him, what with the trappings of Shubhi's home so similar in many ways to our own. In a country overrun with wild, often rabid dogs, the Singhs dote on an obese golden retriever, a yellow Labrador, and a demented terrier mutt, which slinks around the house, peeing on carpets and chair legs. Shubhi has her driver shuttle us from the Red Fort to Connaught Circle to the palatial Imperial Hotel for cappuccino and an American-priced lunch among the potted palms. Howie has a relieved yet wary look on his face. Notwithstanding the elephant we see lumbering around a downtown traffic circle, he doesn't expect Delhi to feel so much like London. All I can think is: ha. The guy is really in for it. Just as he has yet to be dazzled, he has yet to be horrified. It is not possible to set foot in India without experiencing both.

I met Shubhi on my first visit to India, in 1992. I was traveling alone. Though I managed to see a lot of the country, from the tropical Malabar Coast to Darjeeling in the foothills of the Himalayas, much of the trip was devoted to researching a magazine piece about a Madras surgeon who procured donor kidneys from the poor. At the same building housing a dilapidated dialysis clinic, hundreds of men and women from surrounding villages would queue up hoping to qualify medically to trade a healthy kidney for the equivalent of $1,000 in rupees. It's a huge amount of money for most Indians. But the payment rarely elevated the donors' living standard. Most of the money goes instead to paying off dowries or gambling debts. K. C. Reddy, a charismatic surgeon trained in Great Britain, defended the practice by citing the constraints of treating end stage renal failure in India — the lack of cadaver donors, for one. Whether he truly felt this way I don't know. I wondered what was in his heart when he spoke of donating a kidney as a manifestation of dharma, the Hindu stricture to "do one's duty." Would he allow his son or daughter to stand on that line? Despite the doctor's zeal and undeniable charm, his clinic was an indescribably depressing place. I had a bad cold, I needed sleep, and I must've looked pretty wrecked. As I sat among the jaundiced patients and their families in a waiting room with all the amenities of a prison cell, several Indians asked me if I was there "to get a kidney." Ouch.

I've made about a million "friends" in my travels, but the exchanges almost always feel superficial. Generosity toward strangers is fundamental in Eastern cultures, and Indians seem especially fascinated by Americans. As Octavio Paz writes, "Indians are hospitable and cultivate the forgotten religion of friendship." But in Shubhi I found a soulmate, someone to whom it felt perfectly natural to reveal myself. Though she never grasped the pronunciation I taught her the word *schmooze,* which is what we did together over lunches, drives, and walks among the ruins of ancient temples. "I wish you would come back to India," she once said on the phone, "so we can smooze." We met by lucky coincidence. I was at All India Medical Institute to interview a prominent kidney surgeon who was outspoken on the dire need for donor organs but equally adamant in his feelings that Dr. Reddy was a sleazy profiteer. Dr. Kumar, a strikingly handsome man in his late forties, was a family friend and frequent news source of Shubhi, who was writing for magazines as well as television. "I have a friend who covers this same topic," Dr. Kumar told me as he dunked a chapati in his lunch korma. "Perhaps she can help you. Why don't I give her a call?" He made a few flattering comments about me and handed me the phone. "Here is my address," said Shubhi. "Come for lunch." I liked Shubhi even before I got through her front door. A wiggling golden retriever named Bubka half blocked the way, and I felt instantly at home. Shubhi fixed me real filter coffee. She introduced me to her teenage daughter Panna, and Brijendra served a vegetable korma and a seemingly bottomless stack of hot roti. My new friend and I spent my last days in India poking around Delhi together. Spending time with Shubhi is like riding a tornado. She is an immense woman with long wild hair, a Brahmin's crimson streak in the part, and fierce black eyes thickly rimmed in kohl. Her fingers, wrists, ears, and neck support a pound or two of twenty-four-carat gold and fat semiprecious beads. The earrings are three-tiered chandeliers, the necklaces a tangle of goddesses and talismans. When I traveled with Shubhi I noticed that she changed her rings to match her outfit. And Shubhi is, by anyone's standards, a shopaholic. She pays cash for everything, pulling 500-rupee notes from a wad an inch thick. Whatever guilt she may feel is mitigated by her habit of buying a little something for her shopping companions and the extravagant tips she leaves in her wake. Shubhi is whip-smart, fiercely well read, assertive in that often scary Brahmin way, and a sight to behold. Shop clerks quake in her presence. The pants of her shalwar kameez drape around voluminous hiking boots, which she wears routinely at the insistence of the doctor who monitors her circulation, compromised by severe diabetes. When she worked on a documentary about snow leopards she trekked deep into the punishing wilds beyond Ladakh with her crew, a few porters, a guide, and a doctor in case Shubhi fell ill. Her health is tenuous and both S.P. and her physician routinely read her the riot act. But despite her rotten circulation and two-pack-a-day smoking habit, Shubhi clomps tirelessly through the bazaar from shop to shop, stuffing her shoulder sack with books, CDs, videotapes, bolts of fabric, decorative sandalwood, souvenir T-shirts for her little grandsons. (Six months after I returned home Shubhi e-mailed to say she'd had a serious heart attack, had quit smoking, and was attempting, miserably, to adapt the strictures of Dean Ornish to her native palate.) I once got fed up and abandoned her in a music shop at Calcutta's New Market. I crisscrossed the entire bazaar, bought a few small things, and stopped at a café for a cold coffee. Preparing myself for Shubhi's ire I headed through the bazaar to the exit and happened to glance in the music shop. She was still there, peering at the displays, her arms full of tapes. Shubhi's energy is scary. She worries about me because I need to nap. "You should have your blood checked," she tells me.

Brijendra makes bread three times a day. But he is so neat and precise about it I've never seen so much as a minute poof of flour on his shirtsleeve. There is an opening running the length of the kitchen's serving counter where I take to spying on Brijendra at work. He acts unfazed. But I can tell that servants in India often find Americans' jovial efforts to befriend them bizarre and annoying. Americans cheerfully ask personal questions, speaking slowly and loudly in the hope this will help non-English speakers comprehend them. "Do — you — have — children??" Most middle-class Americans are uncomfortable about making any kind of fuss. "No, no, no," we say to the porter, "I'll do that, don't you bother." We ingratiate ourselves to no one with this behavior, which makes servants livid. We think we're being sensitive and equality-minded. What we're doing is usurping the role of a person whose continued livelihood depends on his performing unskilled tasks you of course could, but shouldn't have to, perform yourself. That said, I confess it turned my stomach the first time I saw an entitled Indian teenager raise his teacup, snap his fingers, and bark only the word "Chai" to an elderly servant. I'm grateful that I grew up in a home where my mother would say, "Go clean your room, the cleaning woman is coming today."

Watching Brijendra make bread is soothing as well as instructive. He has lovely nimble hands. I learn best by simply observing, and Brijendra's silence (he speaks only Hindi) works well for both of us. I can focus; he is free to ignore me. With the exception of nan, the clay-oven bread introduced to India by Muslims, Brijendra's kitchen is, breadwise, northern India in mini-microcosm. It is the enigmatic Brijendra who initiates me into the world of roti, chapati, puri, and paratha. I love to watch his fingers tightly roll coils of dough into paratha. I love the way chapatis inflate into little whoopee cushions when he holds them over a flame. And all this from the simplest dough: finely ground whole-wheat flour, water, and salt. After insinuating myself into Brijendra's kitchen I learn that these breads involve only the subtlest difference in dough and one of two pans, deep for puri, and shallow for chapati and paratha. The roti — essentially chapatis made with a bit of oil or ghee — taste of whole wheat faintly charred from browning on an ungreased, concave cast-iron plate called a tava. Brijendra slaps the rounds onto the hot tava, and the dough is so thin that they brown within seconds. Held over the flame for just a few moments, the roti puff up to resemble tiny pita. In Shubhi's home only Indian bread is eaten, though yeasty, Western-style bread shows up in some Indian markets. Indians refer to this bread, a legacy of colonial Portugal, France, and Britain, as "dubble roti" — the double bread. The renowned chef Madhur Jaffrey writes that "the soft, fluffy part of the (dubble roti) slice would be dug out and discarded — usually fed to the parrots in the garden. The hollow that resulted was filled with meat korma or whatever dish happened to be in the oven."

I feel safe and cozy in this kitchen and in this house. This is a good thing because later we will have to hunker down at Shubhi's after my husband falls into the black hole of Calcutta. But I'm getting ahead of myself.

You can't really know an Eastern country's food unless you eat at someone's home. Because my initiation into Indian cooking — whether in India or close to home — took place only in restaurants, until now I didn't get the full treatment. Most Indians don't eat in sit-down restaurants unless they are doing business or traveling far from home. The whole concept came late to India, where the upper classes believed that food prepared by outsiders was unclean. Brijendra's food is more basic, yet spicier, than what I'm used to.

Dinners at the Singhs are informal, even raucous. S.P. holds forth with his swashbuckling tales and grandiose pronouncements, and Shubhi proceeds to cut him to shreds. They bicker in English for our benefit but when they really get going the channel changes to Hindi. She shouts him down and flicks her hand in exasperation and disgust. He's nuts about her.

After serving each of us, Brijendra sets out the steaming bowls of curries: vegetables, potato, chicken, mutton, or fish. But the bread is shuttled to the table roti by roti. Brijendra must log miles each week marching in and out of the kitchen and rounding the bend to the dining room table to dispatch hot roti as the breads quickly disappear. In the Indian state of

Punjab a man's virility is playfully judged by how many roti he can consume in a sitting. "Ah," someone will joke, "now that is a seven-roti man!" The bread accompanying Indian meals is served fresh from the pan and each is replaced by another until you make a show of pushing your plate away or the world ends, whichever comes first. Brijendra pads into the dining room every three minutes with a steaming roti, chapati, or deep-fried puri bread, which he sets down soundlessly with a set of tongs. It becomes a joke: "Oh no, here he comes again!" and Brijendra's face melts into a gentle smile as we wave our arms in protest: "No, not another!" He retreats, but returns within minutes, wielding his trusty tongs. When the meal is finally over you can't recall how many roti you've consumed. I try to keep track but somehow can't. After the first two you tend to lose count, but the key thing is, there is always another. Leftover roti are fed to the dogs, and not just pets. All over India I saw women tossing roti on to the street, where wild dogs appear from the shadows to devour it. Indians never dispose of food. They pass it along to the less fortunate, human or beast. Though riddled with mange and likely to be rabid, pariah dogs appear well-nourished.

Once at lunch Lenny began to cut a roti with a butter knife. Shubhi grabbed his arm and scolded him. "You must never, ever, take a knife to bread," she said.

I've heard American schoolchildren say only this about India: people are starving there. It is a land racked by hunger, they say, some widening their eyes to ask me, "Did you ever step over a dead person on the street?" I have never, anywhere or at any time, stepped over, or for that matter, seen a dead person lying in the street. Then again, one might find oneself sharing India's hectic city roads with a funeral procession, the body enshrouded and borne on a pallet. It is true that Indians are obsessed with food. What is also true is that most Indians, rich and poor, are always eating. The streets are crammed cheek by jowl with food stalls for all budgets. In Calcutta a man rents or otherwise boldly claims for himself a battered space the size of an exercise mat. A coal fire, a bread pan, and a pot or two, and soon people are laying down the equivalent of a few pennies for a meal.

In Old Delhi an impossibly narrow street is nicknamed "Paratha Row" for its dense chain of bread stalls. Everywhere the nimble hands of men and boys are tossing, stretching, and rolling a pale silky dough of flour and water. At some point in the process they slap the dough like babies' bottoms. The street is barely the width of a rickshaw and Howie, until this day separated from the hoi polloi by an automatic car window, looks apoplectic as he ducks out of the way of a hand-pulled wagon carrying a moaning leper. I recall my first visit to Old Delhi. I wrote in a postcard to my friend Jack: "If there were a hospital for culture shock, I'd be in intensive care." Cows, donkey carts, rickshaws, throngs of men, women, and children are forever going and coming who knows where, their sandals flip-flopping through streams of raw sewage. The air is heavy with smoke and every other brand of pollution. Everyone in India has a cough. Small knots of people gather at snack carts that look like poster art for public health warnings about cholera. In *Days and Nights in Calcutta*, written with his wife, the Bengali novelist Bharati Mukherjee, Clark Blaise describes his young son, on their first visit to India as a family, gazing up at a street vendor and asking, "Daddy, is that man selling flies?" But woven into the slop and squalor are heaps of marigold blossoms for making puja and doting parents holding aloft gorgeous children with kohl-rimmed eyes and jangly anklets on their chubby feet. Women wear saris and pajamas in what has to be the most exuberant palette on earth. In India a pile of rags can startle you with its beauty.

We are slumming, literally. Shubhi's driver, Kanati, and the shiny Toyota await us at a parking lot unfolding precisely where New Delhi thickens and darkens into the Old. Howie wants to get out of here right now. Lenny, as always, fiddles with the manual settings on his too-conspicuous camera. I am squeezing into the bread stalls, excitedly asking questions of men and boys who must think I'm insane. Here a Muslim in a skullcap slaps nan onto the heated insides of a coal-heated clay pot. A thin wall away a boy is rolling small balls of dough into chapatis and slapping them onto a griddle. The chapati maker doesn't stop for a moment, as if he fears not being able to recover his rhythm. Slap, slap, slap. With their hands, paratha makers scoop balls of the dough — which has been rising naturally for at least four hours — and flatten them into patties. He smears the paratha with a layer of clarified butter, or ghee, and proceeds to roll it tightly into a snake. Then, like a child busy with Play-Doh, he coils the snake around and around until the paratha spirals like a mosquito coil or an all-day sucker. He does these things in a flash; you could turn your head briefly to some passing commotion and turn it back to find the paratha already frying. He rubs in a little more ghee and slaps the paratha in the pan, slowly turning it as it browns, then flips it, dribbles a bit more ghee, and browns the other side. I hand over a few rupees for a hot paratha, which is both dense and flaky and unfurls like a buttery cinnamon roll. Slap, slap, he rolls another and another.

At street stalls from Jaisalmer to Calcutta I accept rounds of steaming nan or chapati. But at times I let them fall from my hands moments later to be gobbled up by less fastidious creatures. Ah, street food: to eat or not to eat? It's a persistent dilemma. One voice tells me the bread is benign, fresh out of the pan, still hot in fact. Another whispers reminders of budget travelers battling typhoid. When I first visited Calcutta I saw something I'll never forget. For just a few moments the proprietor of a food cart turned away toward some distraction. That was enough time for a passing cow to glide its tongue across the cart's entire contents.

When I visited Tamil Nadu, in southern India, I watched fervent hands at work mixing a batter of moist rice flour and dal, the Indian staple of crushed split peas or lentils. Left to ferment overnight or longer, the batter grows bubbly and fragrant. Thinned with water, the batter is spooned onto a large oiled pan like a crepe. But the golden, fried result is heartier and in some places so huge the *dosa* cradles its spicy potato stuffing like a hobo bag. Indians I met found it odd and amusing when I tried to order *dosa* for supper. That's the equivalent of a foreign visitor to the U.S. requesting a dinner of French toast. Despite their having the dimensions of carry-on luggage, *dosa* are a snack, to be eaten in the late afternoon. That's what I mean about Indians and food.

The densely packed stalls of paratha row thrive day and night, and their aromas mingle with those from the simple cooking fires of the pavement dwellers. Everywhere you turn something is cooking, if not food than chai, ubiquitous chai. Like bread, tea is crucial to the rhythms of Indian life. Tea is the Indian handshake, the Indian embrace. Journalists touring villages flattened by the Gujarat earthquake reported their guilt and surprise when groups of grieving homeless victims insisted on serving them tea. The chai-wallah is the lifeblood of Indian street life. For me the chai stall is a good place to sidestep the clamor, pause, breathe, take stock, and attempt to answer the question: What the hell am I doing here? But the chai stall is also one of the world's great equalizers. Here I am, just another heartbeat in the human crowd, no better, no worse. To one side a businessman in Western clothes drinks while flipping through *The Hindu*, to the other a ragged laborer in dhoti cloth and sandals. The tea is sweet, milky, and faintly spiced with cardamom, cinnamon, and pepper. At some stalls you drink from clay cups shaped like miniature flowerpots. When you finish you smash them on the pavement, where they join a growing pile of shards later recycled. Nothing in India goes to waste. If it's organic the animals will devour it, if it isn't someone will use it again, perhaps for some wildly unrelated purpose. One man's pajama pant is another man's turban.

In India, being away from one's kitchen is never an obstacle to home cooking. Pilgrims or travelers from distant states congregate by the river or on the parched grounds of an ancient fort and prepare steaming feasts. It's not unusual to see a family plunked down and cooking supper a hair away from the screaming traffic of a busy city street (the only kind) or on the tiled floor of a crowded train station. And no one goes hungry on an Indian train. Even those trains teasingly named "express" stop constantly, and every stop means another snack. Indians love the word "snack." Out of what appears to be the middle of nowhere hawkers surround the car to thrust at the open windows platters of samosas or pakora or spicy nuts. Peer out onto the platform and you see a squatting man frying chapatis, his helper rushing stacks of bread to the train windows. Except for the foreigners, who fear contamination or, more likely, are already suffering intestinal distress, nearly everyone buys something. Out comes a heavily bangled arm with a few rupees in hand, in comes a banana leaf cradling some fragrant seeds. This continues all day long and so does the eating. Their flesh rolling and spreading under their saris, Indian women are fond of nibbling on sweets, like semolina drenched in honey or colored melt-in-your-mouth squares made from coconut milk. As a rule, well-off Indian matrons are at least plump, and often obese. In the company of these women I have, relatively speaking, the dimensions of a bikini model.

In America we're expected to fend for ourselves on a ten-hour bus ride. If we're driving a long stretch of turnpike the only convenient way to quiet the rumbling in our bellies is with a hamburger manufactured God-knows-where and zapped back to life, arranged with a few shreds of wilted lettuce and thrust over the counter in a box resembling something from an intensive care ward. Or the bus driver releases us en masse like livestock, and the whole sorry bunch waits for the chance to shake a bag of stale corn chips from a vending machine. I am always wandering airports forlornly, looking for something wholesome to put in my stomach.

This state of affairs would horrify the typical Indian. Because of a sluggish fog over Delhi, we once faced a seven-hour delay at the Jodhpur airport. The air terminal's only diversions were a closet-sized bookshop and a stall selling tea, bottled water, and packaged biscuits. We settled in with our reading, trying to affect the developing world's innate nonchalance about waiting. At 6 p.m. an airport employee in a pink shalwar kameez began marching around the terminal, rousing each and every man, woman, and child. "The bus is here!" she cried. Uh-oh, we're going to have to get to Delhi by bus? I had a flash of those two-inch wire stories buried in what seems like every edition of the *New York Times*: 28 Die in India Bus Mishap. "Come, come," she bellowed, and everyone in the place began to rise and collect themselves. "You are coming?" We sat there looking perplexed. "If you want to eat, the bus is outside, hurry, it is leaving for the restaurant right away!" We grabbed coats, piled into the luxury bus, and bounced along Jodhpur's main boulevard like expectant schoolchildren. The bus stopped at a modern hotel and we all filed inside to a clean, well-heated restaurant, its tables adorned for some kind of party. The party was for us, courtesy of Indian Airlines. A copious buffet was unveiled. We ate, drank beer, and made friends. By the time the bus got us back to the airport, the plane was waiting.

Shubhi is excited about having us as houseguests. We get the royal treatment. She knows Howie's books and cartoons, and the fact that Lenny is a physician impresses her mightily. They are tickled to be hosting such celebrities from America. Shubhi and S.P. decide to throw a dinner party in our honor. "Would you like to wear a sari?" Shubhi asks. After a few weeks in India one begins to warm to the concept of a sari. What middle-aged woman with creeping cellulite wouldn't embrace a garment that is, in essence, a queen-sized bedspread? All saris are created equal, truly one-size-fits-all, as opposed to Western clothing, which is one-size-fits-everyone-but-you. And when women expand, their saris expand along with them. There is not enough saag paneer in all of India to make a sari dig into one's gut the way jeans do.

"The entire sari depends on this staying put," Shubhi warns me, as she tucks the doubled fabric into the waistband of my skirt. "Feels fine," I lie. She proceeds to circle me with the sari round and round as if I'm a maypole. It's a crinkly cocoa-colored silk embossed with carnelian snowflakes and stripes. "How am I ever going to pee in this thing?" I ask as she makes neat accordion folds in what will be the part of the sari that drapes like the sash of a five-star general. I follow her upstairs on tippy toes, clutching the sari like a billowy wedding gown. "Don't do that!" she commands. A sari demands a bindi, the mark on a married woman's forehead. In her bedroom Shubhi dabs my third eye and hair part with crimson from a small lip-gloss-sized tub, then she selects some rust-colored bangles from the hangers and hangers full in her collection. My long hair is still damp from the shower. "I'll send down a hair dryer," Shubhi says. The hair dryer is a human being. A tiny barefoot Nepalese woman appears with a hand-held dryer and brush and goes to work on me, slowly and gently. When she finishes she clasps her palms together in a bow and a namaskar and tiptoes back upstairs.

"The sari really suits you," a Punjabi guest comments to me later. "I thought you were a blue-eyed Indian." A blue-eyed Indian! Shubhi has told me I have an Indian soul. She takes me to see Nina, her dressmaker, and asks Nina to outfit me in something "that screams India." (Shubhi considers Lenny and Howie, on the other hand, hopeless cases and typical American xenophobes.)

Howie, Lenny, and I plan a weeklong road trip across the dusty desert of Rajasthan. Our ultimate destination is Jaisalmer and its ancient, still inhabited fort, reputed to be right out of *Arabian*

Nights. The initial misguided plan was to travel by train from Delhi to Jaipur, Jaipur to Jodphur, on to Jaisalmer and then back to Delhi. Perusing the map, this seemed to make sense. (The more condensed the map, the more sense it made.) What we wouldn't have guessed is that our neat little rail excursion involved twelve- to twenty-four-hour stretches arriving and departing at painfully odd "timings," as Indians say. The trek would have destroyed us. Even a young, hashish-smoking backpacker would be undone by the grueling regimen: several long days and two entire nights on trains, which were susceptible to delays adding hours to the ordeal. We're unsure how to proceed. But as we slumber one morning, Captain Singh, as his cronies call him, clad in crisp white pajamas, is on the case, pacing with the cordless and issuing stern directives to his personal travel agent. When we appear for morning tea he says the words I will forever associate with him: "It is all arranged." "The train is no good. We have hired you a driver, who will collect you Sunday morning and be at your disposal for the week. No need for worry, it is all arranged." We are in luck, says S.P., the agency is providing an English-speaking driver. Unfortunately, though, all the agency's Toyota Land Cruisers are engaged, so we will bump and grind our way across the Thar Desert in an Ambassador. "You know what they say about Ambies — everything makes noise except the horn," S.P. jokes as the servants stuff our bags in the trunk of the waiting car. A bulbous, anachronistic vehicle, which until recently was the only car available in India, the Ambie, it seems to me, could not be less suited to an odyssey along some of the planet's worst roads. Our driver, Rajkumar, is a skinny, nervous man with thick pomaded hair and acne-ravaged skin. He first displays his fluent English when explaining to me why it's no use fumbling around for the front-passenger seat belt. "Is no good. Is gone!" he says, head bobbing like a dashboard ornament, a tic endemic to the culture. I am the kind of person who fastens my seat belt to change spaces in a parking lot, but somehow the dilemma seems aptly Indian. What can't be cured must be endured. One must be fatalistic and trust in the power of karma. Does it matter whether I exit this body in a human stampede, an epidemic, a train derailment, or a head-on collision with a speeding TATA truck? ("TATA means Ta-TAH," says S.P.) Along the Jaipur-

Jaisalmer route, medical facilities are as rare as rain. Another sound argument against the seat belt: Should the Ambie end up in a smoldering heap of TATA fenders and camel carts, better to be on one's way to the next life than injured beyond recognition in this one.

It becomes apparent soon after we pull out of Sadhana Enclave that Rajkumar understands less English than the average American house pet. No big deal, but it's a little frustrating because we'll be spending so much time together. Already we're doing that screaming thing, as if it will make the slightest difference. In Jaipur we check into the old, romantic Samode Haveli where Lenny and I leave Howie to sketch its tiled courtyards and Mughlai arches. Rajkumar barrels along Jaipur's colonnaded main street awaiting our instructions. Even in its decrepit state, old Jaipur retains its magic. Its broad streets are scaled to suit regal processions of elephant-drawn chaises and camel caravans. The ornate Rajput buildings and artisans' bazaars look as if someone doused them in peach-colored paint. Rolling slowly past the billowing sandstone facade of Hawa Mahal, or Palace of the Winds, the heretofore-silent Rajkumar turns to us in a gleeful outburst. "Jaipur pink sit-eee! Every-sing pink!"

The Ambie lurches inside the city limits of Jodhpur after a grueling seven-hour dust-a-thon, with one break for lunch at a government rest stop. The chapatis were fine. Considering they're always hand-made, chapatis are remarkably consistent across the subcontinent. We should've stuck to bread alone. But Lenny and I scarf down the curries on our *thali* plate even though they're suspiciously luke-warm. Now we've got raging diarrhea. Our heads throb. Our bones ache. Motoring in the Ambie is like being imprisoned in a Cuisinart. We are haunted by these words: "It is arranged." Lenny has a barking cough nurtured by a succession of spewing marble quarries and the rank fumes of a never-ending convoy of TATA "Goods Carriers" emblazoned with the Lord Krishna. Howie wears a bandana wrapped around his face, Jesse James–style. When we stumble into the Ajit Bhawan hotel we are fed up with each other, Rajkumar, and India itself.

The Ajit Bhawan is one of a growing chain of Heritage Hotels. These are former maharajah's palaces or havelis expanded, refurbished, and sanitized to meet the needs of Western tourists with our penchant for marathon showers, luxurious bedclothes, and packaged entertainment. The word "Heritage" has joined "Historic," "Old Tyme," and "Ye Olde" in the list of latter-day synonyms for "We thought you'd be much more comfortable if we added some plastic." Dotted about a lushly landscaped theme park in which every guest is a maharaja, maharani, or rajput, the hotel rooms are separate earthen cottages with names out of Kipling: Jasmina, Parvati. Lenny is led to a great white hunter's lodgings scaled with leopard skins and spears. A teak tree grows in its center, poking through a hole in the roof. Warmed by kettle fires, guests partake of a nightly dinner buffet in view of a stage where dour musicians pounding *dhol* — Rajasthani drums — strumming sitars, and *sirangi,* accompany tribal girls doing the *luvar,* a never-ending line dance. It has the authenticity of a pavilion at Epcot but I'm not knocking it; beyond these walls lies the authentic, unrelenting din and chaos. I attempted a walk "out there" and was mobbed and jostled by street children until a passing driver pulled over to scold them.

At Ajit Bhawan breads are prepared and cooked out in the open on spacious tables.

The setup is similar to a television cooking show. One man kneads and flattens rounds of airy dough for nan, which he presses into the sides of a heated clay tandoor oven. His neighbor is busy frying and flaming chapatis or pressing greased roti into the pan with a square of towel.

"Jodhpur blue sit-eee! Every-sing blue!"

Rajkumar is in a chatty mood when he collects us the next morning. He's had a shave and changed into a crisp new shirt. Jodhpur is, indeed, nearly uniformly blue, its concrete and mud structures coated with a pale indigo wash reminiscent of a swimming pool at an old Catskill resort. Why blue? Most people say it's because blue is a Brahmin hue and lower castes followed suit. Others insist the color repels mosquitoes. So why don't they dump blue paint over every city in India? Or over every city in the temperate, tropical, and equatorial world?

Just as Rajkumar deposits us at the clock tower rising from Jodhpur's old walled quarter I spot my first Indian transvestite. *"Hijra!"* I announce. "Is man wearing clothes of woman," a voice whispers close to my ear. That is how we cross paths with Sandeep Singh Couhan. In truth, he was waiting for us. Handsome, fit, and nattily dressed, Sandeep is one of those confidence men who haunt India's tourist sites, a "university student" on perpetual holiday who is happy to spread cross-cultural good will and make cheerful English conversation while attaching himself to you like a wood tick. Strange how, in a land bursting at the seams with humanity, foreign visitors to Jodhpur inevitably make the same "friend." Everything reeks of subterfuge. As one always does, we realize too late that Sandeep has appointed himself our guide. It's impossible to shake him as he herds us to shops peddling stale overpriced spices and cheaply made Rajasthani turbans. Sandeep is a pro. What the hell, we'll visit his uncle's spice shop and then have him take us to the grain market.

No matter what people read or hear beforehand, nothing prepares a visitor for the real India. Some people fall in love with the place, some do a passable job of pretending to fall in love with the place, and the rest are frankly repelled. Sandeep reads tourists like a Visa card. Some tourists are on the verge of losing it and Sandeep knows to huddle them into his uncle's for a cup of tea and some reassuring chitchat, spiced with soothing references such as "Chicago" or "Delaware." (Howie and I witnessed a tourist meltdown outside a Jain temple in Jaisalmer. The sadhu by the temple entrance motioned for the man to pay. Apparently that was the last straw. Part of a tour group from Britain or possibly South Africa — I couldn't place the accent — the man went berserk in a most un-Indian way right there on the temple steps. "Rupees!" he hissed. "Rupees, rupees, rupees, rupees! Gimme rupees!" He waved his arms menacingly but was soon escorted away by his countrymen, leaving muffled cries of "Rupees! Rupees!" in his wake. For all we know he remains in a straitjacket somewhere, howling "Rupees!" as the nurse murmurs "There, there" and plunges a needle into his arm.)

At the spice shop with Sandeep still in our faces we accept porcelain cups of saffron tea and select candle-sealed packets of garam masala, biryani, and chai spices. The merchant throws in a complimentary packet of white tonic powder called "the Indian Viagra." Spices always seem like the perfect gift idea until they detonate in your luggage and your clothes begin to smell like Curry in a Hurry. But they are laid out so enticingly, stacked Crayola-like in deep red and pink and terra-cotta, with charming instructions such as "The GarlicSpices add extra in the cooking to get a taste in it . . . (1 spoon) mix with some water to make thick paste (sauce) which apply on BREAD OF CHAPATI AND SERVE TO EAT." We listen to the proprietor boast about how his spices are "selling big in Alaska." Then I ask Sandeep to earn his keep. "Take me to the grain market."

Soon we are engulfed by the narrow streets, the usual commerce thinning to give way to the butchers' quarter, ghettoized because Hindu Brahmins will neither consume nor touch beef. Holding our breath through the tunnel of carcasses, we veer onto a quiet cul-de-sac to watch barefoot men gleaning sesame seeds through what looks like a window screen. Largely cleansed of chaff and dust, the seeds are fed into a press hand-cranked by a man squatting in a space scarcely bigger than a refrigerator box. A plump wooden pestle pounds away at the seeds and from a tap below flowed thick, pure sesame oil. Just to inhale it was almost as nice as eating a hunk of halvah.

The old Jodhpur grain market occupies an airy square designed to embrace camel caravans. As it has for centuries the market serves tribal farmers selling rice or grain, and village or city merchants who buy sacks of rice, lentils, millet, wheat and corn flour wholesale at prices fixed by the government. Each open-air stall is festooned with strings of lemon and chile peppers to protect against the evil eye. The grain market is an airy peaceful place, exempt from the spirited haggling common to other bazaars. We sniff at sacks of wheat flour for chapati and nan, lentil flour for pappaduam, rice flour for *dosa*. The rice merchant shows me how to test if the rice is good and fresh. You place a few grains in your palm, then clasp your hands closed, and blow into them. Then smell the rice; the heat of your breath should have activated its perfume.

At ten in the morning Rajkumar returns from doing something either preventive or creative to the Ambie's battered tires, and soon we are bumping along the desert road toward Jaisalmer. A city spilling like lava over and beyond its ancient, still inhabited golden fort, Jaisalmer nuzzles the border with Pakistan. Dotted ever so stingily with green and yellow mustard fields, the Thar Desert is mostly a parched, godforsaken moonscape best suited to camels, smugglers, and Paki spies. In other words, my kind of place. Acacia trees and squares of alfalfa, millet, and wheat, some of which is still winnowed by hand. Freshly harvested wheat grains are shaken in a basket so the straw will be blown away by the wind. The winnowed wheat is poured onto a pile at the worker's feet and carried off for milling by small gas-driven millstones. Women walk by the roadside balancing earthen water jugs on their heads as TATA trucks hurtle past, existing in parallel universes. Along the road scrawny tribal people labor at inscrutable tasks. A woman wrapped in a sari the color of egg yolk, gold dangling from her ears and nose and her eyes rimmed in kohl, bends over a small crater in the asphalt. Is she searching for something and if so, what could it be? Outside a haveli a kilometer or so from Jaisalmer Fort a man spends all day squatting on the dung-encrusted earth, hacking away at stones to make gravel. Why does he labor at that spot, which appears to have been settled upon at random? Is his home tucked among this dispirited string of curio shops? Perhaps he puts down his charpoy at night and sleeps right here by the pile.

There is always something to captivate the senses but I long to be off this road, in light of the fact that for the last forty miles

Rajkumar has been playing chicken with a convoy of rocket launchers. About six inches in front of us, mounted not too securely on a flatbed trailer, is a huge lethal weapon pointed right smack in our direction. "Do you have to, um, stay so close?" I ask. "Ha ha ha," replies Rajkumar, veering to the right in a futile attempt to pass. "Is big army place, ha ha ha." I am impressed by Rajkumar's fearlessness in the face of all this military might, what seems to us like a mini–Republic Day parade. I've been smashed into second-class train cars with Indian soldiers and found the experience unnerving, especially being goosed by rifle butts. But Indian travelers never seem the slightest bit intimidated by soldiers.

"Jaisalmer!" announces Rajkumar, sounding as relieved as we are. There were a few tricky turns in the road, and as we soon learn, he's never been here before. This doesn't stop him from offering a bit of commentary: "Jaisalmer gold sit-ee! Every-sing gold!!"

A clot of camel carts, rickshaws, schoolchildren, and the ubiquitous water-bearers gradually overtakes the road. I had reserved us rooms at Hotel Jaisal Castle, one of many old havelis in the city. But this one is located along the ramparts of Jaisalmer

Fort, which surges from the desert rock like an immense and perfect sandcastle, conceived as the backdrop for some animated *Arabian Nights* cartoon.

The fort is closed to cars except for several hours a day, and this was not one of those hours. Rajkumar angles the Ambie among the traffic jam below the fort's walls, and his eyes gazed skyward in panic as the other drivers point to Jaisal Castle. Some Samaritans pour out of a small travel agency. Uh-oh. Our *Lonely Planet* mentions that Jaisalmer is rife with ambitious touts who will tell you falsely that your hotel is closed. One tout lied to a group of tourists that their hotel had been destroyed by a bomb.

We have no choice but to let them "handle" the situation; Jaisal Castle is way up there and we are down here. So we watch helplessly as three sullen-looking boys yank our roller suitcases out of the Ambie's trunk and began dragging them through the slime and water buffalo dung, up the steep cobbled fort entrance, to a place that may or may not be the real Jaisal Castle. We follow them along a disorienting succession of courtyards and alleyways. Howie is fuming, Lenny is gripped by a coughing fit, I begin to fear for our safety, and even Rajkumar looks apoplectic. But at last we arrive at the immense cathedral-like doors to Jaisal Castle.

It is the real thing, a crumbling but beautiful haveli with a mosaic-tiled court-yard wrapped in columns, framing a succession of latticed windows. Women pad in and out of a shrine performing the holy rite of puja. The smell of incense mixes with curry fumes wafting from a tiny kitchen. We follow the proprietor up a narrow, weathered stone staircase to a ter-race with a desert view that must stretch clear across to Pakistan, and a catty-corner pair of cold dark rooms with hand-carved bedsteads and Rajasthani carpets. I love it. The men are not happy.

"Is no good, this place," snaps Raj-kumar, in an uncharacteristic display of emotion. "Is bad place." Howie finds it charming but shoddy. Lenny declares it unacceptable. So tomorrow we will move. But in the evening we sit in the courtyard under a full moon, beside a roaring kettle fire, scooping a delicious *korma* with dense, chewy chapati. I'm up before dawn to watch the sunrise and the full moon fade, and walk the streets in the stillness before the shops open. I take my first cup of chai sitting on a box by a campfire.

Rajkumar comes later to fetch us. He is so excited he is actually salivating. "I find good place!" We tumble out of the fort behind the porters and watch our luggage roll through fresh mounds of dung. The new hotel is indeed a good place, an immense haveli with a sweeping courtyard full of French tourists dressed for camel safari, Abercrombie and Fitch poster people in head to toe microfiber khaki with those pants that unzip into shorts. The rooms are big and clean. I'm happy. Howie is happy. Lenny is very happy. And Rajkumar, pocketing his hefty commission, is happiest of all.

Lenny and I prepare for our own intimate safari, just two camel drivers and us. It's a long ride out to a village at the edge of the desert and a small rest house where a blanket is laid out on the earth for our meal. I crawl into the cement cookhouse and watch a boy hunched over a propane stove, turning wheat chapatis, and then a batch made of ground millet from the winter harvest. The millet breads are bluish in color, dry and tough. The meal is delicious and accompanied by some "special desert wine" that smells like nail polish remover. To our companions' disappointment we don't drink. In our pasts both

Lenny and I have committed regrettable acts under the influence of such nameless local brews.

The camel drivers — one older and regal in a scarlet turban, the other disheveled and evil-looking, escort us to our camels. I am paired with the evil-looking guy who says precisely two words to me the entire day. Leering at Lenny and then back at me, he murmurs, "Your father?" The two men enjoy loud, incessant conversation as we bounce along, stopping in villages of thatched roundhouses where children surround us and poke aggressively at our shoulder bags. At one point we're led inside a hovel where a toothless woman dripping tribal silver serves us tea in cracked porcelain cups. She glares at us unflinchingly; she will earn a few rupees but we have disturbed her siesta. We sit in uncomfortable silence feeling like idiot sahibs. Then the turbaned camel driver reaches deep in his pocket for a foil-wrapped cube and whispers in Lenny's ear: "Opium?" Our pampered lives flash before us.

When we arrive back in Delhi, Shubhi awaits us with gifts: a red-and-yellow print shalwar kameez for me, cotton shirts for the men. That night, still battered from our week in the Ambie, we fly to Calcutta.

329

We plan to stay five nights. Judging from her luggage, Shubhi has packed enough to last until the monsoon.

There are two types of people in the world: those who love Calcutta, and sane people. There's no denying it's a noisy stinking pit of a place, perilously decrepit, corrupt to the core, and congested beyond belief. Calcutta has the population density of a can of worms. To say there are a large number of "homeless" is like pointing out that in Beijing one is likely to encounter many Chinese people. Calcutta possesses the world's largest banyan tree, a perplexingly clean, efficient subway, and a park just for rats. I adore it.

Shubhi, too, is sentimental about the city. Though she isn't Bengali she grew up in the Calcutta suburb of Hooghly and studied at Santiniketan, the West Bengal liberal arts university founded by the great writer, painter, and Nobel Laureate Rabindrinath Tagore. On my first visit to India I hopped all over the country. But it was Calcutta that captured my imagination and affection. You can safely wander its streets and find your way back, like in Venice. Picture Venice with cows, several million overflowing toilets, and a chorus of tubercular coughs. What also impressed me about that seething mess of a city was the level of individual dependability and efficiency that somehow kept things humming along despite the corruption and decay. The train may or may not appear on time, but the rickshaw-wallah will. In the throes of the near-daily street demonstrations, the riots these become, the power outages, dire epidemics, and floods of biblical proportions, one can count on the prompt return of one's laundry. You may be unable to secure a working telephone or a flight to Delhi but you are always within sneezing distance of a tailor who will cheerfully and expertly hem your shalwar kameez right then and there for next to nothing. My first time in India it took a while to shake that native New Yorker habit of repeating requests over and over, as if to an idiot. Indians' characteristic politeness and reserve will not permit them to say, "Give it a rest, I heard you the first time." But they heard you the first time. My lack of faith came back to taunt me at a hotel coffee shop. "I'd like some tea," I said to the busy waiter, and then "and I'd like some tea." "Some tea please," I repeated as he passed within earshot. Minutes later the waiter appeared with three cups of tea — one for each time I'd asked.

I'd booked us rooms at the Fairlawn Hotel on Sutter Street. It's a goofy, endearing place, Fawlty Towers meets the Raj. Crammed with wicker lawn furniture and strangled with potted plants, the lobby and courtyard are a stage upon which dramas play out daily. The Fairlawn was built 218 years ago by a European, its deed describing it as a "Pukka" building — one built of brick. The ruling Nawabs of that time allowed Bengalis to build only from coconut palm and mud. Along with her husband Ted, Mrs. Violet Smith has lorded over the place since 1962. When she was a toddler Vi's Armenian parents brought the family to India via Pakistan. In 1942 she met Ted, a major in the British Army stationed in West Bengal. Vi will tell anyone who'll listen how she played host to Tom Stoppard, Sting, Dominique Lapierre, Patrick Swayze, and the cast of the movie *City of Joy*, parts of which were filmed in the hotel. Bewigged, her face painted, the gregarious and lovable Vi still makes an appearance every night at the Fairlawn's family-style dinners, sodden, tasteless English fare included in the room price. The last time I stayed at the Fairlawn she was strutting around with an obese toy poodle. Day and night in a chair by the reception desk sat the doddering Ted, dressed as if he expected to be called off to a tiger hunt, his lips frozen in a disdainful pout. The waiters at the Fairlawn wear turbans and cummerbunds and sneer at you as they dish out boiled potatoes and greasy mutton. They put an end to it — "It upset some of the guests," says Violet — but until recently the Fairlawn served "bed tea," a Victorian custom whereby a servant enters the room before dawn and sets down a tray of tea so memsahib will have it when she wakes. The Fairlawn is crumbling, the beds are hard as rock, the plumbing is deplorable, and the rooms are noisy and haphazardly furnished. But I'm convinced there is no place like it and I want Howie and Lenny to experience the Fairlawn before its likely demise. Howie tries to keep an open mind. Shubhi is pining for the marble splendor and Brahmin comforts of the nearby Oberoi Grand. Lenny thinks the place is a dump.

Violet turns eighty the day after we arrive, and for her birthday someone overseas has sent her what we all believe to be the first Big Mouth Billy Bass to hit the subcontinent. Violet flips the switch for the servants, who watch the crooning, flopping fish with a look of bewilderment. "My but isn't that just sooooooo clev-ah," chirps Violet. I remind her I've stayed here before. "Oh yes, yes how are you, darling?" she asks me. She cups her hands around my face and jiggles it. "Such a sweet, lovely girl." I love this hotel.

Shubhi phones her college friend Anu, who comes to the Fairlawn with her daughter Ritoo to collect us. For the duration of our stay in Calcutta we have a driver at our disposal, thanks to S.P. ("It is all arranged.") I was looking forward to walking, but here we were smashed into yet another Ambassador and crawling in the city's horrendous traffic to the Oberoi. (It takes five minutes to walk there.) Anu is a sweet, well-meaning but lonely woman who lives with her teenage daughter and a servant in a fortified apartment complex, which, like Sadhana Enclave, is meant to cushion the very rich from the harsh realities of the street. But Anu's cramped, nearly windowless apartment with its multiple deadbolts seems suited to a city under military siege, more war-torn Beirut than Brahmin Enclave. Her husband, the captain of an oil tanker, is home only for occasional visits. Ritoo, who would fit right in at any American shopping mall, is finishing private school and cavorting with a young

German ecologist. Even with her loud saris, high-volume Carol Channing voice, and diamond-studded baubles, Anu strikes me as a defeated woman, a virtual prisoner. She's recovering from thyroid surgery. Mostly, she just sits. She sits at the club, sits in her parlor, sits in her friend's parlor. It's an expression wealthy Indian women use. "I'm going to go sit with Anu," says Shubhi.

My impatience with Anu soon melts into gratitude, for without her Howie might be maimed for life. At the Fairlawn, at New Market, among the beggars working Sudder Street word spread about "the American who fell in the hole." In the night, in my bed, in my home, the scene still replays in my head sometimes, and I reach for Howie beside me. Here is what happens:

The ladies have mapped out an evening for us. We meet at Anu's and walk next door to the Dalhousie Club, a seemingly deserted network of what look like the lobbies of chain motels. The air is a sauna spiked with car exhaust. Shubhi and Anu lead us outside to the "garden," a fetid patch of dead grass with a lawn tennis court that has seen better days. They are thinking: tea and pakoras. We are thinking:

malaria. Two platters of pakoras later we return to Anu's apartment and drink wine while Howie goes off with the driver to fax his weekly cartoon to our hometown newspaper. By the time he returns, Ritoo has joined us. We sit and make idle chatter. "Why don't you have a manservant?" asks Shubhi. "This is a woman's house now," says Anu. "What happened to the driver you used to have?" "I had to fire him. He was chasing my maid and I can't have that."

In keeping with her campaign to impart the complete Indian experience Shubhi suggests we dine in a Calcutta suburb called Tangra. Tangra is a community of Chinese tanners, who reside in a homogenous clump because of the Hindu stricture against handling leather. Packed into the grimy streets of Tangra are three hundred tanneries and a string of Chinese restaurants. I find that combination unsettling, but say nothing as we settle into two cars — Howie with Shubhi and Ritoo, Lenny and I riding with Anu — and proceed along streets that grow darker and darker until we find ourselves in a hellish no-man's-land lit only by the embers of street fires. The restaurant signs flicker in the gloom, except for Kafulok, the ladies' choice. It is closed on Mondays. For a moment I think we are off the hook, but the women leap out of the tandem cars, confer and decide on another place.

I am an earthy babe and no germophobe, but as we pull up I wonder, is it okay to ingest the food in this godforsaken place? That's what I am thinking when Anu lets out a deafening shriek: "Oh God, he's fallen!" Oh no. What atrocious scene awaits us? This is India — anything can happen, likely to prove far worse than one can imagine. The other car has pulled up behind us. Lenny and I get out, reluctantly. The first thing I see is the brown patina of Howie's jacket, crumpled and sinking. Howie is falling to the ground. Is he having a heart attack? Oh God. Oh shit.

Howie has plunged into an uncovered drainage canal, mistaking it for a shadow on the pavement as he stepped aside to let Ritoo and Shubhi pass. Pulled to safety by a gaggle of pavement dwellers, he is disoriented, dizzy, and covered with slime. His glasses are splattered with toxic muck. The hole is five feet deep. He could have drowned in there. More pavement dwellers appear, seemingly out of cracks in the walls. They are barefoot, clad only in filthy dhoti cloths, and hovering solicitously over

337

Howie, who is trying to stand. Shubhi is standing back and away in stunned silence. Ritoo weeps. Lenny is searching for Howie's pulse. And Anu is barking into her cell phone in Bengali. Who is she talking to?

We manage to walk Howie to the larger car but he sinks beside it and sprawls onto the foul pavement. He will die here, I think. I dragged him to India and he will die in this putrid hellhole and I will return home without my husband and live the rest of my life in guilt and sorrow. I remember from my nurse's aide days how to make a human stretcher. The pavement dwellers are staring at me with their sad black eyes, waiting to be told what to do. I extend my arms, palms up, and they instantly follow suit. We clasp hands under Howie and slide him awkwardly into the back seat of the car. Lenny gently arranges Howie's arms to close the door. We all see now that one of those arms is snapped and pointing in the wrong direction. Inside the car Howie's arm flops around as if it isn't even attached. Anu tells the driver: Assembly of God Hospital. We head out of the darkness onto the noisy clogged streets of the city, and inch our way along. Howie is talking and making jokes — for my benefit, he tells me later. Because I believe he is dying my behavior must be incredibly strange. A beggar approaches the car and raps on Howie's window. He can't see Howie but he's looking right at me. Lenny rolls the window down and passes the man a coin.

When we finally pull up to the hospital we see the fruits of Anu's frantic phone calls. Waiting for us, standing shoulder to shoulder like some elite force, are the chief of cardiology, the chief of neurology, the orthopedist, and the house staff. A private paying hospital, the facility reveals few of the high-tech trappings of a Western hospital. But it is immaculate. Before we go on the ward we must remove our shoes. Minutes after Howie is carried up to intensive care he has received a tetanus shot, his arm has been arranged in a protective sling, and he is rolled off to X-ray. The chief of cardiology is the most senior doctor at the hospital, and Anu's personal physician. He will stay with Howie through the night.

The accident happened at about 8 p.m. By midnight Howie is out of surgery, his arm encased in an immense plaster cast. It was a bloodless procedure. Once Howie was anesthetized Dr. Chakraborty popped his arm back in place. Shubhi draws a Kali goddess on the cast and writes in Hindi, "I fell into the Black Hole of Kolkata." We go to catch some sleep at the Fairlawn, where Violet and her desk man work out the logistics of moving Howie and me to a room on the first floor. Shubhi is inconsolable. She blames herself: "I never should have come with you to Calcutta." Anu is distraught and babbling. She blames herself: "I should have had my cook prepare a dinner for us." Vi is clucking and sighing. She blames us: "See what happens when you don't dine here at the hotel?"

By the time we return to the hospital in the morning Howie is alert and upbeat. He has also fallen madly in love with Shidi, his nurse. "You pronounce it *shitty*," she tells him. She is young, slight, and dark and her prim nursey whites and stiff cap make her look like a career girl doll dressed by a child. "I'm taking you with me," Howie jokes. "Good," she says. "I like go with you." When Howie refuses his breakfast Shidi shakes a tiny finger at him and says, "You must eat for your strength, and in India we don't waste food." I think it is here, in this hospital with Nurse Shidi, that Howie finally falls a little in love with India.

After we get Howie settled in the hotel

room I set out for a walk to the chemist to fill one of his prescriptions, and the resident beggar greets me. He is permanently bent in half and slowly gains ground by swinging his body to one side and then the other. His limbs were probably deliberately broken when he was a child, to make him a more effective beggar. He swings close to me, looks at me with unmistakable tenderness, and asks, "Madame, how is your husband?" And I, too, fall in love with India, all over again.

It's our last day in India and we're all falling apart. Limping and lugging the weight of his immense plaster cast, Howie's exhausted. Shubhi has come down with a bad cold. I'm suffering post-traumatic stress flashbacks of that dark street in Tangra. What will make us feel better? It occurs to me what I must do.

I will make a pot of Jewish chicken soup. Shubhi loves the idea, and offers her driver Kanati for the trip to INA, Delhi's most versatile market. The narrow ranks of Delhi's yuppies make a point of shopping here. "Whatever it is you will find what you need," Shubhi tells me. Dill, turnips, egg noodles, bouillon, she assures me they'll have it all. I'm expecting Fairway or

Balducci's with an Eastern cast. I'm not disappointed. With a barefoot porter trailing after me I pop from stall to stall in search of the ingredients for my soup. I must appear very determined because English-speaking merchants ask to know what I'm cooking. "Jewish-style chicken soup with noodles," I tell them, and they nod and laugh, happy to get in on the act. One man escorts me the length of the market to a stall where I can buy parsnips. I forage for fresh spinach, red and yellow bell peppers for a salad. I don't have to buy the chickens, which is a good thing, since the ones in the market are still alive and clucking. Brijendra will take care of that. I find a package of egg fettuccini, which will work out fine.

Back at Sadhana Enclave, out of habit I grab a bag of groceries to bring in the house. I felt Kanati's hand just barely alighting on my shoulder. He has a stern expression I hadn't seen before. Of course. Only servants unload packages. I wash up, chat with Howie awhile in our room, and come out to see what's doing in the kitchen. I don't recognize my groceries. They've been scrubbed, pruned, and artfully arranged in huge bowls. Shubhi gives me an apron and I get to work. Now

Brijendra is the pupil. Standing back a bit with his arms folded, he watches me. I can't read his expression. How does he feel about this foreign woman usurping his kitchen? I chop one carrot. In a flash Brijendra swipes the others and begins chopping them. It is not proper for a guest of the mistress to be in here like this, doing the prep work. I quickly come to understand that I am not cooking this soup, I am teaching Brijendra how to cook it. Feeling a bit embarrassed I dredge the greens in bottled water before arranging them in a big salad bowl and topping them with sliced bell peppers and the toasted almonds Lenny and I bought at the Calcutta bazaar.

The meal is a hit. Panna and Sunny, Shubhi's daughter and son-in-law, drain several bowls of soup and chomp away at the salad, declaring all of it "so unusual and delicious." But no one is happier than my weary, one-armed Howie, draped in his new shawl and slurping away. "You should have baked a challah," he remarks, inhaling the tail end of an egg noodle. I could have, but I didn't have the heart. As we speak Brijendra is busy at the tava, having regained rightful control of his domain. As it turns out, hot roti and chicken soup seem like they were made for each other.

As we embrace and say our good-byes S.P. tells us not to worry, at Delhi airport there will be men to greet us with a wheel-chair and they will take us straight through to check-in. "It is all arranged," he says. And so it is.

Brijendra's Roti

INGREDIENTS:
Water

Two cups chapati flour (from Indian
   grocer) or one cup unbleached white
   flour mixed with one cup sifted
   whole-wheat flour

Roti are meant to be served immediately.
Brijendra prepares the roti last, after the rest
of the meal is ready to eat. He cooks roti
while the family eats and serves hot bread to
each person throughout the meal.

Add enough water (between a half and
three-quarters cup) to the bowl of flour so
it can be formed into a soft dough. Knead
the dough until it is smooth, adding very
small amounts of flour if dough is too thin
or runny.

Form the dough into a ball and cover it
in the bowl with a damp cloth. Set aside
for at least a half hour.

Form dough into ten to fifteen small
balls. Heat tava or cast-iron griddle for a
few minutes. Leaving remaining dough
balls covered, flatten each with hands, dust
it with flour, and roll it into a very thin
circle. Slap the roti onto the hot (un-

greased) tava or griddle. Cook briefly (a minute or so) until bubbles form, then flip the roti swiftly with your hands and let it cook for half a minute or so on the other side.

Light another burner (gas stoves only) and with tongs, hold the roti over the flame, turning it until the roti puffs up like a balloon. Remove roti from flame, place it on a plate, and cover with a clean cloth. Add each roti to the stack.

An Army's Greatest Ally:
The Bread Project;
Natick, Massachusetts

*Bread is an army's greatest ally:
the soldier marches no farther
than his stomach.*
— RUSSIAN PROVERB

*Studies have shown that the morale
of soldiers is significantly increased
when fresh bread is provided.*
— U.S. ARMY OVERVIEW OF
"SHELF STABLE POUCH BREAD,"
THE FIRST BREAD EVER INCLUDED
IN ARMY FIELD RATIONS

I am on my way to meet a woman who may be one of the world's most knowledgeable people when it comes to bread. But first I must identify myself to an armed, poker-faced officer at a military security gate. My source has warned me about this and made the appropriate arrangements so I will be waved through. Still, the guard takes a long pensive look at my driver's license. He hands me a page on a clipboard to sign. He nods almost imperceptibly, steps back, and I'm on my way.

I'm just outside of Boston at the U.S. Army's Natick Research, Development and Engineering Center, one of the military's largest proving grounds. I'm here to poke around the kitchen of a researcher named Linnea Hallberg. She's not a soldier herself but a longtime civilian contractor who is referred to alternately as a food technologist, a microbiologist, a molecular biologist, and a biochemical engineer. To these she likes to add, with pride, the title "baker." After all, Dr. Hallberg knows just about everything that can be known about bread.

In a low nondescript building among tens of equally drab structures, I search for Hallberg's office. I wander along a corridor in what feels like a generic middle school and find Hallberg huddled in a room the size of a walk-in closet and three times as crowded. Hallberg is not a small woman — she is broad and beefy and looks at least six feet tall. There appears to be just enough room for her person among the stacks and stacks of books, the chotchkes, and walls blanketed with children's drawings and family photos and mementos of her Army career. Many colleagues have come and gone. But for years, Hallberg has been the enduring force behind what insiders call, simply, The Bread Project.

Just as any beginning botany student can spout the formula for photosynthesis, any serious baker can describe the chemical process known as fermentation. The vocational baker knows, as he knows his own reflection, the physics of heat and moisture, the delicate moods of commercial or wild yeast. But Hallberg probes deeper. She routinely gazes upon the bread molecules themselves. She is intimate with their quirks, their sensitivities, and the fate of their more or less volatile components. She can predict fairly accurately what those molecules will do tomorrow and the next day. She's injected special dyes in sandwiches to scan the microscopic migration of water molecules over time.

Guided by the lens of an electron microscope and the occasional laser beam, Hallberg has, in a sense, traveled through morsels of bread. It's a wild ride. There's a universe in there the rest of us can only imagine, a spongy moonscape of craters and plateaus, ridges, valleys, caves, and eerie air pockets. The prevailing humidity of this world is 35 to 40 percent. Herein lie the secrets to life — shelf life, that is. Hallberg's science goes beyond the prosaic chemistry of additives and preservatives. When Hallberg says she is intimate with bread, she is referring less to its visceral feel or aroma and more to its molecular, even atomic structure. Hallberg is to bread what polymer scientists are to Gore-Tex ski parkas. To make the bread perform the way she is paid to make it perform, Hallberg must know things that would make most bakers' eyes glaze over. As an engineer her approach might be called holistic. Instead of treating the problem — staling, for example, or flaking — she seeks to reinvent the system.

"That's why I loved chemistry back in school, years ago," says Hallberg, "because it can explain so many mysteries in our lives, and we can use it to improve the quality of our lives." As a food technologist in the delectably named Combat Feeding Program, the lives she improves may not be ours, or those of anyone we know. But it can be said that by making our troops a little happier, by perhaps putting a little extra bounce in their step, we civilians owe her a debt of gratitude. She has delivered the ham sandwich to the foxhole. Hallberg's years in the bakery have culminated in the patenting of a bread which in some circles would prove so unappealing any self-respecting yuppie would be scandalized were the stuff presented at a dinner party. She couldn't care less. Her individually wrapped white breads will never grace the pages of *Gourmet* or fly off the tables at the Union Square Greenmarket. If her recipe should appear in the *New York Times* it would most likely be in the science section. Her recipe resides in a military specification manual. Ingredients include: water which "shall conform to the National Primary Drinking Water Regulations." The bleached hard wheat flour "shall have a protein content of not less than 12.5 percent and a maltose content of not greater than 0.2 percent. Amylolytic enzyme activity, as determined by the falling number method, shall not exceed 240 seconds."

Food engineers are funny people. We live in a land of specialists, and the change bread undergoes as it stales has triggered a lively, if narrow, tributary of scientific inquiry. The science of staling is as old as large-scale commercial baking, which suffered extensive "staling losses" right from the get-go. In *Six Thousand Years of Bread*, H. E. Jacob writes that in 1923 a team of scientists investigated stale bread losses for the Food Research Institute at Stanford University. They found that factory losses ranged from 6 percent to as high as 25 percent. As Jacob, no doubt a budding market researcher, asserts, "The consumer invariably chooses fresh bread in preference to old bread." In a cruel twist, unsold breads returned to commercial bakers were fed to the ovens to bake new bread. During World War II the U.S. government, like a looming grandmother-figure proclaiming the loss to be a sin, actually forbid stale bread returns. "To our children or grandchildren, stale bread may be unknown," Jacob wrote sixty years ago. "For staleness is a chemical problem that someday will certainly be overcome."

He had no idea just how daunting the problem can be. Like many aspects of food science, staling is subjective. It is impossible to quantify with scientific precision. Stale means different things to different people. So do "smooth," "crunchy," "bitter," or "sweet." For this reason, scholarly literature on food science strikes the lay reader as silly. In graduate school, a professor of mine who learned of my fascination with obscure scientific journals would present me with gifts of back issues of rags like *Turkey World* and *Food Product Development*, which had articles exploring phenomena such as "creamy mouthfeel." My former teacher and I lost contact with each other years ago, but I thought of him as I perused a report by the Quartermaster Food and Container Institute for the Armed Forces on the "Feasibility of Producing Non-Staling Bread-Like Products." Um, please pass the bread-like product. Blessed art Thou our Lord, King of the universe, Who bringest forth bread-like product from the earth.

John Corcoran, my professor, would have gleefully read me the following passage from the report, which notes that, ". . . changes in bread as it becomes old have been a subject of interest and inquiry for as long as man has been concerned about means of improving the quality of food he eats." The report contains nothing about the evolution of croutons or dried bread crumbs — leave that to the culinary historians — but it does attempt to assess annual losses due to bread staling. Who knew? Though strides have been made, today "stale bread returns of commercial bakeries in the U.S. have been estimated to be 3.5 percent of total production." The report continues, "This does not account for the bread that is wasted in many homes because the members of the family refused to eat stale bread [Good luck to the guy who sets out to measure that!], nor does it account for reduction in bread consumption in organized groups, such as the Armed Forces. The value of being able to retain bread freshness for extended periods of storage is obvious." In other words, the same military willing to shell out a thousand dollars for a toilet will not tolerate a significant percentage of stale uneaten bread to disappear down that toilet.

For decades Hallberg's professional life has been consumed by bread, and in certain circles she receives well-deserved, if woodenly worded, credit for her creations. The shelf stable bread was many years in the making. Each bread resides in a hermetically sealed mud-colored pouch labeled: BREAD SHELF STABLE. *Ce n'est pas le pain Poilâne.* But biochemically speaking these breads are a thing of rare grace and beauty.

Consider the particular challenges Hallberg faces. When it comes to feeding field soldiers taste is just one of a litany of concerns. The same is true for the food engineers at the National Aeronautics and Space Administration. A croissant in space? *Quelle catastrophe! Petit déjeuner* at zero gravity means airborne crumbs, and the risk of a crew member asphyxiating on a wayward flake. The field soldier has a different problem. Of course he or she would like the food to be delicious, but in his or her skewed expectations the soldier craves food which, at best, rivals the least appetizing found in the civilian world. To a soldier crouching in a desert cave as mortar fire crackles overhead, a reconstituted chicken patty is filet mignon. But even compared to, say, a vending machine burrito, what hope is there for a freeze-dried meal that has cowered for God-knows-how-long in a vacuum-flattened pouch in the pocket of a flak jacket?

Imagine a serving of ordinary bread incessantly rattled, chilled, heated, and chilled again, soaked in perspiration and mud and otherwise pummeled and mutilated. It's easy, then, to appreciate what Hallberg has wrought. Her individually packaged breads have a shelf life of at least three years, emerging unscathed and springy to the touch even after being stored in strongboxes at 140 degrees Fahrenheit and surviving the subzero arctic freeze. Where is the *pain levain* that could withstand days, much less years, in the Arabian Desert or the fetid muck of an equatorial swamp? Linnea Hallberg's bread is, in truth, something to write home about: it is the first in history to be included in the "ready-to-eat" rations of U.S. Army field troops. And like its less technologically fine-tuned counterparts from Baltimore to Bièvres, Hallberg's bread was born of flour, water, and yeast in a place not very different from the corner bakery.

I first heard of Hallberg's work while chatting with the admittedly "bread-obsessed" Pavinee Chinachotti, a University of Massachusetts food technologist and Hallberg's mentor. An effervescent Thai immigrant who'd been chosen by something called the Eastern Food Science Conference as 1999 Professor of the Year, Chinachotti told me her former graduate student was doing some stupendous things with bread over at the Natick Center. Did I know, Chinachotti asked, that an entire science is devoted solely to the process of staling?

Army research is a very big deal. Weapons aside, soldiers' needs are special, urgent, and various. At the Natick labs, divisions of enlisted men and women are also serving their country by marching around in circles or immersing themselves in mud puddles to test the battle-readiness of boots, pants, flak jackets, stoves, tents, even bedrolls. Most of the so-called active wear or technical clothing selling for a small fortune at Eastern Mountain Sports or Paragon evolved from breakthroughs in military garb. Those Everest-worthy anoraks investment bankers wear to get from the lobby to a waiting cab owe their existence to plastics engineers with government contracts. They gave us microfiber, and long underwear hasn't been the same since. Natick is the kind of facility where scientists are as likely to be developing a better combat boot insole or field remedy for jock itch as they are to be tinkering with the next generation of tactical weapons. Here is NSC's official motto: "We are deeply committed to making our soldiers . . . the best equipped, best clothed, best fed, and best protected in the world."

We also have the military to thank for the technology behind the condensed slop so brazenly labeled "beef bourguignonne" or "cilantro-lime chicken" that backpackers can purchase — and these "meals" are not cheap — at camping supply stores. In 1997 the Natick labs joined research and development forces with Nabisco, Inc., to develop shelf-stabilized grain and cereal-"based" products. Who knows, if things go according to plan, the line between food and "rations" may be blurred beyond recognition.

The Natick campus has a museum featuring a display of field rations dating back to 1932. This is right up my alley. I love odd museums (Two of my favorites are the Hungarian Paprika museum and the Ava Gardner museum). So I'm transfixed as Hallberg walks me through the displays, sighing at the pathetic lineup of nourishment over the years and the wars. I recall my father's tales of shit on a shingle. He taught me a silly marching song I committed to memory at the age of five: "The biscuits that they give you they say are mighty fine. One rolled off the table and killed a pal of mine." The packaged fare in these exhibits was nasty right from the start. If you cracked the glass and took a bite, the taste probably wouldn't differ much from what it had been on the Western Front. There were crackers and biscuits but never bread. "The Army only had dry bread in a can, like hard tack," says Hallberg. The U.S. has long been the world's leading innovator in field rations and field kitchens. Our soldiers never go hungry. From freeze-dried fruit to beef jerky to what evolved into the processed garbage America feeds its kids, there was no shortage of long-life foods. During the Vietnam conflict the Army tried out an improved canned bread. It was coated with a chemical preservative that tasted horribly bitter, and inside the cans the breads had a tendency to collapse. "The soldiers are always going to complain about the food in the field," says Hallberg. "It's never going to be like home."

Still, the Army is proud of the variety and particularly the longevity of its rations. As for the notion of appetizing names, the military must believe its attention and resources are better directed elsewhere. As a result, menus offer such mouthwatering possibilities as "Grape Beverage Powder," "Ham Slices," and "Cheese Spread." Army ration specialists are constantly refining their repertoire. Field delicacies come and go. Today's Army is the first to breakfast on shelf-stable waffles. In 1998 the powers that be eighty-sixed the pork with rice in BBQ sauce, ditto the tuna with noodles.

But soldiers can say hello to chicken strips in salsa, pasta with vegetables in Alfredo sauce, oriental chicken and honey nut granola bars. Hallberg is putting the finishing touches on a field-worthy version of Parker House rolls.

Before the pouch breads made their debut the only home-style bread offered soldiers emerged from the diesel-powered ovens of makeshift field bakeries. These breads weren't bad but they were enjoyed only by troops who were staying put for a while. In full-scale wars fought in temperate climates the bakeries served the Army well. In more recent conflicts they proved to be a logistical nightmare. "The field bakeries consisted of several trailers put together under a bunch of tents, and these turned out thousands of pounds of bread a day," says Hallberg. "In World War II it worked very well, but it just wouldn't work today. The last time the bakeries were used was in Grenada and it was a mess. It was too muddy there to level the trailers, and the bakeries got sucked into the mud." In the Falkland Islands conflict the bakeries set up by the British fared even worse. In the rugged terrain and fierce winds a makeshift bakery made as much sense as a hibachi in a typhoon. "They had plenty of sheep in the Falklands," says Hallberg. "But no bread."

At one point Hallberg and her colleagues were put to work trying to reinvent the field bakery. "We revisited the field bakery with the hope of shrinking it down," she says. "We tried to put all the components into one trailer, but there were so many logistical problems getting the raw materials in, supplying the fuel." Hallberg shows me a mockup of the latest, state-of-the-art field kitchen. It's got an oil-fueled oven and heating trays warmed by hot water. Compact and a snap to clean, it's basically a system for reheating sealed meals. This latest greatest field kitchen is called the "chuckwagon." That should tell us all we need to know.

It became as obvious as moldy Wonder Bread that field bakeries were no longer the answer. But the Army remained intent on providing its troops with bread. That's when Hallberg and her colleagues shifted their focus to MREs (Meals Ready-to-Eat), or prepackaged rations. They knew biology, physics, and the expectations of the human palate would be working against them. They mulled over their options. "We addressed the subject, and asked, should we go with an A ration — a shelf-stable bread — or a B ration, which would consist of some kind of bread mix to which you just add water?" recalls Hallberg. What about C rations? I wondered. And the bane of my father's World War II career, K rations? "They're gone," Hallberg informs me. "Those don't exist anymore. These days it's A versus B." I'm grateful to be clear on this point, though I can't say why. I suppose it's because I like knowing obscure things. I'm thinking how the next time the subject comes up at a dinner party I will be able to say with authority that there are no more K rations. The subject hasn't come up yet, though. It probably never will.

A powder or a loaf? Rolls or slices? How thick or how thin? The world's most ubiquitous food is also, militarily speaking, the most problematic. The military might have abandoned the notion of bread altogether, conceding that for soldiers on patrol carrying bread makes as much sense as carting around fresh cantaloupes. But several years ago a study commissioned by the Army found that when soldiers have bread to eat they fare much better emotionally. Unlike ice cream, whiskey, or conjugal visits, bread is a morale-booster the Army believed is within reason. And so Hallberg and her colleagues in the Bread Project began baking. They baked and they baked and they baked some more. With each newly modified recipe they subjected the results to quantitative analysis at the hands of this or that scope or scale. But mostly they tested the bread as you or I would. "We tasted it," says Hallberg.

The project was great fun at times, but always a far more complicated affair than one might imagine. The results were either edible but not field-worthy, or field-worthy but unappealing as cardboard. Some of the bakers' efforts seemed fine until they were exposed to extremes of temperature or humidity, whereupon they disintegrated, melted, or exploded. After a succession of sometimes comical flops the poetically dubbed ready-to-eat-shelf-stable bread MILB-44360A was born. During the Gulf War, ground troops consumed 250,000 pounds of the stuff. And recently troops have begun dining on the very latest: pouch sandwiches. If Hallberg can come up with one that doesn't turn into a molten nightmare, those sandwiches will include peanut butter and jelly.

An unfrivolous, solidly built woman with short cropped hair who spends her spare time cycling country roads, Hallberg is one of those career research scientists who easily lapses into the numbing language of a chemistry text. "We can do a thermal curve and keep scanning periodically over time to measure the rate of staling; it's very important to keep the moisture content equal over time or you'll see crystallization of sugars, glass transition of the gluten and starches. . . ." She can go on like this. Transcribing the interview tape, at one point I hear myself yawn loudly.

A food enthusiast outside the lab as well, Hallberg can hop from, "Yum, that's delicious," to a mini-dissertation on the rheology of Cheese Whiz. In a subculture in which scientists have come up with ways to quantify everything, even pleasure, civilian and military tasters ranked the bread an average of eight-point-one out of nine on something called the "hedonic scale." What, I wonder, would constitute a nine? Hot fudge? And a one? Cod liver oil? Pleasure is a relative term, and hedonically speaking, one man's two is another man's seven. The bread fared well nonetheless. Everyone seems to like it.

When Hallberg unfolds her Swiss Army knife to slice one of the ready-to-eat breads "fresh" from its mud-colored packet, she could be serving up homemade apple pie.

She rips open the bread packet and shaves off a few dainty slices, sociably popping one into her mouth. The bread has an appropriate consistency — food technologists call it mouth feel — and it tastes sweet with a very faint bitter aftertaste. Hallberg explains that each packet contains not only a single shelf-stable bread, but a tiny pouch of something appetizingly named Amosorb. It's an oxygen scavenger concentrate, and its adoption to food packaging won the Natick team a prestigious Dupont Award in 1996. Oxygen and food spoilage — engineer types call it "degradation" — go together like bagel and lox.

The bread, a lightly browned oval about as long and thick as a travel packet of Kleenex, looks unremarkable. Aside from that hint of bitterness it tastes unremarkable. And that is the remarkable part. Hallberg explains that the bread could not be any larger — a loaf wouldn't be feasible — because the necessary moisture level would sabotage the bread's shelf life. The taste conveys little evidence of the distinctive, potentially unpleasant "notes and flavors" of the bread's life-extending ingredients. It's soft as a bakery roll and offers that roll's familiar resistance when you take a bite. This is no big deal, of course, to you or me. But imagine how the bread tastes to a soldier hunkered down in a jungle patrol hut for many long days. Imagine the way this bread, however odd or misshapen, feels as it works its way to the soldier's growling stomach.

Hallberg's roomy, whitewashed test bakery resembles any commercial bakery with a few random high-tech touches. These include a gas chromatograph, electron microscope, and something called an oscillator, which examines the molecular motion of the bread's components. But much of the work is baking, plain, if not so simple. When he became terminally ill, Irwin A. Taub, Hallberg's beloved late colleague, worked on the bread project with her, laboring in his home kitchen. "He was home sick and going crazy so he started baking and sending me samples," Hallberg recalls. "He was a very creative person and he never gets any credit." Her recent experiments aim to improve on the patented bread. "I want to extend the bread's shelf life and give it a more homelike flavor that will survive over time," says Hallberg. Extend its shelf life? Right now, a nonrefrigerated bread pouch is still edible after three years. That's three years in the permafrost, three years in the Sahara, three years in a tropical rain forest.

"What I do here combines every discipline," says Hallberg. "I look at the physical aspects of food, rheology of food — the way it flows, like ketchup from a bottle. I look at food on the molecular level, study its molecular composition through a microscope. I look at food kinetics, the effect of heating on microbes, food packaging, food chemistry, food microbiology. When it comes to food technology you get every walk of life." To gain an appreciation of the impact of food technology, or food engineering, or whatever you call it, on contemporary life, the lay person need only visit the local supermarket. Every processed food, all packaged foods, commercial dairy products, all things boxed, bottled, or canned — somebody, says Hallberg, "had to figure it out."

Hallberg sends me home with a gift of two bread packets. How comforting to know I have until June of 2004 to eat them.

Bread, Long Shelf Life, Patent 5059432

Military Specification Manual, U.S. Army Natick Research, Development and Engineering Center

INGREDIENTS:

Flour, 50.53 percent total ingredients, by weight

Emulsifier, 1.0 percent

Water, 28.96 percent

Shortening, 8.50 percent

Glycerol, 6.34 percent

Yeast, 2.25 percent

Salt, 1.29 percent

Gum arabic, .50 percent

Calcium sulfate, .25 percent

Xanthan gum, .25 percent

Encapsulated sorbic acid, .10 percent (can substitute with encapsulated potassium sorbate)

Cream flavor, .03 percent

Blend emulsifier with dry flour. All ingredients shall then be combined and sufficiently mixed to develop the dough.

The mixed dough shall be sufficiently proofed. The proofed dough shall be divided into pieces of sufficient weight to assure compliance with finished product net weigh requirements.

The proofed dough shall be fully baked until the exterior is a uniform, typical bread crust color corresponding to the bread color labeled B in the photographic standard provided to the contractor and inspector, USDA, FGIS. The bread shall be baked in rectangular molds, which may be tapered top to bottom for ease of depanning.

The bread shall be placed into heat sealable polyethylene or other FDA-approved food packaging material for an interim period not to exceed 48 hours prior to repackaging.

DON'T TRY THIS AT HOME!

The Biscuit Lady:
Huntsville, Alabama

I come from people whose concept of the Deep South is Baltimore. Sadly, mine was a late initiation into the TUMS-popping splendors of butter-drenched grits, real Southern-fried chicken, and barbecue not conferred by an MSG-fortified bottle of Heinz. On rare occasions something resembling a biscuit appeared in a restaurant breadbasket spinning curls of steam, and I would bite into it hopefully. Inevitably the thing tasted like a pig-in-a-blanket minus the pig.

My first meaningful encounter with a biscuit was somewhere in Kansas. It was the mid-seventies and my former college roommate Nancy and I were driving cross-country from Boulder, Colorado, where she was attending graduate school. We had less than three days to get to New York so we drove through the night making ourselves hoarse from belting out the ballads of Woody Guthrie and Tom Paxton, the type of music that comes to mind when America is rolling by your window. Somewhere east of St. Louis we crooned the refrain to "Hobo's Lullaby" and pulled over at a truck stop. As was our habit, we sat in the car until we'd finished singing the song. "Can't you hear those steel rails hummin'? That's the Hobo's Lullaby." Overtired and dazed, we found the last two seats at the breakfast counter and debated whether the queasy feeling in our bellies was hunger or nausea. As we stared at the menu with glazed expressions a squadron of waitresses appeared to dispense to each and every trucker a plate of . . . what? To our left, to our right and directly opposite were men lustily plunging their forks into plates filled with vomit or something that looked a lot like vomit. It was biscuits and gravy, of course, but the closest thing I'd seen to it, appearance-wise, was vomit. This was culture shock equivalent to a white-bread gentile friend's when she saw my family start the day by tearing into a whole smoked whitefish.

"You girls havin' biscuits?" the waitress chirped. "Yes, please," Nancy and I replied. "Butter and honey, or gravy?" "Butter and honey!" we cried with relief. The biscuits were amazing. Flaky but not shedding, moist but not buttery, crusty without offering the slightest resistance. The separate but equal halves wore their respective pats of melting butter like frosting on a cupcake. After devouring about five each we concluded that the feeling in our bellies had, most definitely, been hunger.

Surely biscuits like these are born of a few simple ingredients. Why do so many Northern kitchens, if they make biscuits at all, rely on a cloying mix or ready-made dough entombed in a cylinder? And why did I — why *do* I — even care? My biscuit fixation dates back to my early teens, when I curled up on the living room couch with John Steinbeck's *The Grapes of Wrath*. I spent the weekend in that spot, raptly turning the pages, pausing only reluctantly to eat or visit the bathroom. The Joads' misfortunes captivated me and managed, as few things had in those days, to make a mockery of my own grievances, however sincere. As it would be later with the novels *Nectar in a Sieve* and *Down and Out in Paris and London*, my chief fascination was with the cuisine, or stunning lack thereof. I could imagine what it must feel like to be forlorn, bone-tired, hot or freezing without relief. But real hunger was beyond my comprehension, fond as we all are of complaining we're "starving." While my brother, sister, and I were sitting down each evening to plump chickens and weighty slabs of brisket, I followed the Joads in their travails. Day after grueling day they squeezed some kind of sustenance from lard and flour. To this sad table the rare windfall delivered a hunk of moldering salt pork. But the ever-resourceful Grandma Joad always came through. The woman could've penned a lard-and-flour cookbook. Tonight, flour with lard! Tomorrow night, lard with flour! Flour on a bed of lard, fried lard with a dash of flour, flour balls fried in lard, lard balls tossed in flour, lard-and-flour pie!

To folks of a certain geography and vintage who grew up poor the biscuit was a daily staple in good times and bad. That's how it was for Eunice Merrill, one of twelve children of a cotton farmer and part-time minister whose earnings were so meager the family, she loves to say, "couldn't afford to pay attention." "Aunt" Eunice came to my attention thanks to Don O'Briant, reporter and food critic at the daily *Atlanta Constitution*. He'd written a book titled *Backroad Buffets & Country Cafes: A Southern Guide to Meat-and-Threes & Downhome Dining*. Who, I asked him, most embodies the craft, the lore, the spirit of the Southern biscuit? O'Briant sighed. Well, I can tell you where to get some damn good ones, he replied, or words to that effect. He named a few places. One of them caught my interest immediately. It was Eunice's Country Kitchen in Hunstville, Alabama. Mostly, people come to Eunice's for her country ham and biscuits. By all accounts Eunice's Country Kitchen is to biscuits what Bach was to the cantata. Eunice's is the handmade biscuit that sends otherwise reticent citizens into legendary feeding frenzies. It is the biscuit for which the indoctrinated will drive the two hours up from Birmingham. They eat, then turn around and go home. That's about four hours round-trip for *breakfast*. I had to meet this lady.

"You just come on down whenever you like, honey." It didn't seem to surprise Eunice one bit that a woman from Massachusetts was planning to fly all the way to Alabama to hang around in the kitchen of a breakfast joint on the highway out of Huntsville. "Don't come Tuesday," she said. "I'm closed on Tuesday." (That's the day she gets her hair done.) "I'll call you and let you know the exact dates," I said. "To make sure you're in town." "Well, you go ahead and call if you like," Eunice replied, "but I'm not goin' anywhere. Never do." I asked Eunice to recommend a place to stay. "Depends if you're payin', sweetheart," she replied. "Hell, if you ain't payin', you stay at the Hilton." I was, in fact, payin', but I booked a room at the Hilton anyway. I felt Eunice's charismatic powers, even at this great distance.

After a brief layover at Raleigh-Durham, the only airport in the U.S. that appears to encourage smoking, I filed onto the plane to Huntsville in the company of tidy-looking people in pastel crewneck sweaters and comfortable shoes. Despite its growing prominence as one of NASA's most important bases of operation Huntsville is an intimate place, its values arrested in the *Apollo* days. Many passengers on the flight knew each other vaguely and quizzed each other warmly to figure out how or why. The first question they asked was "Which church do you belong to?"

I arrive in Huntsville in the humid dusk, rent a car and find my way to the Hilton. "How're ewe?" drawls the receptionist. Southerners are look-you-in-the-eye friendly and it's hard to be mad at one even as she insists you do not exist. In exotic locales such as New Delhi there's no problem, but I've yet to arrive at an American hotel that manages to spell my name right. "Ah, here it is. They had you under Samuelson." "Thank ewe ever so much," I say. My head is throbbing. I let myself in the room, undress, and collapse. Aunt Eunice is expecting me the next morning before things get too crazy. That would be at opening time, 5 a.m.

When the wake-up call catapults me out of a REM action feature my headache is even worse than the night before. Because my room at the Hilton is rigged with air-conditioning stuck on sub-arctic I am unprepared for Huntsville's ambient air, stifling as the inside of a vegetable steamer. I follow the route to Andrew Jackson Way on my complimentary Hilton point-of-interest map. A few turns guide me out of the dense, modern metropolis of downtown Huntsville. Tucked away between the blocks of cold granite and glass are still a handful of unassuming places with names like Bubba's, but Huntsville's old cotton-town ambience has been largely bulldozed and paved over to make way for the space program, a growing state university, and hundreds of high-technology firms. It's the kind of downtown that grows eerily still after business hours. Aside from the quaint "cotton-pickin' " knickknacks for sale at its smattering of downtown gift shops, the old Huntsville endures along the leafy residential streets branching out from downtown. Ornate bungalows, Victorian and stately Federalist homes strut their charms in the dappled shade of willow, cherry, pecan, and horse chestnut trees. There appears to be a law mandating a rocking chair on every porch.

I drive past auto body shops, a barbecue joint, a Baptist church. When you first set eyes on Eunice's place you know the food has to be damned good. Her "country kitchen" is plopped forlornly on a gravel lot along a dreary stretch of commercial highway that feels like anywhere and nowhere. Like so many others must do, I drive right past it at first and wait for a legal U-turn to get me back. The modest sign — EUNICE'S, HOME OF COUNTRY HAM & HOME MADE BISCUITS — is perched beside a Coca-Cola logo and a disembodied ham that looks cut and pasted from a child's word primer. Encased in brick and smaller than a convenience store, the squat rectangular bunker doesn't even look like a place I'd pull over for out of desperation, much less enthusiastic premeditation. I take my time getting out of the car. I'm still feeling nauseated from the "Stroganoff" I foolishly polished off on yesterday's flight. And I'm beginning to feel ridiculous for actually boarding an airplane and booking a room at the Hilton, for this.

Except for the nausea, these feelings vanish when I step inside. The contrast is jarring. If Dollywood had a fallout shelter it might resemble Eunice's. The bunker door opens to a busy hive of gingham and knotty pine, wainscoting and walls crammed with memorabilia. The air is suffused with the aroma of frying oil and coffee. Eunice knows me immediately and extends her plump arms like a televangelist gathering me in to be saved. She is wearing a faux taffeta blouse the color of Hawaiian Punch, black slacks, and one black glove.

Probably never a beauty, Eunice has the kind of looks one can't help but describe as "grandmotherly" — a generically-styled helmet of silver hair, thick glasses, strong, slightly wizened features compressed around a wide mouth with lips that purse tightly when they aren't stretched into a disarming smile. Though she rises to greet "the girl from Massachusetts," most of the time Eunice stays enthroned in a specially designed chair to accommodate the arthritis that has stiffened her joints and left her in constant pain. A cross between a bar stool and a therapeutic walker, the chair keeps her propped up and towering over the tiny restaurant's liveliest table. Eunice has cheerfully endured five joint-replacement surgeries. Her doctors bring their families over for ham and biscuits.

Front and center opposite the coffee station, Eunice's round table is impaled by a supporting post, without which, she informs me, the building would collapse. Here and at the neighboring "Liars' Table" longtime regulars join her to eat and everyone seated at the surrounding booths stops by Eunice's table to pay tribute, exchanging news and a hug. "Some of these people grew up here, and now they bring their own kids to show them what real country cooking is." Eunice's operation is cash-only. After the newfangled cash register pooped out one too many times Eunice dug up an old gunmetal cash box and now customers pay her directly and politely wait for her to make change with a gloved hand. One after another the guests pay their respects: Eunice's internist and his family, an assistant district attorney, a contractor, Huntsville's best known watercolorist. There are hugs all around: "We love ya," she tells them. Eunice has two daughters, a son, and six grandchildren, but she'll be the first to tell you that this is the center of her life: this restaurant, these people, day after day of news and gossip and political banter and saying "We love ya," and really meaning it.

"Go on back," says Eunice, motioning toward the kitchen. "Janie's waitin for ya." The kitchen is small, T-shaped and spare, consisting of a four-burner stove, an oven, some cupboards, and sack upon sack of White Lily Self-Rising Flour. The kitchen hasn't changed in the half-century since Eunice moved her place here from another part of town. Eunice peddles a tasty ham but it is her biscuits that made her famous. These are nothing more, or less, than the biscuits Eunice's mother baked for her preacher husband and twelve offspring, most of whom picked cotton for a few cents a day. They're baked from the same recipe Eunice's grandmother used when she baked for Eunice's mother. The day Eunice's husband walked out the door for good she said to herself, "I've got to do something, so what do I know how to do?" What Eunice knew best, she says, was simple home cooking. That was hundreds of vats of Crisco ago, and Eunice still loves her work, even more since she became a celebrity. If Eunice didn't exist Huntsville might have had to invent someone like her. She is the old, sleepy, low-tech Alabama, now the backdrop for manned rockets routinely sent hurtling into outer space. Eunice is a good sport about being reported on and packaged as the state's down-home sweetheart but there is nothing patronizing or cute intended when the mayor comes to seek her endorsement or state, even national, legislators seek her seasoned wisdom.

Stirring the contents of a large saucepan, a short-order cook named Mary cheerfully shares the ingredients of genuine red-eye gravy: pork fat drippings and instant black coffee. I peer into the pan and face my reflection in what looks like a crude oil spill and smells not much better. "People say, oooh, gross, but it's good stuff," says Mary. My stomach does an ominous flip. I am a stranger in a strange land, with a strange and uncharacteristic urge to convert to veganism.

A dark-haired, weary-looking woman, Janie has toiled in Eunice's kitchen for only a year. Like that of her predecessor Janie's existence in this kitchen is the sum total of the "secret" of Eunice's biscuits: a live human working the dough by hand. "Most places don't want to hire someone so they use frozen dough," says Janie. Her job is to make the biscuits, and that task alone keeps her busy from 4:30 until closing time, 11:30 a.m. She goes through about twenty-five pounds of flour on Eunice's busiest day, which is Saturday. Like all cooks south of the Mason Dixon line she uses only White Lily. Perfect for biscuits, cakes, and piecrusts, not so great for bread, White Lily uses only soft, low-protein winter wheat and grinds and sifts it again and again into a powder-fine light baking flour. Janie's biscuit recipe is so simple, so fundamental, it owes a debt to a century of Mama Joads. The ingredients are White Lily Self-Rising Soft Wheat

Flour, vegetable shortening, and milk. Period.

Where is the buttermilk, lard, salt, baking powder? "Aaah," waving a dismissive hand. This is how Eunice's mom made biscuits. "This is how my own mom made biscuits," Janie tells me as she measures five pounds of flour into a huge stainless-steel bowl. "My mom always had fresh biscuits for breakfast and supper," Janie tells me. "You don't get too far away from your raising around here." Into the flour goes two pounds of Crisco, a basketball-sized blob of it. Then Janie goes to work with her hands. "You work it until the shortening is dime-sized and leave it all crumbly like that, then add the milk." Janie pours in a half-gallon of milk, turns the bowl with one hand and turns the dough with the other, cupped hand. "This is the country way to make biscuits." The dough shouldn't be thin but it shouldn't be thick either, she says. It should be moist but not too moist. "You get a feel for it."

Janie gathers the dough in her hands and presses it onto an old kitchen table coated with flour. She flattens it until it's the size of a large pizza, then kneads it in a flattening and folding motion. She flattens and folds, flattens and folds, and then she's ready to roll. In swift confident motions Janie rolls the dough out about a quarter inch thick. To cut out the biscuits she uses an empty juice can. The biscuits are two inches in diameter, almost precisely the size of the proverbial hockey puck. They'll bake for eight to ten minutes. With the hungry mouths just outside the kitchen door and the morning's list of takeout orders for ham'n'biscuit, every batch is spoken for before it emerges. A typical male adult will consume four or five biscuits at a sitting. "We had a man here say he ate twenty-one biscuits, though we only counted seventeen," says Eunice. "He was an evangelist from Texas. Just kept asking for more." The thing about the biscuits, one patron tells me, is you lose all sense of proportion. "If she gives me two I'll eat two," he says. "If she gives me three I'll eat three."

Under Janie's and Mary's tutelage I learn my concept of gravy is completely misguided. I thought that nearly all gravy, by definition, is made with drippings, juices, reductions, giblets, or some other by-product of a substantial hunk of meat. But the gravy of Eunice's biscuits and gravy is essentially a molten variation on the biscuit itself. The milk gravy recipe is nearly identical to the biscuit recipe. It's that Joadian ingenuity again. All you've got is flour, milk, and fat. From that — ta-dah! — a platter of baked something with a sauce on top. Posted at the stove, Mary elaborates. "You add about three pounds of flour to an oiled skillet, let it brown, then add milk and some water."

Though Crisco is a fixture in most Southern kitchens, the lard versus shortening debate is far from dead. "We had lard when we were kids, but not too many people are killing pigs anymore," a fiftyish woman named Reba Gordon tells me. We met in the Misses Dresses boutique of the Parisian department store at the Huntsville mall. Reba uses White Lily, of course, along with Crisco and buttermilk. "Got to have buttermilk," she says. But just then another customer, a woman who looks slightly younger than Reba, pipes in. "I couldn't help overhearing," she tells us. "And let me tell you, lard makes a huge difference. Using lard is the only way to have moist biscuits."

The stomachs congregating at Eunice's would respectfully disagree. In a kind of perpetual instant replay a tired-looking middle-aged waitress named Ramona emerges from the kitchen with plates of ham and biscuits. But refilling coffee is the customers' responsibility. "You get up to pour your own, you've gotta go around pourin' everyone's," explains Eunice. "You havin' regular or decaf?" asks a customer as he makes the rounds. "It don't make no difference," says Eunice, miles away from the grande-skinny-half-decaf-no-foam-latte crowd. The coffee-pouring rule applies equally to NASA brass and checkout clerks from the Publix. One morning newly elected U.S. Representative Bud Cramer showed up and Eunice asked him to help clear the table. The Liars' Table is designated, so the overhanging sign says, FOR POLITISHINS, FISHER FOLK AND OTHER BAREFACED LIARS. Its flip side welcomes WIMMEN, BIZNESFOLK AND PREECHERS. The walls are crammed Sardi's-style with signed photographs of astronauts and politicians, team banners, commendations for community service, and quirky testimonials, From Jessup and Associates, a framed antique pocketknife with the inscription, "Aunt Eunice, your kitchen is as memorable as a person's first pocketknife." A tiny photograph of the restaurant peeks out from a framed page of a Japanese guidebook. And my favorite, a framed group photo of uniformed men over the inscription: "To Aunt Eunice from your friends with the good appetites, U.S. Army Space and Strategic Defense Command Sensors Directorate." Well, everyone's gotta eat.

When visiting dignitaries are so high falutin' that the logistics of proper security make a meal at Eunice's impossible, Eunice will dispatch her food to them. "We had an international delegation at the space center, and we sent 'em home on the plane with ham and biscuits," she tells me. In Huntsville with his Secret Service entourage, President Jimmy Carter's son Chip arrived for a breakfast meeting at another restaurant. When he declined breakfast and explained that he already ate at Eunice's the young Carter was given a standing ovation.

"I'll leave 'em all to the Huntsville Library when I go," says Aunt Eunice, eighty-two, who is emphatic that the end of Aunt Eunice will be the end of Aunt Eunice's. "I bet I've had somebody here from every country in the world. Jan Davis the astronaut is a Huntsville girl — she's been eating here since she was fifteen, and now she brings the boys from NASA over." The Russians love the place. Next to me a local contractor attacks his biscuits and gravy. "Eunice has been in business as long as I've been alive," he says. In the mornings I park myself at Eunice's table. I see her greet her physician, her minister, Huntsville's best-known watercolor painter, and the owner of the city's biggest hardware store. Huntsville's mayor Loretta Spencer stops in for breakfast as often as she can. She and Eunice are good friends. "When she was deciding whether to run for mayor she consulted with me," says Eunice. "She wanted to know if she could count on my support." If the office were purely a popularity contest Eunice would be Spencer's biggest threat. The EUNICE FOR MAYOR posters for sale are the legacy of a fund-raiser that got out of hand, in a good way, of course. Several years ago a collection of Eunice's admirers launched her tongue-in-cheek mayoral campaign. Eunice held a televised press conference promising a "liars' table" in the city council chambers. Her posters and bumper stickers were big sellers and she handed the $3,300 over to the Arthritis Foundation.

Eunice orders a plate of food for me. Its content shocks and horrifies me. From the land of croissants and bagels, I am staring at a slab of fried ham the color of a magenta Crayola, biscuits smothered in "gravy." A humongous tattooed, pony-tailed man stuffed into a Harley Davidson shirt sets down his motorcycle helmet and takes the seat across from me. Eunice flashes her maternal smile at him and he introduces himself to me. "Dave Roberts, nice to meet you," he says, wagging my hand. Roberts is an aeronautics engineer — yes, that would be a rocket scientist — at the NASA center. Within minutes I learn that he's done some consulting work with the Israeli Defense Forces, and that is how an Aunt Eunice for Mayor poster came to grace the wall of a coffee shop in Tel Aviv. When he's in town Roberts always eats at Eunice's. He's working on some kind of missile system and blabs about it. An unpublished fiction writer, when he waxes poetic about Eunice's cooking he looks down at his medicine ball of a belly and gives it an affectionate pat. Roberts offers advice on what to eat with what. "Let me do that for you," and before I can make a sound he's mixing a soup of margarine and sorghum and proceeds to drown my plain biscuit in the stuff. Then he "fixes" my grits for me, a process involving another half cup of margarine and a hefty portion of salt.

Eunice reminds me of a Eudora Welty

character. She is a woman whose world, though it rarely exceeds the boundaries of a one-story building smaller than the average dry cleaner, is a warm and richly populated world, a world ripe with possibility. In a culinary culture increasingly dominated by pricey braised or deglazed this on a bed of wilted or pureed that, a kind of magic happens when you feed people the most simple, honest foods. Eunice tells me she believes her biscuits remind people of the safest moments of their childhoods and they want their own children to experience the same thing. Eunice herself was born on a cotton farm near a place actually named Piney Woods, in Madison County in 1919. Also a preacher, her father, Joseph Franklin Jenkins, married Mary Magdalene Hornbuckle, and the couple had six girls and six boys, all named after biblical characters. The family traveled to church, piled into a two-horse wagon. The family raised nearly all its food and Eunice would carry her lunch — ham and biscuits — to school in a tin bucket. Her mother made most of the children's clothes out of flour sacks and fertilizer bags. The first time she went to town, Eunice was twenty years old. "It was the end of cotton-picking season and as a special celebration Daddy took us to the county fair. I had never seen so many lights and so many people."

It's hard to restrain an "Aw, shucks." Then Eunice tells the rest of the story, which isn't exactly the script for *State Fair*. To feed her own family she took care of other people's kids for six dollars a week. Later she took a job as a waitress at her brother-in-law's restaurant, a place where the sheriff and local politicians would hold court in a backroom, pocketing the cash bribes of the waiting restaurant patrons. As Eunice puts it, this was where she learned how to pour coffee and keep her mouth shut. Eunice opened her own place, the Butler Grill, with seventy-five dollars borrowed on her life insurance policy. Open from dawn until about nine at night, the place was across from the now-defunct Butler High School. The kids loved Eunice's place enough to nickname her Aunt Eunice, but they weren't big spenders and Eunice was going broke. She moved to the present location in 1952 just as the city began tearing up the highway to widen it. The whole area was a war zone. Every time it rained faithful customers of Eunice's Country Kitchen had to slop around in six inches of water. Eunice talks wistfully about those times. The customers would simply sit on the tables. Hell, they would've dangled from the rafters if they had to. For these fierce displays of loyalty, Eunice credits not herself, but her country ham and biscuits — especially her biscuits.

Eunice has been routing a never-ending procession of biscuits to the bellies of mayors, legislators, district attorneys, presidential hopefuls, and astronauts for half a century. It is the unfailing fluffiness of the handmade biscuits and the exuberance, generosity, and mischievous intelligence of Eunice herself that attracts. And the fact that Eunice is always there, six mornings a week from five to eleven-thirty. When she unlocks the door at dawn, there are people waiting. Eunice's is closed on Christmas, Easter, and Mother's Day. "I like being at work better 'n being at home. I like people," says Eunice, who lives alone. "Moving around is good for the arthritis."

Eunice arrives at the restaurant at four in the morning, an hour before the place opens, but that's just a concession to safety. For decades she let herself in the place at three. Then one morning when she was on her way from her house to the car, Eunice was severely beaten by a pair of robbers. They were father and son, and they pummeled Eunice so mercilessly she was left for dead. "I came to and pulled myself down the steps," says Eunice. "I got myself to the car and started honking the horn."

The next morning Huntsville awoke to front-page news about the assault on one of its most cherished citizens. Local television news teams kept a vigil outside the hospital, where the recovering Eunice was inundated with flowers, gifts, and thousands of get well cards. "I got a call from the White House. It was just unreal. It was just something else." There was a huge celebration the day she was released. Huntsville wanted Eunice.

It also wanted her attackers' blood. On the testimony of a female accomplice who received probation, the forty-two-year-old man, the one who did the beating, was convicted of attempted murder and robbery and handed two life sentences without chance of parole. His eighteen-year-old son got fifteen years. Eunice's wounds are healed but she still suffers. "I'll never feel safe anywhere," she tells me.

I'm about to hit the road when Eunice pops up from her throne. "Wait, honey," she said. "Gotta get you your liar's license." Eunice settles back in her chair to make the license official. It reads:

This is to Certify That Susan Seligson, having by reputation and long practice, coupled with a vivid imagination exhibited all the proper requirements therefor, is hereby empowered to Lie, Prevaricate, and to show every other recklessness with the Truth, considered expedient by him in connection with all matters for current year, subject however to conditions and the state he is in. Lies may be told at any time or place without notice.

In Witness Hereof is attached the Grand Signature of Eunice. She hands the license to me and I see it is signed "Love you, Aunt Eunice." "You sure we can't wrap up a few ham biscuits so you can eat 'em on the plane?" "No, but thanks so much," I say. What I don't say is that I plan to go home and eat nothing but broccoli for a few days. We hug one last time. Eunice wraps her plump polyester draped arms around me, and says, "We love you," and I say, "Love you, too." And that, despite the new powers vested in me, is no lie.

Aunt Eunice's Country Biscuits

INGREDIENTS:

Two cups White Lily Self-Rising Soft
 Wheat Flour

One-quarter cup Crisco vegetable
 shortening

About three-quarters cup milk

Preheat oven to 500 degrees. Place flour in mixing bowl. With fork, cut in shortening until mixture resembles coarse crumbs. Blend in just enough milk with fork until dough leaves sides of bowl. Turn dough onto lightly floured surface. Knead gently about ten turns.

Roll out dough ½ inch thick. Cut out biscuit rounds with small empty can. Place biscuits on ungreased baking sheet about an inch apart.

Bake for 8 to 10 minutes. Makes 12 biscuits.

La Fête du Pain:

Paris, France

Il y a beaucoup de quelque chose
which is something
Oooooooooo I absolutely love quelque chose
— *ELOISE IN PARIS*,
KAY THOMPSON

Le pain se leve!
— FRENCH PEASANTS' RALLYING CRY

All I ever want for breakfast is a fresh baguette, crispy without and chewy within, spread with sweet creamery butter, and a cup of café au lait to wash it down. I want to partake of this breakfast not in my kitchen but in a pleasant café with the scent of wood and coffee and a view of the street. I want the bread sliced not in dainty diagonals but in halves like twin longboats, butter smeared on each. I want the man who places the bread on my table to wish me *"Bon appétit."* I

396

want the buttered bread to be called *tartine*.

I want to be in Paris. When it drizzles, when it sizzles, when it fizzles, I'm not picky, I'll go there any old time. To me, Paris is the antidote to an America in which lunch is a canned protein cocktail, people discuss fat grams at the dinner table, and dogs are left at home. Part of me longs to see as much of the world as possible, from Santorini to Samarkand. The other part would just as soon keep going to Paris.

We have good friends in London and Howie routinely proposes that we return there. I reply, how about we save some money and you go alone? My thinking is, why London? Forget the friends; let them come here. Why not Paris? What I'm really trying to say is, why a dark pub, why not a bright airy café? Why a crumpet, why not a croissant? Like places of worship to the itinerant believer, the cafés of Paris lighten my heart and soothe my soul. Add some fragrant fresh bread, coffee, a hearty salad, and I've got all the sustenance I want or need.

On the Paris streets it's invigorating to be alone. Unless you're half of a pair of lip-locked twenty-year-olds, better to dispense with domestic chemistry; it only numbs the senses to the ambient drama. In Paris Howie and I smartly go our separate ways during the day. He stalks off with his shoulder bag and his own agenda, bound for museums, bookstores, and art supply shops. This is a man who can spend an entire afternoon perusing fountain pen nibs. Paris was made for such a man. Howie likes to park himself at Les Deux Magots for a horrifically overpriced lunch and an afternoon of sketching the patrons as they come and go. I just give myself over to the streets. On a whim I choose a direction and wander all day, resting occasionally at cafés as they beckon. If I'm wearing decent shoes and packing a field-tested umbrella I can easily log eight to ten miles in a day because there is something new — a carved doorway, a garden, a shop devoted to paper, silks, music boxes — to admire or learn from at every turn. And you can always count on the Métro (its plan akin to "Sesame Street" for this girl who grew up riding the New York City subways) to zip you back to where you began. I crisscross the Seine and loop around to explore narrow lanes and cobbled mews. I was born to poke around and Paris is a poker's paradise. I once spent an entire day at Père Lachaise cemetery communing with the likes of Molière and Chopin. I wasn't hungry; I'd brought along a loaf of bread.

Paris embraces you. A friend and mother once told me, if, God forbid, something should happen to her girls Paris is the only place she can see herself going on, actually enjoying some kind of sentient life without them. It's not just the elegance and beauty of the city but the little touches that charm me. I get a kick out of the way shop clerks lovingly wrap a $4 purchase, the way secretaries put you on hold with the words: *"Ne me quittez pas."* I love how the French treat children as full-fledged members of the human race. I marvel at the French in their devotion to beauty. Like those people with a knack for casually crafting the kind of sandwich that makes you want to throw your own on the floor, the French have a way of rendering all things scrumptious. Of course, few sights on this planet are more tantalizing than the window of a patisserie, but almost as delicious-looking is a shop that sells cutlery or writing paper.

Most of all, I love the French for their relationship with food. Like the best marriages it's an enviable one, affectionate and freewheeling. The French palate remains unmarred by righteous overtones of "good" foods (anemically fat-free) versus "bad" (substantial and robust). How inspiring to see Parisians dig into their *gratin dauphinois* with joy and gusto. It's a gusto that carries over to other pleasures and, despite all the obsessing (and I'm no exception) this side of the Atlantic, seems not to prevent people from being reasonably trim.

Next to the iconic Eiffel Tower, the cartoonist's shorthand, the glyph that screams Paris, is the baguette. French for "stick," the baguette is as cliché as La Vie en Rose, as emblematic as "ooh-la-la." Like an umbrella or lapdog the baguette is a Parisian accessory. The motion of tearing off the bread's heel to have a nibble while riding the Métro or moving along the streets seems almost innate; it's as if the hand reaches for the bread of its own accord. And as Kay Thompson's Eloise noted, where toddlers are concerned, baguettes make wonderful skis.

But when it comes to the culturally enshrined baguette, all is not exemplary in the City of Light. For the last two decades France in general and Paris in particular have been coping with a bread crisis. Crisis is a relative term, of course. This time around the situation has triggered no riots. There has been no lynching of hapless *boulangers* or corrupt grain merchants, no storming of ancient prisons. It is a crisis of quality, what writer Rudolph Chelminski called "one of the saddest aspects of the ransom paid to progress."

The situation is steadily improving, though, and in spite of it Paris remains, *sans doute,* the bread capital of the world. My status here as roving scribe, however, is on a par with a frozen dinner roll. Lionel Poilâne, the most famous bread baker in the world, doesn't answer my e-mails, letters, and faxes. Why should this surprise or disappoint me? The man is up there in the firmament, *le roi du pain,* the Caesar of sourdough. In the last few years the baker has gone global with the June 2000 opening of a London branch and sales over the Internet. Poilâne isn't stingy with his artistry and expertise, but at this point, with an operation that delivers handmade breads as far away as Tokyo and Manhattan, he prefers to impart his wisdom through his books and a Web site that incorporates a gazette and bread library. (Poilâne has managed something that's possibly unprecedented: the franchising of a credible, unadulterated traditional enterprise. The commercial wood-fired bread oven is London's first since such hearths were prohibited in the wake of the Great Fire of London in 1666. From the Périgord-walnut flour to the butter, all ingredients come from France.) I thought it would be interesting to talk with the slightly less lofty Jean-Luc Poujaurans, creator of the *baguette biologique,* ostensibly the first organic loaf in Paris. He doesn't want to be bothered either. In the resounding silence I conclude that it's easier to meet and camp with Bedouins than it is to interview a high-profile Parisian baker.

We are in Paris for one day, then another, and my phone calls continue to go unanswered. *"Est-ce qu'il y a des messages?"* I inquire hopefully, incessantly, at the hotel desk, and the kindly faced manager replies *"Non, madame"* with an unmistakable tinge of pity. Paris and bread, this is heavily trod-upon territory. What, I ask myself, do I hope to learn? I find myself fixating not on the good bread, but the mediocre. Who knew there were many places in Paris where the bread is not much better than the loaves at our ubiquitous Au Bon Pain? I've plunked myself down at the most enticing cafés only to bite into bread a faint notch above those half-baked creations from Sara Lee. Though dinner baguettes still nest in countless armpits and poke out of every other tote bag bobbing along the boulevards of Paris, the French consume less than a third the amount of bread they gobbled at the turn of the century. After centuries of vigilance and characteristic cultural purism, the French began in the sixties to do something unspeakable. They began mass-producing inferior, overprocessed bread. Aggravating the downhill slide are commercial yeast, mechanical kneading that's more like pummeling, and flours emasculated by high-volume, standardized milling. A lifting of price controls on the ubiquitous baguette in 1988 paved the way for cheap, industrial breads, what food critic and Paris chronicler Patricia Wells calls "flabby impostors." But unlike America's quiet rebellion, waged in the rarefied circles of people with the cash and wherewithal to pursue alternatives, enough French citizens are dismayed about this *horreur* that simple, if slightly more costly handmade bread is staging a valiant comeback. Fearing those processed "imposters" were detracting from their exalted status, French bakers themselves launched a "good bread campaign," a call to arms against mediocrity. The government has reinforced its standards so not just every Jean or Jacques can label his bread *artisinale*. In the fall of 1993 it issued a decree distinguishing *les vrais boulangers* from producers of industrial bread. The decree stipulates that bread called *pain maison* must be mixed, kneaded, baked, and sold on the premises, and that the only bread that merits the proud label *pain traditionnel de France* is that which has not been frozen, extended, or spiked with unnatural or unapproved additives. The days of shame are fading. *Le pain se leve* . . .

What constitutes real French bread? For one thing, the bread is relatively salty. French bakers use a 2-percent or more ratio of salt to flour. Unlike the Italians, who first made do without salt four centuries ago in the face of a crushing salt tax and have been baking salt-free bread every since, the French consider salt a nonnegotiable component of legitimate loaves. The requisite salt and purity laws are the reason French bread triumphs over Italian. It isn't just taste; beyond its role as a flavor enhancer salt retains moisture and keeps bread fresh longer. By law legitimate French bakers can't go dosing baguette dough with preservatives. The only improvers bakers can legally use include a wheat, yeast, an enzyme agent called levit, vitamin C, and rye or fava bean flour.

I'd read that the number of French youths wanting to be bakers is declining. That's no surprise. The work is hot, lonely, and physically demanding. The hours make trash collectors look pampered; first shift begins as early as two in the morning. Who is choosing this career today? I hoped to meet some budding bakers. Back home I'd arranged a visit to l'École de Boulangerie et de Patisserie de Paris, but that isn't for a few days yet. For the time being my research amounts to eating as much bread in as many locales as possible. It's a tough job but I feel up to it.

We've settled in at Hotel de Buci off the Boulevard St. Germain, a four-star hotel of understated elegance with a cheerful staff. The place is amazingly quiet considering the activity on the short but buoyant Rue de Buci, a string of cafés woven into a cavalcade of bustling specialty food markets. It's May and everyone, as if by legal decree, is out on the street. By eight in the evening packets of cigarettes, glasses of beer and wine vie for space on the tiny tables at the cafés, each of which disgorges those tables so far a passing car must proceed at a turtle's pace or simply give up. Out on a spring night Parisians constitute both the audience for a grand pageant, and the pageant itself.

Though we secretly prefer it, we didn't plan to stay at a hotel. We intended to be more frugal and less touristy this time around, and rent an apartment. To hear our friends talk about it, renting an apartment makes a person feel as if he's staked a little claim to Paris. We allowed ourselves to be bullied. What self-respecting subscribers to *The New York Review of Books* would stoop to stay in a *hotel* like Frommertoting package tourists? The renter isn't just "staying," he's "living," albeit for a measly two weeks.

There are more short-term Parisian rental agencies than there are benches in the Bois de Boulogne but did we use any? Nope. On the recommendation of one of these proselytizing friends we contacted an academic apartment rental service, agreed to a place, and mailed a deposit. The agent described the place but we'd seen nothing, not even one of those photocopied interior photos rental agents favor, the kind that look as if they were taken by a malfunctioning satellite. When we arrived, jetlagged and dyspeptic, we felt as if we'd fallen victim to a cruel prank. Or maybe something was lost in translation. I am an earthy gal. I've slumbered in fallow fields, in cars, on concrete rooftops. But this place was disgusting, prohibitively so. It was dark, filthy, and arranged with the kind of sagging, moldy furniture you'd find in the gutter with a FREE sign. Except for some stains with possible forensic implications the walls were bare. The lone table listed despondently, the place reeked of roach killer, and I've seen nicer bathrooms in Texaco stations. A dead roach bobbed in the toilet bowl. At times like these I'm usually the one who kicks into gear with my signature, chirpy optimism. I despise confrontation and I possess a reflexive tendency to say, "It's okay," whatever It may be. I was exhausted and I dreaded schlepping our stuff back to the rental office. We could buy lots and lots of flowers, I thought. Then Howie peeked under the bed and calmly said, "Let's get out of here." I knew enough not to look there myself. What was odd was how blasé the agent was. He refunded our money without so much as a twitch of indignation. It was over faster than a bad dream. We hailed a taxi and got ourselves to Rue de Buci, where we'd stayed before. We love Rue de Buci. Even in the absence of cooking facilities it's comforting to be in the embrace of so much tantalizing meat, fowl, and cheese, such glowing produce.

We were relieved to be back.

Yet here it is, day three, and I am feeling *un petit peu* sorry for myself. Under a rare blue sky Howie and I stroll aimlessly along the Rive Droite past Châtelet. As we round a bend toward the plaza at Hôtel de Ville we can see some sort of ruckus involving huge white tents, their roofs floating across the square like swales. Crowds course in and out. "Something's going on," we say in unison and quicken our pace. Because "something" is to the tourist what nectar is to a bee. We hone in on a sign and make out a word: *Pain*. "Pain?" says Howie. What kind of gathering would be about pain? Silly Howie and his anemic French. As he puzzles over the notion of a carnival devoted to analgesics I am thinking, there is a God. For we have stumbled upon *La Fête du Pain*, the Festival of Bread.

We enter the nearest tent and pluck an English brochure from a wide selection of languages. This is the first day of a four-day annual event, newly expanded from a strictly French affair to an event welcoming exhibitors from *tout l'Europe*. We follow a chain of placards depicting the story of flour, from the sowing and harvest of wheat, to threshing, winnowing, gleaning, and milling. It's a user-friendly exhibit, which invites visitors to grab a handful of whole grains from a basket or run their fingers over a sheaf of wheat. A line of women in white caps are stationed at a dais slicing baguettes, whole-grain loaves, cheese breads, and *pain de campagne* into sample chunks, which people are stuffing into their mouths as if they are starving to death. One can only assume they are tourists seeking a kind of justice for the daunting cost of that morning's croissants. So far, this *affaire* is nothing to write home about.

Then we slip into the bakers' tent. This is where the action is. Like figures on a calliope, a bevy of bakers in their toques pound dough, roll baguettes, genuflect before ovens, and balance trays. A narrow counter stretches from one side of the tent to the other, and here, elbow to elbow, are at least a hundred apron-clad schoolchildren rolling mutant baguettes as a team of bakers offers words of instruction and encouragement. Visiting from schools all over Paris, the children are eight to ten years old, a teacher tells me. Now in its fifth year, the festival will bring about a thousand kids, a small minority of whom, it's hoped, will be inspired to take up baking as a career. Though the supervising bakers are all men, I notice that the girls are far more adept than the boys are. The girls work the dough with confident but delicate hands. The boys just pound the hell out of it. The girls present lumpy but passable baguettes. At best, those "baguettes" beaten into submission by the boys look like socks filled with tennis balls.

Bakers celebrate *La Fête du Pain* in small ways all over France. In the Loire Valley and in the more residential neighborhoods of Paris we will encounter tables set outside bakeries offering samples, informational pamphlets, and fist-sized heart-shaped breads meant to be saved as a keepsake, one baker told me, for one year. But here in the main festival tent, *"Tout les enfants sont boulangers,"* according to my *"Petit passeport du pain,"* obtained at the information table. The baker "works while the rest of us sleep," the *passeport* tells us. "He creates with love the bread that we will eat." There is a small description of *"un grand mystère, le goût du pain."* Why bread tastes the way it does is a mystery rivaling that of the precise contents of the atmosphere on Mars. Researchers have identified 150 odors contributing to the taste of bread, as many as the scent of a rose. I find this information gratuitous.

Couldn't the same be said for a pickle? But I am pleased to learn there is a division of France's ministry of commerce devoted to compiling and disseminating all manner of arcane details relating to handcrafted bread.

Oddly, in a culture sometimes referred to as "painivorous," *La Fête du Pain* is part of a sweeping public relations campaign to incite French citizens to eat bread. As if the French, of all people, needed convincing, the bread brigade at the ministry of commerce trumpets slogans such as *"Le pain pour tous"* (bread for all), and *"Le pain, l'atout santé,"* bread as a health food for children, athletes (*"Bon pain, bon sport"*), for the pregnant, the diabetic, and those seeking to curb obesity. *"Le pain doit trouver sa place dans chacun de nos repas,"* counsels the bread and health pamphlet. Bread has a place at every meal. It goes on to elaborate, noting that *"deux tartines de pain . . . c'est le menu ideal du petit déjeuner à la française." Excusez-moi,* but this information strikes me as being about as useful and overdue as a campaign urging the Japanese to drink tea or pressing upon Italians the virtues of red wine. I'm perplexed. It appears that the guardians of the culture actually fret about the day when *les*

Français start requesting cornflakes for breakfast. Or worse — the French will take a liking to the processed sliced bread-like product ubiquitous in America and the U.K.

From the spirit of *La Fête* and the indoctrination of its attendant schoolchildren, one might conclude the baguette is at least as old as the Republic. But it is a relative newcomer to the French table. Until the early 1900s France's signature bread was a five-pound round loaf, or *miche*. A serendipitous, elongated variation of the daily bread proved crustier and, according to bread historians, had consumers clamoring for more crust and less doughy innards. It was probably consumer demand that inspired bakers to gradually lighten the standard loaf to eight ounces. Increasingly long and svelte, the bread became today's baguette, of optimum crust-to-flesh ratio and ideal for dunking in *chocolat*. Though historians fail to note it, I can't help concluding the baguette was also a winner because its weight and contours so well suit the bicycle basket, the school bag, and the armpit. As breads go, it's the most user-friendly of the lot.

As the throngs of *petit boulangers* at the festival so graphically illustrate, crafting a baguette is a skill requiring considerable practice and an intimacy with the dough. I think about this when I meet France's legitimate future bakers at L'École de Boulangerie et de Patisserie de Paris. A seventy-year-old institution that began with seven students and now graduates 200 bakers each year, since 1996 the school occupies the renovated Anciens Chais de Bercy. A chain of single-gabled stone buildings standing edge to edge like Monopoly houses, the school's glass doors open to a gleaming cavernous lobby and a network of broad corridors of working kitchens. My guide Danielle Laurent explains that the students range from young "apprentices," to those pursuing diplomas to adults learning to bake just for fun. There are students from Japan and Africa as well as from Europe but all are committed to learning the craft of artisan baking and join in reversing the trend away from the much-maligned *pain industriel*. Within these corridors fledgling bakers use only natural *levain* and learn, as Provençale student Bernard Leblanc put it, "to bake the bread with love." This approach is relatively recent, and the idealistic young bakers here consider themselves craftsmen rather than technicians. A full-time student, whose father was a baker in Tours, Leblanc dismisses with a scowl the "cafeteria" bread being thrust upon the French masses. Boulanger-hopefuls come to this spotless, fluorescently lit institution to learn the ways of the traditional village baker. "We come to learn all about the fire, how to get the temperature just right," says Parisian Laurent Sarrazin, soon to receive his baccalaureate Professionnel Boulanger. Like Leblanc, Sarrazin speaks of the nation finally emerging from the dark days of the eighties, when, to hear him describe it, industrial bread spread across France like a latter-day plague. "One gets to know where the bad bread is," he says. "That bread is baked without love, and with far too much yeast. But the bread is getting better all the time," he says. "People have better taste now."

Will the French truly be able to unring this bell? With the possible exception of Lionel Poilâne, whose main bakery in Bièvres, outside Paris, calls into service a phalanx of wood-fired ovens, enough to churn out *pain Poilâne* for the world market, what we call progress is an anathema to the French baker. But the finest traditional bakers say that more and more Parisians are staging their own protest against mediocre bread. Just notice, they say, how Parisians are increasingly willing to venture out of the orbit of their neighborhoods to buy bread at boulangeries a considerable walk or even a Métro stop away. Witness the line snaking out of the original Poilâne bakery on Rue Cherche-Midi, where it has stood since 1932. I trekked along Boulevard St. Germain to Rue Monge, up past the flea market, the Islamic institute, and the museum of natural history, to Place Monge. There I nudged my way into the fragrant, impossibly crammed corner bakery of S. Hervet, whose varied and exotic sourdough loaves attract their share of lines, too.

The Hervet family have been bakers for two generations and their shop has existed in this spot since 1959. "Twenty years ago we just made baguettes," says Madame Hervet, a silver-haired woman with bangs falling haphazardly around warm, pale blue eyes. The Hervets have gained a reputation as innovators. Their natural sourdough loaves, in addition to a hearty baguette, include ten-grain loaves, fougasse with olives, rye and cumin bread. "Much fewer people want the baguette," says Hervet, mopping the sweat off her brow as we lean against the storeroom shelving, hidden from the commotion of shoppers. "Today we make varied breads and we look for the best flour, the finest grain. We buy from the small millers. There was lots of *pain industrielle* in the postwar period but we're going back to the traditional ways. It's a good time for bakers." Hard living, though, requiring lots of strength and punishing hours, which is why women don't bake bread, the women bake the patisserie. "*C'est un petit peu difficile pour les femmes.* In at four in the morning, six days a week."

I take another route back to Boulevard St. Germain and pass several bakeries with *Fête du Pain* tables set up on the sidewalk and arranged with samples of *pain au levain, pain biologique.* The message on the accompanying Fête literature echoed the seemingly redundant message, "Parisians, eat lots of bread!"

I had given up completely on Lionel Poilâne, and confess being relieved the man snubbed me. I'm afraid I'd be struck dumb in his hallowed presence. But there is another esteemed baker in the family. He is Poilâne's brother Max, a colorful, passionate character reputed to be an eloquent polymath who brings to his baking training as a research biochemist. He is, I have read, an unflinching purist, a fanatical bread lover who eats bread for dessert, a baker with a loyal adoring clientele and little interest in fame or fortune. To me, at this point, one of the most compelling things to recommend Max Poilâne is his willingness to meet with me. Monsieur P. not only sounds delighted about the prospect, he is already courting me on the telephone. "Shall I call to remind you?" I ask in French. (He speaks no English.) "No, I'll remember because it's a special day." Oh? "*Mais oui,* the day is already memorable because I will be meeting you."

Though he has three shops including a small branch in Place Constantin Brancusi near Gare Montparnasse, Poilâne does all his baking on the place du Marché St. Honoré not far from the Tuileries gardens. I am nervous about finding my way so I allow far too much time for the Métro ride, and arrive early. When I find the bakery, which sits on a corner at the bottom of a quiet residential street, Poilâne had not yet arrived, and from the ensuing chatter among the clerk and a man I learn is Poilâne's son-in-law, I conclude he's forgotten all about me. I hear the clerk reminding him of my existence. And I am thinking, *Mon Dieu,* that's that, another strikeout. But the bakery clerk, a gentle-faced woman with flame-red hair and a pinafore apron, senses my desolation and assures me all is well. I am expected. "He said you should wait for him at the café," she tells me, and proceeds to herd me across the street with a solicitous hand on my back. She explains to the proprietor and waiters that I am a guest of Monsieur Poilâne, and after a chorus of *"ah ouis"* I am welcome to anything I like. *"Alors, madame, asseyez-vous et Monsieur Poilâne, il arrivera bientôt."* Everything is, finally, going swimmingly. And I can't help congratulating myself on my fluency in *la langue.* In this place, a good ten Métro stops from the tourist hordes of St. Germain-des-Prés, little or no English is spoken. But as I make small talk with the waiter I feel at home. My oh my, do I love Paris.

It is a neighborhood place, a lovely old café with etched glass windows, lace curtains, and a tiny bar. I make peekaboo faces at a giggling toddler circling the café tables and soon enough I am face-to-face with Monsieur Poilâne, that would be Max. The *other* Poilâne. It is a kind, expressive face, dimpled with a trace of mischief. He sports a thick but neatly trimmed sandy mustache. Set off by a red bowtie, the face is reminiscent of a mime's. Poilâne is a small, wiry man who doesn't so much walk as skip. Constantly in motion, he has a habit of leaning into your airspace when he speaks, and resting his hand on yours to make a point.

"*Je vous en prie,*" Poilâne says, lurching forth to take my hand, and launches into the story of where he's been and why he is delayed. Then he greets the other patrons, all of whom happen to be his employees, relations, or both. My little peekaboo friend is Poilâne's grandson, who gets a good all-over tickling in greeting.

While brother Lionel touts a creed of "retro-innovation," a large-scale, cyber-dependent operation that honors and pre-serves old hand-baking methods, Max is the embodiment of retro, period — every-thing from his professorial garb to *les fours,* the bakery's five wood-fired ovens, the *pain au levain* perched willy-nilly, the crystal chandelier that crowns the bakery's small tiled reception area.

"Ah, so you are looking for a dissertation *sur le pain,*" says Poilâne, settling into a chair opposite me and the small table. He apologizes for his lack of English. "Everyone in my house speaks English but me," he says. Poilâne gestures to the waiter to bring us glasses of white wine. As we sip — the wine is cool and faintly sweet — Poilâne, whose father was also a baker, tells me he is a happy man: *"J'aime bien la vie!"* "I'm very attached to tradition," he says, "because in tradition lies wisdom. I believe in what I do, in the quality of my bread."

Poilâne has traveled a bit in the United States. The country impressed him, especially Chicago, which he found very European. But when I ask him about the quality of the bread, he makes a sheepish gesture. "I don't eat the bread," he says. "I never do — *ce n'est pas du pain*." That's not bread. He compares it to bad caviar. "I can't eat bad caviar because I've tasted good caviar," he says. "It's sad, actually. The sensibility suffers." It's not bread because the wheat is inferior, the water isn't pure, and with very few exceptions the bread is baked in ovens fired by gas or electricity, when it is wood — *le bois* — that imparts the vitality essential to fine bread. In his five hearths Poilâne uses only untreated white wood, *le bois propre*. It's very expensive, burns slowly, and is regulated by government quotas. "But the product," says Poilâne, "is so much more agreeable." But his bread isn't perfect, says Poilâne. "Perfect? McDonald's makes things that are perfect. I make *le vraie pain,* the true bread, always a little different."

Poilâne laughs at the notion of toiling under the vast shadow of brother Lionel. "I have no competition," he says with a naughty wink. "All the locals come to me. There are two other bakers on the street, and one of them buys his bread at *my* bakery. As for my brother and me, it is good that there are two of us because we learn how to carry on in peace. *Il faut absolutment avoir la paix.*" And Jean-Luc Poujaurans? "I love him!" says Poilâne. "He is unique, a most interesting man!"

According to Poilâne, the supremacy of French bread was one of the countless casualties of World War II. "Ah, *la guerre,*" he says with a sigh, lifting his wineglass. "I must tell you that the war did a lot of damage to everything." And it was after the war, in the prosperity of the fifties, that white bread began to edge out dark bread on the bakery shelves. "Dark bread was considered poor bread, mediocre bread having all the connotations of the bread of soldiers, *le pain sale,* dirty bread. "All that dark bread ended with the war," says

Poilâne. This is lamentable because it's the "dirty" bread that's most nourishing. And Poilâne should know; in his former life as a research scientist his field was gastro-enterology. "I bring to my work the sciences of physics and biology," he tells me.

Poilâne compares the wheat in his bread to an egg. At least I think he does. I have nearly polished off a second glass of wine and, in truth, I don't know what Poilâne is saying. I haven't eaten much lunch, and it's nearly seven in the evening. I am famously incapable of holding liquor. I feel my facial features losing their taut alertness, that eyes-wide-open interviewer mode ceding to alcohol, gravity, and bewilderment. I am, in a word, drunk. And at this moment Monsieur Poilâne's French is as comprehensible to me as Cantonese. Never mind how I will make sense of the loopy scrawl in my notebook. I don't even know how I'll make it back to quai des Grandes Augustins, where Howie and I are to meet for dinner. Or is it Rue Dauphine? And what was the name of that restaurant, anyway?

"One is animal, one is vegetable, it dies to fertilize the next generation. One rediscovers the earth in the egg of a bird or a chicken."

Comment?

Uh-oh. Now I'm in big trouble. Deep *merde*. Chattering away about God-knows-what, Poilâne is leading me across the street to the bakery. We descend to where a shirtless man, his skin slick with sweat, tends to the fires in the gaping hearths. See how he pours water over the coals to distribute the heat, says Poilâne. He thrusts a basket under my nose, smell that beautiful dough! It is that now familiar *parfum*, a sachet of fermentation fumes. At a moment when I could really use some fresh air the smell nearly knocks me down.

Poilâne calls for a taxi and guides me solicitously into the seat. I mumble something about quai des Augustins and actually doze off during the brief ride through the clogged Paris streets. By some miracle I recall the name of the restaurant and find Howie there, eager to hear all about my interview with the unsung brother of the bread king. But it will have to wait because my head is this close to flopping into my plate of lamb shoulder speared with smoking twigs of thyme. "You should have eaten some bread," says Howie.

As we gather our luggage to check out of the sweet embrace of Hotel de Buci, I go to shake hands with the manager, who I decide looks like a svelte Theodore Bikel. "For you, madame," he says, and presents me with a gift: a rhinestone-studded Eiffel Tower pin. "Come back to Paris soon," he says, strolling over to replace the key. He looks inside one last time and says, "So sorry, madame. Still for you no messages."

Basic Baguette

From Lora Brody, author of
The Kitchen Survival Guide, Bread
Machine Baking: Perfect Every Time,
and The Cape Cod Table

INGREDIENTS:
For Poolish (Starter):
1¼ cups (5¼ ounces) unbleached
   all-purpose flour
½ cup + 3 tablespoons (5¼ ounces) cool
   (approximately 60°F) water
a pinch of active dry yeast

For Dough:
2½ cups (11 ounces) unbleached
   all-purpose flour
1½ teaspoons active dry yeast
½ cup + 3 tablespoons (5¼ ounces) cool
   (approximately 60°F) water
all of the poolish
2 teaspoons (⅓ ounce) sea salt

The Poolish: Combine the flour, water, and yeast and mix until well blended in a medium-sized mixing bowl. Let the poolish rise for 12 hours or so (overnight is usually just fine). It should dome slightly on top, and look aerated and just plain goopy. Try to catch it before it starts to fall, just as bubbles begin to form on the surface, as it will be at its optimum flavor and vigor when it's at its highest point.

The Dough: Place the flour and yeast in a mixing bowl, the bucket of your bread machine, the work bowl of a food processor, or the bowl of an electric mixer. Pour some of the water around the edges of the poolish to loosen it. Pour the poolish and water onto the flour. Mix the dough till it's sticky, but has started to come together and form a ball. Add the salt and knead the dough till it's cohesive and elastic, but not perfectly smooth; the surface should still exhibit some roughness.

Transfer the dough to a lightly oiled bowl (or oil your mixer bowl and leave it in there). Cover it, and let it rise for 2 hours, folding it over after the first hour (or more frequently, if the dough is very slack or wet; this folding helps strengthen the gluten).

Divide the dough in half and gently preform it into rough logs. Let it rest for 20 minutes, then shape it into long, thin baguettes. Let the baguettes sit, covered in the folds of a linen or cotton cloth until they're about 85 percent risen, 30 to 40 minutes. If you don't have a cloche, place them on a lightly greased or parchment-lined baking sheet, and cover them lightly with greased plastic wrap.

Preheat your oven and baking stone to 500°F. (If you don't have a baking stone, that's okay; baguettes baked on a stone will have a crispier crust, but those baked on a pan will be just as tasty, if not equally crunchy.) Just before putting the loaves into the oven, slash them several times at an entering angle of about 45°. Fill the oven with steam by spraying water into it twice in the first 5 minutes. Reduce the oven heat to 475°F and continue baking the loaves for 20 to 25 minutes. Remove the loaves from the oven when they're a deep, golden brown, and transfer them to a wire rack to cool.

Yield: 2 baguettes

Bibliography

Abu-Lughod, Lila, *Veiled Sentiments: Honor and Poetry in a Bedouin Society*, University of California Press, 1986.

Ahmed, Akbar S., *Living Islam*, Facts on File, 1994.

Alford, Jeffrey, and Naomi Duguid, *Flatbread and Flavors; A Baker's Atlas*, William Morrow, 1995.

Allen, Brigid, ed., *Food: An Oxford Anthology*, Oxford University Press, 1995.

Blaise, Clark, and Bharati Mukherjee, *Days and Nights in Calcutta*, Doubleday, 1977.

Denzer, Kiko, *Build Your Own Earth Oven*, Hand Print Press, 2001.

Dupaigne, Bernard, *The History of Bread*, Harry N. Abrams, 1999.

Guinaudeau, Madame, *Traditional Moroccan Cooking: Recipes from Fez*, Serif, 1994.

Hensperger, Beth, *Breads of the Southwest*, Chronicle Books, 1997.

Jacob, H. E., *Six Thousand Years of Bread*, Lyons Press, 1997.

Jaffrey, Madhur, *A Taste of India*, Atheneum, 1988.

Jhabvala, Ruth Prawer, *Out of India*, Simon & Schuster, 1987.

Lonely Planet Travel Survival Kit, *Jordan & Syria*, Lonely Planet, 1997.

Mackintosh-Smith, Tim, *Yemen — The Unknown Arabia*, Overlook, 2000.

Mernissi, Fatima, *Dreams of Trespass*, Addison Wesley, 1994.

O'Brien, Edna, *Mother Ireland*, Plume, 1976.

Ortiz, Joe, *The Village Baker*, Ten Speed Press, 1993.

Paz, Octavio, *In Light of India*, Harcourt-Brace, 1995.

Sonnenfeld, Albert, *Food: A Culinary History*, Columbia University Press, 1999.

Trager, James, *The Food Chronology*, Henry Holt, 1995.

Ward, Sue, Claire Clifton, and Jenny Stacey, *The Gourmet Atlas*, MacMillan USA, 1997.

Wells, Patricia, *The Food Lover's Guide to Paris, 4th ed.*, Workman, 1999.

Wing, Daniel, and Alan Scott, *The Bread Builders: Hearth Loaves and Masonry Ovens*, Chelsea Green, 1999.

Wood, Ed, *World Sourdoughs from Antiquity*, Ten Speed Press, 1996.

The employees of Thorndike Press hope you have enjoyed this Large Print book. All our Thorndike and Wheeler Large Print titles are designed for easy reading, and all our books are made to last. Other Thorndike Press Large Print books are available at your library, through selected bookstores, or directly from us.

For information about titles, please call:

(800) 223-1244

or visit our Web site at:

www.gale.com/thorndike
www.gale.com/wheeler

To share your comments, please write:

Publisher
Thorndike Press
295 Kennedy Memorial Drive
Waterville, ME   04901